A Game of Brawl

A Game
of Brawl

*The Orioles, the Beaneaters,
and the Battle for the 1897 Pennant*

Bill Felber

Foreword by
Senator Edward M. Kennedy

UNIVERSITY OF NEBRASKA PRESS · LINCOLN AND LONDON

Library of Congress
Cataloging-in-Publication
Data

Felber, Bill.
A game of brawl : the Orioles,
the Beaneaters, and the
battle for the 1897 pennant /
Bill Felber ; foreword by
Senator Edward M. Kennedy.
p. cm.
Includes bibliographical
references.
ISBN 978-0-8032-1136-0
(cloth : alk. paper)
ISBN 978-0-8032-2636-4
(paper : alk. paper)
1. Baltimore Orioles (American
Association : Baseball team)—
History. 2. Baseball—Maryland—Baltimore—History.
3. Boston Red Sox (Baseball
team)—History. 4. Baseball—
Massachusetts—Boston—His-
tory. 5. Baseball—United
States—History—19th century.
I. Kennedy, Edward
Moore, 1932– II. Title.
GV863.M32B354 2007
796.3570973—dc22
2007005161

Set in Minion by Kim Essman.
Designed by R. W. Boeche.

*This story is dedicated
to those engaged in the invigorating
and occasionally noble field of newspaper editing,
and particularly to the people of the
Associated Press Managing Editors.*

Contents

Illustrations

Foreword

Senator Edward M. Kennedy

Before there were the Boston Red Sox or the Boston Braves—or even Fenway Park or the World Series—there were the Boston Beaneaters, a powerhouse baseball team at the top of the National League at the end of the nineteenth century. Before there was an American League, before there was the proud and widespread Red Sox Nation, there were the loud and fiercely loyal Boston baseball fans called the Royal Rooters.

My grandfather, John Francis Fitzgerald ("Honey Fitz" as he was called because of his beautiful singing voice), represented Boston in the U.S. House of Representatives from 1895 to 1901, and he was proud of his role in 1897 in creating the Royal Rooters, as the Beaneaters' fans were known during the wild and wonderful early years of Boston baseball.

Growing up, I heard countless fascinating stories from Grampa about the Royal Rooters—how he helped create them with "Nuf Ced" McGreevy and other fans; how the Rooters would parade in the outfield and sing rousing renditions of "Tessie" and "Sweet Adeline" (Grampa's favorite song) to get the crowd cheering before a big game; how the Beaneaters went on to become the Braves; how the Red Sox arrived after the creation of the American League in 1900; how as mayor in 1912 he threw out the first pitch at the first game ever played by the Sox at Fenway Park and the first pitch at the first World Series later that fall.

His tales of the Rooters and their excitement were as ingrained in us as his love and knowledge of politics.

It was easy to see why he cared so much for Boston's teams in all the years when I was growing up. I've always felt the Braves didn't dare leave Boston until after Grampa died in 1950, for fear of disappointing him. I'm sure he's smiling down on the Red Sox every time they take the field today.

Baseball was also the favorite sport of my father, Joseph P. Kennedy. He was captain of his team at Boston Latin High School and he made the team at Harvard. Everyone in my family inherited a love for the Red Sox. Their long, glorious, and often heartbreaking story is special for all of us.

Grampa, though, was an equal opportunity fan of Boston baseball. My cousin, Tom Fitzgerald, loves to tell the story of the day the Braves clinched the pennant in 1948. Tom had just turned fourteen and was ecstatic when Grampa invited him to the decisive game, but he got more and more upset when Grampa took so long getting to the ballpark. Grampa had opinions on everything, and he stopped for fifteen minutes to talk to a newspaper reporter about his favorite subject of baseball, keeping poor Tom from his seat at the game for what seemed like an eternity.

The game was a cliffhanger, and Tom loved every minute of it. Suddenly, at the start of the ninth inning, with the Braves clinging to a 3–2 lead over the New York Giants, Grampa took Tom by the hand and said, "Let's go." Tom couldn't believe it, but he quickly realized that they weren't leaving the park but were heading for the locker room to be the first to congratulate the Braves. Grampa had faith that they would win, and he was right.

Tom was overjoyed. In the locker room, Grampa shook hands and congratulated the players, and Tom met them all. Grampa was soon approached by the Braves' sportscaster, Jim Britt, who asked him for his reaction to the game. The words rushed out: "You know, baseball has meant a lot to me from the time the Red Sox won the pennant when

I was mayor in 1912. I remember Babe Ruth. I remember the troubles we had with baseball following the Black Sox scandal." After a while, Britt cut Grampa off and tried to move away, but Grampa took the microphone. "I'm not through yet," he insisted, and he went on telling everyone what was on his mind. That was Grampa when it came to Boston baseball, and we loved him all the more for it. I still love to go to Red Sox games, and I always think of Grampa when I do.

I remember the "Impossible Dream" season of 1967, when the pennant race came down to Boston and the Minnesota Twins. My brother Bobby and I were serving together in the Senate, and late in the season we invited Vice President and former Minnesota senator Hubert Humphrey to a critical game between the teams. We gave him a hard time after the Red Sox won, 6–4, and then clinched the pennant the next day. Jose Santiago, Boston's pitcher that day, gave me the game-winning ball, which I still have on display in my Boston office, along with Carl Yastrzemski's MVP and Golden Glove Awards for that year.

Bill Felber's *A Game of Brawl* is like sitting and listening to Grampa's greatest stories again. It's a wonderful history of early professional baseball and the intense rivalries that made the game so exciting in those days. I'm sure Grampa would love it.

Sources and Acknowledgments

Ah, the old Orioles!

During a mid-1890s game at the outset of their championship run, Louisville's Pete Browning reached third base, the domain of chief Oriole trickster John McGraw. With one out, the next batter lifted a medium-depth fly ball to left field. Tagging up, Browning felt McGraw virtually on his back. He broke for the plate on the catch and slid safely home. Then, as he rose, the savvy runner laughingly pointed back at McGraw, who stood at third holding the incriminating evidence—Browning's belt. McGraw had grabbed the belt to thwart Browning's effort to score; Pete outsmarted him by surreptitiously unbuckling it.

On another occasion an opponent laced a drive into the gap between center field and right field. Willie Keeler dashed toward the ball—which was rolling between him and center fielder Steve Brodie—retrieved it, and without looking, heaved it back toward the infield. There it almost collided with the ball Brodie had dislodged from deep in the center-field grass, where the Orioles had hidden it for precisely such occasions. That Keeler story is even better known than the one recounted to reporter Fred Lieb in which Keeler climbed a slanted wooden fence and then dashed atop the fence posts to snare a would-be home run.

Then there was the time an opposing first baseman chased a thrown ball down the steps that led to the Orioles clubhouse. But he did not return with the ball until it was too late, because groundskeeper Thomas

Murphy closed the gate to the steps. The batter and all the Oriole base runners could have crawled home.

The stories are recorded in Oriole legend. Today we cannot be sure whether any of them actually happened. Newspapers of the era do not report them. Browning died in 1905, decades too young to refute the tales passed along from men such as McGraw and Hughie Jennings to often gullible newspaper reporters. In their senior moments, old Orioles McGraw and Jennings, along with Wilbert Robinson and Joe Kelley, loved to regale friends with stories of their own and their team's exploits . . . and they were good storytellers.

That doesn't make such stories false. But it also doesn't make them true. In preparing this tale, I've tried to shy away from retelling yarns for which no verification is available. In a couple of instances—notably the legend-infested Louis Sockalexis story—I have noted the various moments when fact departs from legend. The reality is that the story of the baseball season of 1897 doesn't require gilding; it's gilt-edged enough as it is. This was a season when documented instances of fights among players, fights between players and umpires, forfeits, fan insurrections, and published accusations of collusion, bribery, game-fixing, and efforts to cut or maim occurred almost daily.

The primary sources for the events described herein are contemporary newspaper accounts. In every major city in the United States there were plenty of newspapers in the final decade of the nineteenth century, and most of them covered the local team. In Boston, the *Globe*, *Herald*, *Post*, and *Journal* all devoted plenty of inches to the doings of the Beaneaters. In Baltimore, the *Sun* and the *American* are the best sources. The *Sporting News* and *Sporting Life* are, of course, broader references, and the whole is supplemented, as needed, by accounts published in Philadelphia, Washington, New York, Chicago, Louisville, Cincinnati, and Pittsburgh.

I do not mean to suggest that if something was mentioned in a newspaper account it should perforce be taken as truth. For the cause of selling more papers, reporters were encouraged to embellish their stories, and readers and historians must be on the watch for those embellishments. But through a process that might be described as trian-gulation—cross-checking descriptions against competing accounts in the newspapers of both involved cities—one eventually arrives at a notion of which descriptions can be accepted.

Increasingly, that notion is supplemented with excellent secondary research. Plainly the best work on the Royal Rooters is *Boston's Royal Rooters*, written by Peter Nash and published by Arcadia Publishing in 2005. And by the way, if you're ever in Cooperstown, make it a point to visit Nash's authentic recreation of 3rd Base saloon just a short dis-tance from Doubleday Field. Nuf Ced McGreevy is no longer there, but his spirit infuses the place.

Due largely to their élan, the Orioles are a particular favorite of baseball historians. Charles Alexander's biography of John McGraw, now nearly twenty years old, is the standard, although his acceptance of some of McGraw's taller tales is beginning to come into question. Burt Solomon wrote a brilliant recollection of the team in 1999; it is called *Where They Ain't* and was published by the Free Press. Other player biographies—for example, *Ee-Yah* by Jack Smiles (McFarland, 2005), which is about Hughie Jennings, and *Uncle Robbie* by Jack Kava-nagh and Norman Macht (University of Nebraska Press, 2000), which is about Wilbert Robinson—flesh out aspects of the broader portrait. Robert L. Tiemann and Mark Rucker's *Nineteenth Century Stars* (So-ciety for American Baseball Research, 1989) is a useful resource for bi-ographical backgrounds on many of the players: Marty Bergen, Bill Hoffer, Fred Klobedanz, Ted Lewis, Dutch Long, Bobby Lowe, Jack Stivetts, and Fred Tenney. The library at the Baseball Hall of Fame has extensive files on many of these players as well as on sometimes over-looked players such as Dirty Jack Doyle, Jimmy Collins, Kid Nichols, and Joe Kelley.

Ancillary aspects of the era have also received excellent treatment. The Louis Sockalexis story is a recurring topic and is best told by Ed Rice in *Baseball's First Indian: Louis Sockalexis: Penobscot Legend, Cleveland Indian* (Tide-Mark Press, 2003). Jerold Casway's *Ed Delahanty and the*

Emerald Age of Baseball (Notre Dame Press, 2004) provides an exquisite ethnic context to the era. *Sunday Baseball* (McFarland, 2003), by
Charlie Bevis, includes an extensive look into the 1897 fight between
the Cleveland Spiders and Cleveland's establishment over whether to
open the fields on Sundays. Every tale needs a skeptical fact checker,
and nobody's been more assiduous in that regard than Howard W.
Rosenberg, whose *Cap Anson 3* (Tile Books, 2005) puts most of the
handed-down claims through microscopic scrutiny.

For their assistance at various stages of the project, I am indebted
to Peter Nash; Tim Wiles and his staff at the A. Bartlett Giamatti Research Center at the National Baseball Hall of Fame; staff members
at the Enoch Pratt Free Library in Baltimore; Ned Seaton of the *Man-
hattan (ks) Mercury*; and the Library of Congress. I also would like to
thank my editor at the University of Nebraska Press, Rob Taylor, and
copy editor Sandy Crump, who saved me from several embarrassments
of fact, clarity, and attribution in the preparation of this text.

The extensive and remarkable compilation of material available on-
line—particularly the wondrous files of Project Retrosheet—must be
noted. Although Retrosheet's work hasn't yet reached the point of re-
constructing box scores for every game of the 1897 season (give them
time), the site is an absolute must for keeping tabs on day-to-day events
such as scores, winning and losing pitchers, and standings. Its files on
games worked by particular umpires were invaluable in the preparation of this book.

Together these sources comprise what I believe and hope to be a secure network of checks against embellishments to a tale that needs
none. In other words, Joe Corbett really did let two runs score by fling-
ing the ball into the stands in disgust; Boston fans really did beat their
own first baseman senseless; and Tim Hurst really did hurl that beer
stein back at the fan.

Finally, it is necessary to say a few words about names. To preserve
the historical tone of this book, I have used the spelling of the city of
Pittsburgh that was in use in 1897—that is, without the *h*. The name

of the fellow who owned the 3rd Base saloon, that popular Boston tavern that figures so prominently in the organization of the Boston Rooters, is a matter of some dispute. Peter Nash, who wrote the book detailing the history of the Royal Rooters, spells the name as "Mc-Greevy," and that is the spelling I have used as well. However, when McGreevy donated his collection of artifacts and papers to the Boston Public Library, it was called at the time and continues to be identified as the "McGreevey Collection." Both spellings are found in contemporary accounts.

Several players who factor into the story of the 1897 season had names that might be confusingly similar to fans not familiar with nineteenth-century baseball. What follows is intended as a reference for those readers. None of the following persons are thought to have been related to one another:

Bill Clark was a first baseman for the New York Giants.

Fred Clarke, a future Hall of Famer, was player-manager of the Louisville Colonels.

William "Boileryard" Clarke was a catcher for the Baltimore Orioles.

Willie "Dad" Clarke was a pitcher for the New York Giants.

Fielder Jones was really named Fielder Jones.

Joe Kelley was an outfielder for the Baltimore Orioles.

Kick Kelly was an umpire.

John O'Brien was a second baseman for the Washington Senators.

Tim O'Brien was a utility infielder for the Baltimore Orioles.

Heinie Peitz was a catcher for the Cincinnati Reds.

Heinie Reitz was a second baseman for the Baltimore Orioles.

Jim Sullivan was a lightly used pitcher for the Boston Beaneaters.

Mike Sullivan was a lightly used pitcher for the New York Giants.

Bill Wilson was a catcher for the Louisville Colonels.

Parke Wilson was a catcher for the New York Giants.

Introduction

This is a story about good and evil, right and wrong, heroes and villains—or at least people's perceptions of them. It also touches on religion, racism, chicanery, rationalization, idealism, greed, mad genius, boosterism, and hooliganism, with a brief detour into murder.

Or, if you prefer, it's about a danged good pennant race.

The fight for the 1897 National League championship says a lot about our cultural values at the turn of the century. Baseball is often that way. In the 1890s Andrew Freedman's maniacal effort to run New York's franchise—and by extension the entire National League—as a Tammany Hall fiefdom mirrored attitudes in the broader business world. By his more or less constant battles with umpires and other players, John McGraw personified the fears of the age's nativists. On the field, winning was everything.

While the issues are different today, the themes recur. In his imperial approach, Freedman could manage any of a half-dozen franchises seeking public funds for construction of a new ballpark and threatening drastic steps if their demands are not honored. John McGraw has morphed into Barry Bonds, defying or simply disdaining common understandings of fair play in the pursuit of on-field excellence. The Boston team continues to fight the Evil Empire, occasionally gaining the upper hand.

Debates regarding the ethics that apply to the pursuit of "victory" are confined neither to baseball nor to sports in general; they enliven politics, business, and probably most other modern endeavors involving humans. The names and settings may have changed since 1897, but the core question remains. What can you do in the name of victory?

In 1897 that question crystallized around baseball because baseball was one of the few activities that bound an otherwise disparate and distant nation. As a commonality of urban life, it cut to the core of the process of assimilation into American society. But merely learning baseball, of course, was not good enough. Acceptance came through winning. Winning in turn—under the rules by which the game was played—made tacit allowances for fighting, cussing, cheating, and rowdyism.

Simply put, the ballpark was a pretty nasty place.

John Morrill knew a lot about ballpark atmospherics. By 1897 the forty-two-year-old sportswriter for the *Boston Morning Journal* had invested half his life in the game. An infielder for fourteen seasons, most of them in Boston, he played on three championship clubs. He took that resume to Boston's Newspaper Row, where over the next seven years he became one of the most respected voices concerning the status and conduct of the evolving game. When John Morrill said baseball was in good shape, fans believed him. And when he said it was not, fans believed that as well.

By August of 1897, this was what John Morrill was saying: "The game of baseball will not long continue if this kind of work continues. . . . I don't want to see baseball lose its popularity. It is the only sport on earth played by professionals that is generally looked upon as being on the square, and I hope to see the time when all the petty points will have ceased." He was not alone in this concern; you could hear the same refrain from Lewis Meacham and Hughie Fullerton in Chicago, from Joe Vila in New York, and from Ren Mulford in Cincinnati. Although the problem was widespread, any proper fan—certainly any proper Boston fan—knew the location of the deepest, rankest decay.

It was the home field of the hated three-time champions—the dirtiest, cheatingest, most conniving team ever put together, the Baltimore Orioles.

In the eyes of Morrill and many in the sporting world, Oriole baseball corrupted the game, legitimized underhanded tactics, and compromised virtue in the Machiavellian pursuit of victory. Given baseball's prominence as the only major sport, many even remotely familiar with it believed that corruption on the ball field, left unchecked, must inevitably dilute the public ethic as well.

Nowhere, perhaps, was the feeling more strongly held than in Boston, whose own club's domination of the league ended with Baltimore's ascension. By 1897 the interest in Boston's ball field heroes—widely viewed as clean by contemporary standards—coalesced around a loyal and dedicated collection of regular "Rooters." That coalition marked the birth of the organized fan movement we see everywhere in the United States today, and it rose with a purpose. That purpose was to cheer the restoration of the game's proper order and ethic. The "Royal Rooters," as they came to be called, rose as a direct challenge to the organized malevolent atmosphere, both among players and fans, at Baltimore's Union Park, where the championship banners of 1894, 1895, and 1896 all flew.

As far as the Rooters were concerned, what the Orioles needed was what bullies often need: a good thrashing. As is often true in sports and in life, the problem was how to give it to them.

A Game of Brawl

1. Baseball's Original Evil Empire

John McGraw took his accustomed position near the entrance to the Diamond Café, greeting each entrant warmly. McGraw was a novice businessman, but he had the sense to recognize the value of a paying customer. So ever since the day earlier that year that they had opened the combination restaurant, bar, and sports parlor, he and co-owner Wilbert Robinson made this their practice: Be friendly. Be happy. Make the patrons feel welcome. Let them enjoy spending money.

At the Diamond Café, McGraw and Robinson offered plenty of opportunities to spend money in a leisurely setting. The bar was one of the longest and finest in Baltimore. The dining room, which featured exquisite oak décor, spared little expense in catering to those who planned an evening at the theater next door. The menu was pure Wilbert: plenty of hearty meat-and-potatoes dishes.[1]

Those envisioning something a bit more active could test their skill on one of the bowling alleys, each equipped with the latest ball-returning device. Upstairs, billiard tables hosted polite gaming—McGraw's favorite pastime. He and Robinson kept a nearby reading room stocked with the most recent copies of the *Sporting News*, *Sporting Life*, and other sports-related periodicals. A gymnasium and workout area on the third floor allowed for more vigorous pursuits.

It was, if McGraw said so himself, one of the finest entertainment palaces in downtown Baltimore. And it should have been; together, he

Fig. 1. Ned Hanlon, brainy manager of the widely reviled Baltimore Orioles. (Transcendental Graphics, Boulder co.)

and Robinson had sunk ten thousand dollars into it, about two years' salary for each of them. Had the Diamond Café failed, they would have been ruined.[2]

To the contrary, the café proved to be one of the most popular spots in town, especially among the sporting set. Within two years of opening the café, McGraw would report making five times more money at the Diamond than he had on the ball field. But why shouldn't the Diamond be a hit? Where else could you enjoy a drink, a fine meal, pleasant surroundings, and the company of two of the most renowned and affable athletes in all of America?

To the patrons who filled the place, the fact that McGraw would show up, greet the crowd, and make them feel at home—on this night of all nights—demonstrated the kind of regular fellow he was. Off the field, McGraw had the reputation of a consummate gentleman. On the field,

Fig. 2. Four future Hall of Famers who comprised the heart and soul of the Baltimore Orioles. *Back*: Willie Keeler and John McGraw. *Front*: Joe Kelley and Hughie Jennings. (McGreevey Collection, Boston Public Library, Print Department.)

the same McGraw was widely judged by those outside Baltimore to be a blackguard. Orioles fans had been endeared to him—and to the entire team—by that trait. That and their penchant for winning. As they had for three successive seasons, the Orioles took the field in September 1897 with one thing and one thing only in mind, and it had nothing to do with pleasantries. Like McGraw, they would show their visitors from Boston a good time this weekend at the Diamond Café. On the Union Park diamond, however, war was afoot.

The Orioles' cutthroat style of ball was comfortable to Baltimoreans. That was natural enough; the history of the city was a rough and often contrarian one. In an otherwise Protestant country, Baltimore and Maryland traced their heritage to John Carroll, who founded the colony as a haven for immigrant Catholics. Baltimore had been—and largely remained—southern by culture. It was in Baltimore in 1861 that the first blood of the Civil War was spilled when Southern sympathizers attacked a Massachusetts troop en route to defend the nation's capital. Since then, Baltimore had struggled to establish its own refinements. After the war's end, whites from the ravaged areas of the Confederacy joined freed slaves in coming to Baltimore. The whites were trying to recoup lost fortunes, while the freed slaves were trying to establish working identities as day laborers. Immigrants poured in as well.[3]

Baseball as She Is Played

The city braved the realities of an 1890s America that was often far less "gay" than the surviving phraseology might suggest. Malaria, diphtheria, diarrhea, and consumption were constant threats, especially in Baltimore, a growing city of a half-million people that was the nation's sixth largest. McGraw himself had beaten back a malaria attack—barely, his doctors believed—in 1895.[4] The 1890 U.S. Census described some of the reasons why those diseases were feared, noting the absence of any type of municipal septic system. "House wastes are carried into large cesspools," it reported, "while the water from the kitchen and butler's pantry pours into the gutters." There it mixed with the manifest droppings from the city's population of horses, still the preponderance of the transport system. Fortunately, the report noted, "owing to the large amount of cobblestone pavement . . . nearly all of this matter percolates into the soil."[5]

Baltimore was a bustling, burgeoning city that loved the rough game the Orioles had mastered—"baseball as she is played," their manager, Ned Hanlon, called it.[6] The cutthroat tactics that had made the Orioles hated everywhere else in the league did not originate with them. For more than a decade, big leaguers schemed, cussed, and maneuvered in search of an edge. Under Hanlon, Baltimore players simply schemed, cussed, and maneuvered more frequently, more aggressively, and better. That especially applied to arguments, or "kicking," as the fans called it. Attempting to browbeat umpires, McGraw told the *Sporting News*, was not only acceptable, it was essential to a team's success. Before his marriage that spring, and even occasionally afterward, he and his teammates would spend evenings in rooming houses or hotel rooms conjuring new and more effective strategies, many of which incorporated some element of intimidation. Winning teams, he believed, always had "good kickers"—that is, players who could browbeat umpires into changing calls—just as they had good bunters or good base stealers. By keeping the umpires alert, he contended, "an artful kicker could gain his ballclub as many as 50 additional runs a season."[7]

Orioles fans believed in McGraw, Robinson, Willie Keeler, Joe Kelley, and all the rest. They especially believed in Hanlon, the mustachioed thirty-seven-year-old former center fielder who had assembled the team. You had to give Harry Von der Horst, the well-known local brewer and team owner, credit for seeing in Hanlon the leadership qualities that nobody else recognized. As a player, Hanlon had been merely capable: a .260 career batting average over thirteen seasons, topping out at .302 in 1885. He played center field and led off for the champion Detroit Wolverines of 1887, stealing sixty-nine bases. But that pennant had less to do with Hanlon than with his intimidating teammates, sluggers Dan Brouthers (.338) and Big Sam Thompson (.372).

A leg injury that reduced Hanlon's value as a player made him obtainable as a manager in 1892. He was earning a salary of five thousand dollars when he fell early in the season and severely strained a tendon. When the Pittsburg Pirates looked at him thereafter, they saw a highly paid center fielder with a gimpy leg. When Von der Horst interviewed Hanlon, he saw something else: a serious professional who had always made the most of his talent. Hanlon was by no means an imposing fellow. At less than five feet ten inches tall and 170 pounds, he looked less like an athlete than a businessman. He said little and thought about what he said before saying it. But what he lacked in physical talent and personality he had made up for in drive and intellect. Hanlon had acquired a reputation as a brainy center fielder, one who could scheme his way through a ballgame. He had developed the habit of mentally cataloging every opponent's strength and weakness. From the cut of his suit to the wax in his immaculately trimmed handlebar mustache, from his positioning in the field to the way he cut first base to stretch a double, he was precise. That, Von der Horst decided, would be a valuable leadership quality.[8] Thus, in May of 1892, Ned Hanlon came to Baltimore . . . to command one of the worst aggregations of talent that had ever taken the field.

The Orioles, in fact, were fortunate even to be able to take the field. As members of the American Association (the other major league) during the 1880s, they had never finished in contention, much less won a pennant. The so-called Brotherhood War of 1890—a labor-management dispute that presaged those of recent vintage—had hurt them as much as every other American Association (and National League) team. In 1891 their Union Park grounds rarely hosted any crowd approaching its capacity of eight thousand, and the Orioles finished twenty-two games out of first place. Nevertheless, when the American Association collapsed and the National League agreed to swallow four of its teams for the 1892 season, Baltimore was one of the four. The wreck of a lineup Hanlon inherited won just forty-six games all season, finished fifty-four games behind the champion Boston Beaneaters, and became only the second team in the history of the National League to lose one hundred times.

The Master Tradesman

McGraw never doubted much about himself, but he must have wondered how he survived what Hanlon did to the Orioles between his hiring and the following spring. Oh, McGraw's batting had been all right, he supposed; a .279 average didn't embarrass him. But his work on the field was another matter. For starters, he had no position; Hanlon used him at second base more often than anywhere, but he also frequently played right field and occasionally played short, third, left, or center. It wasn't that the cocky nineteen-year-old was versatile. Hanlon simply wanted to find the place where McGraw would do the least damage.[9] Even at a time when gloves were rudimentary, if they existed at all, his .897 fielding average was horrible. Bobby Lowe, second baseman of the Boston champions, had fielded .928, and Cincinnati's Bid McPhee, generally acclaimed as the game's best at that position, fielded .948.

Yet when Hanlon finished his makeover of the Orioles roster for 1893, McGraw was one of only four returnees (Wilbert Robinson, third baseman Billy Shindle, and pitcher Sadie McMahon being the others). Even better, when McGraw reported to training camp that spring, he saw two things he had not seen in the Orioles previously: talent and hustle. If the Orioles had a star in 1892, it was George VanHaltren, a twenty-six-year-old from St. Louis with a mustache even more full than Hanlon's own and the speed to run down anything a human could catch in center field. But Hanlon judged that VanHaltren lacked the competitiveness he saw as an essential quality. So in September, with VanHaltren on his way to surpassing .300 for the fourth straight season, Hanlon was willing to listen when the Pirates called about a trade.

In addition to the asking price of two thousand dollars for VanHaltren, Hanlon wanted Joe Kelley, a twenty-year-old rookie. Other than Hanlon, no man in the game saw anything in Kelley, who came to the Orioles with a .239 batting average in part-time duty. Hanlon had not managed Kelley in Pittsburg—the kid didn't arrive until Hanlon had left Pittsburg for Baltimore—but he'd seen the reports. "I've had my eye on him for a long time," he told the *Baltimore Sun*'s baseball writer when the transaction was sealed.[10] The outfielder fit the mold Hanlon himself had set, which would become the hallmark of his acquisitions. Kelley was young, smallish, extremely fast, intelligent, and daring, and had a baby face that served two purposes—it made him attractive to women, and it fully masked the intensity of his drive to succeed. It was a description that would be applied to a host of arrivals—Willie Keeler, Hughie Jennings, and Jack Doyle included—and certainly to McGraw as well.

In Hanlon's mind, Kelley filled the gap left by VanHaltren's departure. But there were plenty of other problems. On a gamble, he took a friend's tip and invited a kid named Heinie Reitz to training camp. Reitz had started in semipro ball with his hometown team, the Chicago Whitings, in 1889, and he had worked his way through one minor-league stop after another until being spotted by Hanlon's friend in California in 1892. At twenty-five, Reitz was older than Hanlon's ideal, but he possessed most of the other attributes, including quick hands, a prime asset at second base. He made the team.

When Louisville came to Union Park for an otherwise uneventful early season series between also-rans, Hanlon made time to explore one or two personnel moves. The Colonels held the contract to a first baseman they had been trying to unload all spring. Harry Taylor, who had not played since the season started, was demanding a trade to an eastern team to be closer to his New York home. In exchange, they asked Hanlon for outfielder Tim O'Rourke. Hanlon had no special use for Taylor, but he had no use for O'Rourke either. The trick, then, was to acquire something of true value as a disguised sop for taking Taylor off the Colonels' hands.

The Colonels had such a player. He was young, smallish, daring, handsome (in a red-headed sort of way), fast, and intelligent. The player, shortstop Hughie Jennings, couldn't hit a lick; a career .230 hitter, he was batting only .136 when the Colonels came to Baltimore. From Louisville's perspective, Jennings was an easy throw-in.

Hanlon may not have realized it—nobody else did—but within a couple of months he had obtained—in second baseman Reitz, shortstop Jennings, and center fielder Kelley—the defensive backbone of a championship team. Even better, he had done so at no significant cost.[11]

Of the three, Reitz proved the most game-ready. Stepping into the middle of the infield at season's start, he hit .286 and fielded well. It was said that Hanlon himself worked almost daily to improve Kelley's batting stroke. From .244 as a rookie and .235 in 1892, Kelley raised his average day by day to finish at .305 in 1893, driving in seventy-six runs while showing grace in center. Jennings took longer, in part due to an illness that he contracted almost immediately after the trade and that sidelined him for two months.

Brothers in a Cause

In some respects the friendship that developed between McGraw and Jennings did not make sense. Both had fiery personalities, and they were essentially competing for the same position. Having flunked tests at second base and in right field during the previous season, but with too many offensive skills to sit down, McGraw had been handed the shortstop position for 1893. The results were no different from 1892: a .321 batting average offset by a fielding average in the .890s. Even Mc-Graw could see that Jennings was obtained to challenge him for his job. Yet the commonalities—their Irish background, their determination, their aggressiveness, their youth, and their size—created something of a musketeers' bond. Malcolm Bingay, a Detroit sports reporter when Jennings managed there, described Jennings in terms that could have been applied to McGraw's temperament as well: "a red-headed Irish-man who would fight at the drop of a hat."[12] Like McGraw, Jennings was pleasant off the field, to the point that he was sometimes described as saintly. He regularly attended church and was known as an affable dinner companion and a deferential cardplayer. Why such a cutthroat approach on the ball field? "Baseball is different," he explained once. "In professional baseball, one must concede nothing."[13]

The two men boarded together at home and roomed together on the road, strategizing away most of their free time. McGraw adopted Jennings as his assistant in the off-season job he had taken coaching the baseball team at St. Bonaventure College in upstate New York. There they worked hour after hour on the flaws in Jennings's technique, especially his tendency to pull away from tight pitches. In the 1890s pitchers threw plenty of high and tight fastballs, and the player who bailed was doomed. It was said that McGraw taught his teammate to overcome the tendency by standing him against a basement wall and firing fastballs in on his hands. McGraw might get more credit than he actually deserves for Jennings's improvement. The mere change of atmosphere from Louisville to Baltimore had done a lot to add vigor to Jennings's bat. After the trade, he had hit .255 for his new team. But there is little question about McGraw's contribution to improving Jennings's nerve. Hughie led the league in being hit by pitches in five consecutive seasons during the mid-1890s.

Perhaps McGraw did not view Jennings as a threat because he anticipated that he would be moving to third base for the 1894 season. If so, he knew something that Hanlon hadn't finalized yet. In fact, the Orioles manager came close that winter to trading McGraw to Washington in a deal that fell through only because the Orioles wanted both a player and cash in exchange; the Senators insisted on a straight player-for-player swap.

Instead, Hanlon traded Shindle in one of the most one-sided trades ever completed. The two players Hanlon acquired cemented the lineup that would dominate the league through the mid-1890s and dictate the game's new style as well.

The initial offer, to Brooklyn's Charley Byrne, was simple: Hanlon would give the team known then as the Bridegrooms (because so many of their players had recently married) George Treadway, a competent outfielder with a strong arm, in exchange for Dan Brouthers, the aging slugger from Hanlon's Detroit days. Seven years earlier, Brouthers had been the most feared batter in the game, posting averages well up in the .300s and driving across more than one hundred runs. Approaching his thirty-sixth birthday, he was still a threat and he could play first base capably. But Byrne needed a third baseman as well, so he asked for Shindle. Hanlon agreed but wanted a throw-in. Nothing much, just an undersized kid with less than forty games of experience. The Bridegrooms had picked him up the previous summer from the New York Giants, who, like everybody else in baseball, thought him too small. Who ever heard of a five feet four, 140-pound regular, anyway?

So to ensure Shindle's presence in the deal, Brooklyn agreed to Hanlon's request that they toss in William Henry Keeler.[14] Thus was third base opened for McGraw; and thus were the essential components of the Orioles' combustible assemblage completed.

It did not initially combust. These new Orioles were green. Other than Brouthers and Robinson, the starting lineup—McGraw, Jennings, Reitz, Keeler, Kelley, and left fielder Steve Brodie—averaged less than two seasons of big league experience. Then there was the matter of age and bulk. They looked like an undersized and undernourished high school team. Again, with the exception of Robinson and the six feet two, 210-pound Brouthers, the average profile of the team amounted to a five feet eight, 162-pound twenty-three-year-old.

So Hanlon worked them. The Orioles trained that spring in Macon, Georgia, developing a routine that was virtually round-the-clock. In the mornings, they ran to the field, where they drilled on individual weaknesses. The drills included base running, a skill at which Hanlon remained better than almost all of them. Tirelessly, he schooled them on reading outfielders—their arms and their body positions—until each knew when an opponent could and could not get to a ball and when a throw to third could and could not be made. It was repetitious and exacting. But the Orioles, who wanted to win, bought into it.[15]

They drilled on hitting, especially place hitting and the hit and run. Today some historians believe that the Orioles invented the hit and run that spring, although the evidence indicates that Hanlon borrowed it from his playing days of a decade earlier and that Baltimore merely refined and perfected the tactic. Neither McGraw nor, as it turned out, Keeler needed much urging to work long hours, especially when they could see the benefit. What McGraw, the lead-off hitter, soon found was that if he could get on base, Keeler could find virtually any hole in the infield created by McGraw's movement toward second.

They drilled on bunt placement to the point where it was said that McGraw could draw a ten-foot circle midway between home and third and stop the bunt within it. In those days, a foul ball wasn't counted as a strike unless the umpire determined that it was fouled deliberately,

so the Orioles practiced "inadvertently" fouling the ball. They practiced slapping the ball into the dirt directly in front of home plate, then
racing to first before it could be fielded; the stroke became known as
the "Baltimore chop." When the Orioles executed properly, their offense became close to impossible to stop.

The Cerebral Game

But it wasn't just their offense and it wasn't just their practice during
the daylight that made them such formidable opponents. Evening after
evening the players congregated in Hanlon's room for what later might
have been viewed as "chalk talks." The topic was winning strategies—a
broad subject with a specific meaning that we can only guess at. We do
know this: Years later McGraw would say that Hanlon did "masterful
work in building up a team," although others said that McGraw was as
forceful and outspoken a contributor as any on those evenings.

The 1894 Orioles are believed to have been the first team to consistently use the pitcher to take the throw at first on ground balls hit
down the first base line, a strategy that probably grew out of those
bedroom sessions. They also polished first-and-third double steal de-
fenses. Among their variations—some still in use today—were an apparent throw to second base that actually went to the mound, a hard
fake throw to second followed by a toss to third, and a full throw cut
off by Jennings in front of second and quickly returned to Robinson
at the plate.

Perhaps with Hanlon's blessing, possibly behind his back, they perfected other strategies too. They schooled one another on how to run
while keeping one eye on the game's only umpire. If the ump wasn't
watching, they practiced all manner of larcenies with the artistry of
pickpockets. Players had cut bases virtually since the National League's
inception, but the Orioles made it their calling card. The outfielders—
Kelley, Brodie, and Keeler—became deft at knowing where they could
hide spare baseballs in the tall outfield grass and when they could retrieve them to cut a triple to a double or a double to a single. The in-

field—especially Reitz, Jennings, and McGraw—virtually choreographed their abuse of base runners with a retinue that included hip checks, held belts, and if the opportunity warranted it, an outright fist. They did not need to practice the language they used to upbraid an umpire whose calls went against them; that came naturally.

Teams played far fewer actual games during those springs, but the Orioles got the chance to practice their craft against local and minor-league clubs. The results often made them notorious. Following a game against New Orleans, a local newspaper described McGraw this way: "A rough, unruly man who is constantly playing dirty ball. He has the vilest tongue of any ball-player . . . has demonstrated his low training . . . adopts every low and contemptible method that his erratic brain can conceive to win a play by a dirty trick."[16]

The Power of a Glare

Now and then, being assaulted by the fans was an even greater danger than being assaulted by the press. Locals, after all, had little use for big-city folks trying to hoodwink them . . . or their baseball team. The Orioles knew this from intimate experience. During an 1896 exhibition in Petersburg, Virginia, Jennings got into a fight with a local player, causing much of the crowd to come onto the field. When that happened, even the toughest players fled. The Orioles tried to escape, but the crowd roughed up both Keeler and first baseman Jack Doyle before they could get away. Even the anticipated safety of the hotel proved illusory; a mob found the team there, stormed in, renewed the fight, and essentially ransacked the place. It took a police escort to get the two-time defending champions to the railroad station and onto a train.[17]

Nor were the Orioles immune to feuding with each other. The oft-told story of a scrap between McGraw and Keeler during the 1897 season illustrates how combative life could be. Supposedly, McGraw cursed Keeler's failure to make a play that McGraw felt had cost Baltimore a game. "What did you mean by cursing me like that today?" Keeler asked, as they headed toward the shower. "Play ball," McGraw sharply responded. Keeler jumped him, and the two players—both naked— fought it out on the dressing room floor.[18]

Day after day, week after week, there was no letup in Macon that spring of 1894. Only three breaches of the baseball immersion were tolerated: meals, sleep, and Sunday morning church.

Their preparation extended beyond Macon and back to Baltimore. McGraw and Jennings took up residence in a boardinghouse a block from the field. "We talked, lived and dreamed baseball," McGraw would later declare of those days.[19] They had developed the habit of arriving on the morning of games and walking the third base and shortstop areas to look for pebbles and lumps. They coached the groundskeeper, Thomas Murphy, on how to contour the foul lines to make them more favorable for bunting and on hardening the dirt around home plate to make the Baltimore chop a more effective weapon. By a few weeks after opening day of the 1894 season, that area was as firmly packed as if cement had been poured atop it. Murphy didn't stop there. With the team's foot speed in mind, he applied a slight downward slant to the first base line. It was said that he laced particular areas around the mound with soap flakes, much to the irritation of visiting pitchers trying to wipe sweat from their faces or hands. The Orioles pitchers knew to avoid those spots.

McGraw's skill at fouling off pitches gave him expert status. With his hands placed six inches apart on the bat, and using a chopping swing, he left pitchers little opportunity to throw the ball past him. During his team's three-year championship run, McGraw struck out only twenty-five times, or once in every forty-six trips to the plate. To defend against the prospect of his fouls being called strikes, he also worked on his intimidation. Keeler swore that one of McGraw's most effective plays was simply to lean on his bat and grin malevolently in the umpire's face at the suggestion of a foul strike. If that failed, Keeler added, McGraw would crowd the plate even more and let himself get hit by a pitch.

The cumulative result was a savvy, nervy, brash ball club that played a style of ball never seen before. By the start of the 1894 season, even Keeler and Jennings were hitting. By mid-June of that year, Kelley stood third in the league in batting with an average exceeding .390, and Keeler was fifth at .372. Winning games at nearly a .700 pace, the Orioles were well on their way to the first pennant in the city's history, a pennant they would eventually claim by three games over the favored New York Giants.

Ladies and Gentlemen, Beware

Both Baltimore's success and its ungentlemanly methods garnered widespread attention, much of it unfavorable.

"Good, clean gentlemanly ball playing is what everybody wants, and they will eventually obtain it," offered the *Sporting News*, which urged the league to "weed out the most brilliant players in the leading leagues in the country to get it." The paper lamented instances that year in which players "purposely interfered or attempted by means of one dirty trick or another to balk their opponents, thereby causing a misplay. This kind of work must stop."[20]

One of the best-known baseball reporters of the age was Tim Murnane, a correspondent for the *Boston Globe*. A National Leaguer himself during its first three seasons, Murnane was an early version of the expert analyst who is viewed as an indispensable contributor to game coverage today. He accused the Orioles of playing "the dirtiest ball even seen in this country" and of being "ready to maim a fellow player for life." Among the tactics Murnane criticized were "diving into the first baseman long after he has caught the ball, throwing masks in front of runners at home plate, catching by the clothes at third base, and interfering with the catcher."[21]

You could see the Orioles' style reflected in the umpires' reports of player ejections, which were far more common in the mid-1890s than they are today. Up until the final week of that 1897 season, seventy-two players had been ejected for one transgression or another, and nearly

20 percent of them had been Orioles. Kelley went four times, more than any player in the league. There was no clearer indication of the contrast between the playing styles of the Boston and Baltimore clubs than that roster of ejections. For 1897 it contained the names of fourteen Orioles and just two Beaneaters.[22]

Ejecting offenders was just one of the tools applied by league officials in the hope of curbing the worst of the game's excesses. They also tried fines, threats of fines, and forfeits. The principal concern was for the sensitivities of fans, especially women, who might be turned away by the effusion of billingsgate. "These patrons pay to see good, clean and gentlemanly ball," the *Sporting News* argued. "If they did not, they would visit vacant lots where dirty ball is put up to their heart's content."[23] In fact, attendance did decline in some cities; but not in Baltimore, where McGraw and his teammates were attracting record draws. From 143,000 in the 1893 season, attendance more than doubled to 328,000 in 1894. Winning always sells.

In addition, the Orioles seemed to know when to draw a line in terms of bending the rules. The mid-1890s were far and away the high water mark in the history of the game for forfeitures. In 1897 alone, umpires declared eight of them. For the four-year period of the Orioles' ascendancy (1894–97), twenty-six forfeits were declared throughout the league, easily the largest number for any four-season period in the history of the game. Yet not a single one of those forfeits was declared against the Orioles.[24]

How to Leave Town on Short Notice

The problem of rowdiness was not restricted to Baltimore. Other teams, envious of the Orioles' success, tried to copy their methods, and the reputations of the Cleveland, Pittsburg, and Cincinnati teams were as bad or (in the case of Cleveland) worse than that of the Orioles. If any team could give Baltimore a run, both on the field and with their fists, it was Patsy Tebeau's Cleveland Spiders, who finished second to Baltimore in both 1895 and 1896. Tebeau himself was an average ballplayer, but his reputation as a ruffian was exceeded by none. An incident at the conclusion of an August 8, 1894, game in Pittsburg between the Spiders and the Pirates illustrated the problems of "Tebeauism." As the game entered the ninth inning, the outcome was certain. Pittsburg led 10–3 and the only question, as far as the Spiders were concerned, was whether they would make their train out of town. Tebeau's solution: Take an inning off the game by forcing a forfeit. And he knew how. He began hurling a string of epithets at umpire Willard Hoagland, virtually daring him to either fine or eject him.

Although it is not clear what he would have accomplished by doing so, Tebeau believed he could "run" Hoagland, who had taken the umpiring job barely two weeks before, replacing a predecessor who had quit in disgust. What Tebeau did not know was Hoagland's background: it was in pugilism. Although never championship material, he had built a reputation for being hard-nosed, both physically and mentally. Instead of yielding, Hoagland ordered Tebeau back to the Cleveland bench, a demand Tebeau ignored. From there the incident simply got out of control. Hoagland issued a twenty-five-dollar fine, prompting Tebeau to tear the umpire's mask from his face, drawing another fine. As the confrontation turned into bedlam, Cleveland's Chief Zimmer, who was on third, saw a chance to steal home while nobody was looking. The Pirates tried to make a play on the runner, but Tebeau regained his composure quickly enough to order batter Jack O'Connor to intercept the throw and heave the ball over the grandstand, which is exactly what O'Connor did. Hoagland issued another twenty-five-dollar fine to Tebeau, gave one to O'Connor as well, and declared Zimmer out for interference, ending the game. Remarked the *Sporting News*, "Many ladies were driven from the stand by the vile language of Tebeau and O'Connor."

Even that did not end the matter. Now enraged, and forgetting that his goal had been to get to the train station on time, Tebeau challenged Hoagland to go under the stands for some postgame fisticuffs. Given Hoagland's background, it is no surprise that the umpire readily accepted the offer. Tebeau got there first and, according to newspaper accounts, was waiting for the arbiter with a baseball bat. But when Hoagland arrived, it was with a willing gang of enraged Pittsburg fans who took off after Tebeau. Hometown newspaper accounts of the day are notorious for gilding their descriptions, but if the mob even approached the published estimates of one thousand, Tebeau had good reason to flee for the team bus. Against such numbers, even that vehicle afforded little safety—and even less when the Pittsburg fans began to stone it. They followed it all the way to the station, hurling melons and other fruit when they ran out of stones.[25]

Hoagland, by the way, lasted two more weeks before he too quit in disgust. The ex-prizefighter's entire major-league umpiring career consisted of fewer than thirty games.

If the atmosphere in Pittsburg is recalled today as being less notorious than Baltimore or Cleveland, it is only because the Pirates were less successful on the field and therefore less visible. During another game that season between the Pirates and the St. Louis Browns, Browns third baseman Doggie Miller accused several Pirate base runners of taking repeated shots at him with their fists and spikes. A correspondent traveling with the Pirates dismissed that allegation as absurd, using what amounted to an "everybody does it" defense. "The Pittsburg team is like all others," the correspondent contended. "They will resort to tricks to win games, but I have never seen them use any but legitimate ones."[26]

League officials who attempted to clean up the game for fans often had to deal with one additional problem: the fans themselves. It is easy to understand how, in an atmosphere rife with gutter language and on-field brawling, a gathering of five thousand could get caught up in the mayhem. Part of the problem was that the nineteenth-century settings were conducive to fan involvement. Even the largest of ballparks, such as Boston's South End Grounds, seated barely more than ten thousand. That is about the size of a typical spring training field today. Surviving images of Baltimore's Union Park show a double-decked grandstand that was only twelve to fifteen rows deep, putting almost all the spectators, including women and children, within easy earshot of the action. Inevitably, as players verbally assaulted umpires, the level of decorum around the stadium declined, with fans feeling freer and freer to join in the conversation. If the umpire would not tell those visiting hooligans off, the fans darned well would. As a consequence, either of their own volition or because they were egged on by the home players, the crowd from time to time could itself become a large part of the problem.

That was the case in 1894 during a mid-July game in Philadelphia involving Boston's defending champions. "The most disgraceful scene witnessed on ball grounds in this city," a correspondent called it.[27] The first seven innings had proceeded relatively uneventfully, with Boston holding a 2–1 advantage. In those days the home team was allowed to decide whether it wanted to bat first or last, and the Phillies frequently chose to bat first. At a time when baseballs were not removed from the game until they were lost or substantially damaged, the goal was to get the earliest and best licks at the hardest ball. In the top of the eighth, as clouds gathered and rain threatened, the Phillies mounted a rally. And what a rally it was. Philadelphia scored seven times, distancing themselves so far from the visitors that Boston realized its only chance was to stall for rain. The Beaneaters knew that if rain halted the game before they came to bat in the eighth inning, the Philadelphia rally would be erased and the game would revert to its score at the end of seven innings, a Boston victory.

What ensued was one of the most farcical scenes imaginable, a circumstance that would be actionable today but that was viewed as legitimate gamesmanship then. The visitors simply refused to field the ball and record further outs. When a ball was hit their way, players avoided it. In time, the umpire warned Boston captain Billy Nash of the possibility of a forfeit, but to no avail. Then the Phillies players reciprocated, deliberately running out of base lines and batting out of turn in the hope that the umpire would call them out. Finally, the game was forfeited to the Phillies.

That may have satisfied the Philadelphia players, but it infuriated their fans, who stormed the field in what amounted to an assault on the Beaneaters. Most of the visitors had the good sense to race to the relative protection of their horse-drawn coach, but Tommy Tucker was caught lingering. "The crowd, which had surged onto the field, gathered about him," a witness reported. "A man jostled Tucker. This was the signal for a riot. Someone in the mob struck Tucker on the left cheek, breaking the bone." Several Philadelphia players tried to inject themselves between the fans and Tucker to prevent further injury.

The fans were not through. As the coach drove down Broad Street toward the train station, a mob of some one thousand men and boys followed it, hooting and jeering. Philadelphia officials were unapologetic for the fans' behavior. At the station, Phillies owner John Rogers upbraided Nash, telling the player, "The Boston team has brought this upon themselves. The Philadelphians will not stand dirty ball playing." The crowd, Rogers warned Nash, was "worked up to fever pitch by the unsportsmanlike tactics of your own players."[28]

McGraw read accounts such as those with a smile. To him it was good baseball . . . and common as well. Charles Alexander, in his biography of McGraw, summarizes the attitude that had been in place for years, which the Orioles had merely brought to a tuned pitch in 1894: "With only one umpire responsible for watching everything that happened on the field, it was accepted behavior for runners to cut inside bases without touching them, for basemen to block, trip and hold runners, and above all for players to assault and revile the umpire with impunity.

"In simplest terms, umpires were [McGraw's] natural enemies, men to be tricked, bluffed, brow-beaten, intimidated any way possible."[29]

Captain Wilbert and Dirty Jack

Before the 1897 season the league reacted to these ongoing discipline problems by imposing new rules that it hoped would curb the worst abuses. One such rule permitted only the team captain to confer with an umpire during a dispute. Other players were required to stand at least ten feet away. The league also limited teams to one coach on the field and banned that coach from bench jockeying, which was viewed as a chief source of fan incitement. These new rules were enforced with great latitude.

Of all the Orioles, the one who never seemed to fit in was the most senior, catcher Wilbert Robinson. When the American Association's Philadelphia Athletics sold him and Sadie McMahon to the Orioles in 1890, he was already a veteran of four seasons. Easygoing by nature, he lacked the external fire so apparent in McGraw, Jennings, and Kelley. He alone among the Orioles appeared to enjoy playing baseball. He lacked virtually any of the physical attributes common to the players Hanlon had acquired. By 1894 he had already turned thirty and topped two hundred pounds; he lacked any foot speed to speak of and had made no particular mark as a strategist. As if that was not enough, he had been married for several years—at that stage, McGraw, Keeler, and Jennings all remained single—and he was an Episcopalian on a club dominated by Irish Catholics.

Yet in his easygoing way, Robinson had proven to Hanlon that he could become one of the most reliable catchers in the game. A consistent .240s batter entering the 1893 season, he strung together consecutive averages of .334 and .353 in 1894 and 1895. True, changes in the pitching rules helped Wilbert just as they helped other hitters. Before the 1893 season, the pitching distance had been increased from fifty feet to sixty feet and six inches. The league responded by raising its collective average from .245 to .280. But the thirty-five percentage point increase accounted for only a fraction of Robinson's sixty-seven point improvement.

With McGraw and Brouthers lending maturity to the otherwise young and volatile team, all the Orioles needed was a reliable pitching staff. In this area and this alone, Hanlon had never succeeded—at least, never in the context of developing one of the game's great mound stars. They all worked in other cities: Cy Young in Cleveland, Kid Nichols in

Boston, Amos Rusie in New York, Clark Griffith in Chicago. Hanlon's answers to these greats came and went almost annually. The two who had come closest to fitting the description of an ace had been inconsistent. McMahon arrived with Robinson from Philadelphia in 1890, having won forty-three games in less than two seasons there, and he won twenty-five of thirty-three decisions for the 1894 champions. But a shoulder injury limited him to only fifteen games in 1895, and he was basically a .500 pitcher through 1896 when Hanlon released him. McMahon's departure left Bill Hoffer, a slender right-hander out of the Eastern League who was signed following the 1894 championship as part of the ongoing pitching search. Hoffer had come into professional ball as an outfielder and didn't even take up pitching until 1891. Once in Baltimore the rookie moved quickly to the top of the rotation, winning thirty-one of thirty-eight starts and presenting a 3.21 earned run average that stood fourth in the league in 1895. He was good for 47 victories the following two years, giving him 78 victories in 106 starts between the start of 1895 and the final week of 1897.

Beyond Hoffer and McMahon, Hanlon scrambled to complete his pitching staff. From St. Louis he acquired journeyman right-hander Bill Hawke early in 1893. Hawke won sixteen games with the 1894 champions in his only decent big-league season. Hanlon got stretches of work out of one-time star Tony Mullane and fill-in Bert Inks, then let both of them go and acquired Kid Gleason, who was off to a 2-6 start with St. Louis. Gleason gave the Orioles fifteen wins in twenty starts. But when Gleason began 1895 by losing four of his first six decisions, he was released and Arthur (Dad) Clarkson was acquired from St. Louis. The far less famous brother of recently retired three-hundred-game-winner John Clarkson, Art Clarkson was 1-6 when he arrived. With the Orioles he won twelve of his fourteen starts.

George Hemming had made a similar turnaround. Picked up from Louisville late in 1894, Hemming had won four Baltimore games to improve his overall record to 17-19. With the Orioles full-time in 1895, he won twenty games for the only time in his career. Hemming returned with fifteen wins in 1896, but by this time Clarkson was essentially through. Literally off the streets of Baltimore walked Erasmus Arlington Pond, a twenty-three-year-old medical student at Johns Hopkins University who as an undergrad had dabbled in pitching at the college level. Pond had no interest in the major leagues as a career, but he was willing to give it a go in his spare time. The result: sixteen victories in twenty-six starts in 1896, and eighteen wins in twenty-eight starts into the final week of 1897.

When McMahon was released before the 1897 season, Hanlon looked to his own roster for a replacement. Two years before, Washington had signed Joe Corbett, the tall, muscular younger brother of heavyweight champion "Gentleman Jim Corbett." The signing appeared to be aimed strictly at building attendance. Corbett pitched mostly in exhibitions, starting only three official games and getting whipped in all three, including his debut at the hands of the Orioles. But Hanlon saw something in Corbett. He signed him for 1896, letting him build experience mostly in the minors and making just eight appearances with the Orioles. Those eight included three complete game victories, enough to justify a fuller chance in 1897. Corbett responded by becoming the ace of the staff, topping twenty victories and working more than three hundred innings. He also beat Boston three times in three tries.

To complete the pitching staff, Hanlon promoted a second 1896 acquisition, left-hander Jerry Nops, who was purchased after making one start for the Phillies. Nops had virtually no professional experience. Like most of his Orioles teammates, Nops did not look like an athlete, standing five feet eight and weighing less than 170 pounds. Despite those handicaps, he had blossomed into a twenty-game winner in his first full season.

With the exception of Hoffer, none of the pitchers had put together as many as two consecutive strong seasons. Yet collectively they had pitched the Orioles to three straight pennants and were poised for a fourth. And the role of these pitchers had hardly been subsidiary. Between 1894 and 1897, Baltimore had consistently been among the league's leaders in fewest runs allowed. (The Orioles had also led the league in fielding during three of the four seasons.) Many looked at Baltimore's batting order and saw a dominant team. That was true, but it was not the entirety of the truth. Through their winning stretch, the Orioles had also been the most balanced club in the National League.

Entering 1896 the team lacked hardly anything, and it certainly did not lack fight. But it was weak at first base. Hanlon had wanted Brouthers for his leadership, but by the time the 1894 pennant had been won, the Orioles were awash with leaders. McGraw, Keeler, Jennings, Kelley, and Robinson—who by then was the team captain—all filled that role. (McGraw would later say of Hanlon that he had the easiest job of all, because if a player did not perform up to expectations, his teammates dealt with him more harshly than the manager ever would have.) Scoops Carey, a rookie, filled in at first for 1895. But Carey lacked the drive to fit comfortably into the Orioles mold. Hanlon found a man who had such fight playing first base for the New York Giants. The player's name was John Joseph Doyle, but everyone knew him by the nickname that epitomized his game: Dirty Jack.

Like many of the Orioles, Doyle was Irish. But he was the real thing, having been born in Kerry County and immigrated to the United States with his parents at age four. In baseball-mad Massachusetts, where the Doyles settled, baseball was what you did to Americanize yourself, and Doyle proved good at it. As a teen he signed his first professional contract with Lynn, Massachusetts, in the New England League in 1888 and then moved to Canton, Ohio, where he became a teammate of the up-and-coming Cy Young. He learned versatility during those early stops, winning a ticket late in 1889 to the American Association's Columbus club, where he played catcher, outfield, second base, shortstop, and third base.

With the American Association teetering in 1891, Doyle signed with Cleveland, where he was schooled by Tebeau and Jesse Burkett in the game's nastier aspects. It was said that nobody could curse in a wider variety of expressions than Dirty Jack, and although the specifics have not been left in written record, his ejections have been. It was nothing for him to be tossed three or four times a season for verbal abuse, fighting, or both. New York team owner Andrew Freedman docked Doyle's pay by $250 just to cover the fines levied against him by the league. But if Doyle could curse, he could also hit. Traded to the New York Giants in the middle of the 1892 season, he had batted .321 in 1893, .368 in 1894, and .313 in 1895. Intrigued by Doyle, the unpredictable Freedman actually let him manage for two months during the 1895 season. When Doyle tired of Freedman's meddling at season's end, the Giants owner accommodated his request to be traded, sending him to the Orioles for Kid Gleason and $1,500.

Although Doyle sounded like a perfect fit for the Orioles lineup, several of his new teammates did not see it that way. Keeler had the best reason of all: money. Doyle had agreed with Keeler before the start of the 1894 Temple Cup postseason series to share winnings on a 50–50 basis, rather than the stipulated 65–35 arrangement. It was a common practice among players on the two teams. But when Doyle's Giants defeated Keeler's Orioles, Dirty Jack welshed on the promise and kept the full winner's share, stiffing Keeler out of about two hundred dollars.[30]

McGraw, Jennings, and Kelley found Doyle irascible, even by Baltimore standards. But they still liked his facility with the bat; Doyle had hit .339 for the 1896 champions, and he was batting .350 coming into the final Boston series. Sure, Doyle had fought it out with most every one of his teammates. But .350 was still .350.

2. The Royal Rooters

As they boarded the train on the evening of September 23, 1897, cries of "On to Baltimore" ringing through Park Square Station, the Boston Rooters had plenty of reasons to look forward to the weekend struggle. They had tickets to the biggest team sporting event in the nation's history. They had rooms at the finest hotel in the host city, meals and transportation included. Those who chose to take it had a side trip tour of the nation's capital led by their congressman. And they had it all for twenty-five dollars a head.

The three games between their beloved "Bostons" and the hated defending National League champion Orioles would essentially decide the closest, most bitter contest in the history of professional sport. Technically, the outcome of the three games to be played at Baltimore's Union Park would not actually settle the race. Each team would leave the field the following Monday with a handful of games to play against lesser foes. But that was a technicality. All season long the two contestants had battled—in both the physical and the metaphorical sense—to a virtual dead heat. They had long since left the competition behind. Whatever the schedule said, the issue would be functionally settled in Baltimore, the pennant honors almost certainly going to whichever team could win two of the three games.

The proper and moral resolution—a victory by the Boston club—was something each of the 130 or so Rooters had envisioned since their com-

Fig. 3. Interior view of the 3rd Base saloon, circa 1900, complete with bat and ball chandeliers. (McGreevey Collection, Boston Public Library, Print Department.)

ing together as a group about a month before. We do not know much about that coming together, except that it probably happened the preceding August at 3rd Base, a tavern situated a short distance from the South End Grounds, where the "Bostons" took the field. (Boston fans never called their home team the Beaneaters, the name by which it was known in the other eleven National League cities.) Catering to the same Irish-German immigrant clientele that saw in baseball a way to prove its American bona fides, 3rd Base ("your last stop before home") was owned by Michael T. McGreevy, one of the Rooters' founding members.[1] The son of an immigrant, McGreevy rose to the status of a successful businessman at age thirty-one and became something of a role model for his own clientele. Short and trim, with a turned-down mustache he sported for most of his adult life, McGreevy looked nothing like the successful amateur ballplayer he had been. Yet his inside knowledge of the game won him the respect of players and fans

Fig. 4. Woodcut depicting the delegation of Royal Rooters entraining at Park Square Station on the evening of September 23, 1897. Originally appeared in the *Boston Globe*, September 24, 1897.

alike. So too did his frequent sponsorship of youth league teams in the Roxbury neighborhood that was his home ground. To underscore that familiarity and to intensify his drawing power among "cranks," as the game's hard-core fans were known, McGreevy festooned virtually every inch of the 3rd Base saloon with baseball pictures, memorabilia, and gadgetry. To walk into it was to enter an early version of a baseball hall of fame. You did not even need to go inside to get the sense of the place; a life-size mannequin of a ballplayer greeted passers-by from a perch above the front entrance. Inside, McGreevy delighted in displaying pictures of his favorite Boston players and their

Fig. 5. "Nuf Ced" McGreevy. (McGreevey Collection, Boston Public Library, Print Department.)

famous rivals; those likenesses, some of them life-size, covered virtually every inch of the walls. The tavern's chandeliers consisted of bats that had been used by the era's stars—stalwarts like Nap Lajoie and Buck Freeman—and through which wires had been strung and lights attached so that they resembled glowing baseballs. On one wall, a pendulum designed to mimic a bat and ball ran the clock.[2]

At the 3rd Base tavern the topic of conversation was always baseball. McGreevy was often at the center of the discussion, but only for as long as he chose to be. When the proprietor judged the debate of the moment to have been settled, he summarily ended it with a two-word phrase, "Nuf ced." So tightly did McGreevy become identified with the phrase that it adopted him; virtually from the start of his public life, which began that summer and continued until his death in 1943, nobody knew him as Michael T. Throughout the baseball world, he was simply "Nuf Ced" McGreevy.[3]

With their loyalty, their enthusiasm, and their money, the Rooters had helped make 1897 the most successful year in the glorious history of Boston baseball. This was especially true from a financial standpoint. The home attendance of 334,000 was a club record, a nearly 40 percent increase over 1896 and the second highest figure in the league, behind only New York. Whether their team won or lost that crucial series in Baltimore, joint owners Arthur Soden, James Billings, and William Conant—known informally as the triumvirs—would clear $125,000. Adjusted for inflation, that would be about $2.8 million today. In 1897 it was a marvelous return on sixty-six home dates.[4]

Hit 'Er Up

The Rooters came from disparate backgrounds.[5] But a few traits, although they were not requirements, tended to show up with regularity, just as they do in modern fan groups. Rooters vocally favored a clean game, although rumors suggested that some were not above a friendly wager in the grandstands (and newspapers in Cincinnati among other towns printed scurrilous suggestions that open gambling could be seen in the Boston bleachers). They were positively rabid for the home team, and they had at least some level of familiarity with the 3rd Base saloon. Rooters also tended to be familiar with, and often active in, the city's Democratic political machine.[6] There was plenty of politics to discuss in 1897. Only a year earlier the U.S. Supreme Court had decided the *Plessy v. Ferguson* case, which established "separate but equal" as a legal precept. In 1897 it was easy to get into a debate regarding the role of Spain in Cuba and what, if anything, President McKinley ought to do about it.

The best-known Rooter was the area's Democratic congressman, John Francis Fitzgerald. At age thirty-four, "Honey Fitz" was a lantern-jawed power within the Democratic machine. Short and with a round face that seemed to glow, he looked like the type of proper gentleman who could be trusted in Congress. But he was far more a son of Boston than of Washington, especially at the South End Grounds when the Bostons took the field. Since Congress did most of its work between December and March, you could almost always find Honey Fitz in his seat just behind the team's bench. By mid-June he had become a visible and vocal presence, so much so that Tim Murnane described him as "well-posted in the fine points and delighted at the (team's) fine work."[7] If you didn't believe Murnane, you could hear for yourself. Inning after inning and game after game, Fitzgerald called out in the thickest of brogues a cheer with which both he and the Rooters came to be identified: "Hit 'er up, hit 'er up, hit 'er up again, BOSTON!"

That being a fan was also good politics was a pleasant side benefit for Fitzgerald, who in time would be elected mayor. His daughter Rose inherited his political instincts, but Honey Fitz at first saw little to recommend Rose's choice of young banker Joseph P. Kennedy as a husband-to-be. Eventually he warmed to the son-in-law and also saw political instincts in his grandchildren, especially the boys: Joe Jr., Jack, Bobby, and Teddy.

Honey Fitz and Nuf Ced were almost certainly the two most identifiable Rooters to board the 6:45 train on September 23, but they were not the only prominent fans. Well-known humorist Augustus Howell was on board. He had been given the important assignment of writing the cheers the Rooters would use in their effort to unsettle the Orioles. Harry Rosenfield was delegated to actually lead the cheers. Many businessmen, members of the clergy, and physicians, as well as seven women, were also numbered among the traveling party.[8]

It would not be a simple trip to Baltimore. Because he was a train conductor, Rooter W. R. Swift assumed responsibility for making the arrangements. The package he put together called for the group to travel by train from Boston to Providence and then board the steamer *Plymouth* of the Fall River line for the overnight trip to New York. They would arrive shortly after 6:00 a.m., in time to catch an annex boat to Jersey City and the 8:12 train for the four-hour ride to Baltimore. Even at 1897 prices the total fare of twenty-five dollars, which included rooms at the Eutaw House, was a steal. Adjusting for inflation, it amounted to a few bucks more than $550 per person today, roughly the price of one scalped bleacher ticket to a World Series contest.

It was a unique journey, the first recorded instance in which fans organized in a significant block to attend a sporting event some distance from home. In that sense, the group that came to be known as the Royal Rooters can be seen as precursors to the fan and alumni clubs that follow professional and college sports teams today. That they blazed the trail could be viewed as coincidental; somebody, after all, had to be first. But such a dismissal would overlook the powerful and particular loyalties that came together in September of 1897 and forged the Rooters.

Foremost was the history of Boston baseball, a history virtually all of the Rooters had grown up with. If, like Fitzgerald and McGreevy, they were in their early to midthirties, their first childhood memories were of the great Boston teams of the early 1870s. Their interest in the game was probably spawned by visits to the South End Grounds. They could have watched such legends as Al Spalding, Ross Barnes, Deacon White, and Cal McVey, the famed "Big Four" who helped Boston sweep to pennants in the first professional league, the National Association, in 1872, again in 1873, again in 1874, and a fourth time in 1875. When that league fell apart before the 1876 season, their interests would have moved with the team to the new National League. As teens they would have watched Boston sweep to pennants in 1877 and 1878, and again in 1883. They probably cheered the purchase of the era's two great stars, slugger Mike "King" Kelly in 1887 and pitcher John Clarkson in 1888.

They might have scratched their heads after the 1889 season—one in which the Beaneaters finished second, just a game behind the champion Giants—when Soden selected the unknown Frank Selee as manager. This should have been a Boston team with championship aspirations. Clarkson, with a league-leading forty-nine victories in 1889, remained the most imposing force in the center of any team's diamond. (Mounds did not come into play until the pitching distance of sixty feet and six inches was adopted in 1893; before 1893, pitches were delivered from inside a 4½ × 5 foot box, the front edge of which was fifty feet from home plate.) The roster was also expected to boast Charles Radbourn, the famed "Old Hoss," who was coming off a twenty-victory season, and Dan Brouthers, the mighty first baseman and the game's most feared hitter. Brouthers's .373 batting average had led the league in 1889.

Victims of War

But the Brotherhood War—the labor-management brawl that sundered every team and led to the formation of an entirely new Players' League—fractured those plans. Boston was especially hard hit. Radbourn and Brouthers both jumped to the city's Players' League team; so did regulars Mike Kelly, Hardy Richardson, Joe Quinn, and Billy Nash. As a result, Selee inherited a shell of the team he expected to find. The Beaneaters wandered through 1890 and finished in fifth place, fifteen and one-half games behind Brooklyn, which won because it held onto more of its core players than the other clubs.

The Brotherhood War ended after a single season, and some of the club's key players returned. Nash was back at third base—the position, not the tavern—and Quinn returned to second. But Brouthers, Radbourn, and Kelly all were gone for good: Brouthers to Brooklyn, Radbourn to Cincinnati for one last hurrah before succumbing to an arm injury, and Kelly to Cincinnati's American Association team.

Nothing in Selee's resume suggested that he was up to the task of resuscitating what remained of the Beaneaters. The thirty-one-year-old came to the nation's fifth largest city with six years of managerial experience at various minor leagues and only the barest professional playing background at a couple of brief minor-league stops. He got his initiation into professional baseball management at Melrose, Massachusetts, near his Amherst home, in 1884, and within a few years he had worked his way into similar positions with Kansas City and then Omaha in the Western League. In Kansas City he and a talented seventeen-year-old pitcher named Charles Augustus Nichols crossed paths. Nichols, whose age, boyish size (five feet ten and 135 pounds), and even more boyish looks inevitably prompted the nickname "Kid," flourished under Selee, so much so that when the manager moved to Omaha in 1889 and then to Boston in 1890, Nichols went along. He cost Boston a mere three thousand dollars extra.[9]

What Selee brought to the Beaneaters was multifaceted. It certainly included an indefinable but precise ability to judge talent. "He was a master of taking unknown minor leaguers and college players and making them into major leaguers," argued Dick Selee, a descendent of the manager, during the 1999 Hall of Fame induction speech he delivered on his ancestor's behalf. Layered onto that skill was the ability to make his players focus cerebrally on the task of winning games. That meant coping with a competition that in the 1890s was—in Dick Selee's characterization—"equal parts barroom brawl and chess match."[10] Selee did it by training his players in the nuances of scoring a run: positioning, timing, bat control, and pitch control. Execution was everything to him, and his teams were said to resemble a ballet on dirt. In addition, he was almost singular in his ability to make those players relax. "Just arrive at the ballpark ready to play," he would say. And they did.

Selee's eye for talent was his most vital asset. He could hardly have missed Nichols, having watched him for three seasons. That final minor-league season in Omaha, Nichols won thirty-six games and lost only twelve. Joining the veteran Clarkson and assuming Radbourn's abandoned place in what was virtually a three-man pitching staff, Nichols started forty-seven games that 1890 season and won twenty-seven of them. (Of the remaining eighty-seven games, Clarkson started forty-three and Charles Getzein started forty. The three pitched all but 30 of the 1,187 innings Boston played that year.)

To the naked eye, it was not at all clear where Nichols mustered his speed. He was not particularly muscular. Nor was he considered especially deceptive. He rarely threw a curve ball, relying instead on location, changes of velocity, and the ability to spot each pitch. Nichols's secret was the effortless nature of his delivery. The combination of location, velocity, effortlessness, and control is a recipe that has stood the test of more than a century of mound experience. A modern example? Roy Oswalt, the Houston Astros star.

For years afterward, Rooters remembered and marveled at the contest Nichols had waged on May 8, 1891, against Amos Rusie, the legendary "Hoosier Thunderbolt" of the New York Giants. In appearance they could hardly have been less similar: Rusie stood a full six feet one and weighed more than 200 pounds. Still a few weeks shy of his twentieth birthday, Rusie, although two years younger than Nichols, was already in his third season and had forty-one major-league victories. He was also considered an even harder thrower than the Kid. The result was precisely what most fans expected when they came to the park: nine innings of shutout ball on both sides, followed by a tenth, eleventh, and twelfth inning. Finally, in the thirteenth, Mike Tiernan's home run settled the game in New York's favor. It was only the fourth hit allowed by Nichols all afternoon; he had struck out ten. For his part, Rusie fanned eleven and allowed just three hits.

Nichols became the centerpiece of Selee's plan to reshape the Beaneaters—the pitcher who could be counted on to pitch every second or third day. But in the early 1890s the nation was awash in untapped baseball talent; the question was where to find it. Selee knew where to look.

In Kansas City, where Selee had managed in 1887–88, the baseball situation was crowded and unstable. The city, still very much a frontier town, had two teams: the Western Association club that Selee had managed and the Cowboys of the American Association, at the time considered a second major league. By 1889, though, the Cowboys had proven such a weak draw that they disbanded and their assets were

sold. Having managed in the city, Selee was familiar with the most talented of those assets, a twenty-three-year-old shortstop named Herman Long. So rangy was Long that fans called him "the Flying Dutch-
man" (later, when Honus Wagner came along to appropriate the name,
Long became simply "Dutch"). Long played shortstop in a way that
it had never been played before. Granted, he committed a lot of errors—more than one hundred in one season with the Cowboys. But
that was the nature of fielding in a time when fielders used only the
most rudimentary gloves, if they used any gloves at all, and played on
poorly maintained fields. Of greater interest to Selee was Long's ability to make plays. He had what we refer to today as range. He could
also run and hit. When he came up for bid, Selee made sure the Beaneaters got him—for $6,500.[11]

Selee mined the Western Association for twenty-one-year-old Robert Lincoln (Bobby) Lowe from Milwaukee. As they had with Nichols, Boston fans took their first look at Lowe and wondered whether
Selee preferred undersized, undernourished players. But despite his
five feet ten, 150-pound stature, Lowe proved to be a tough, rangy competitor. Selee initially used him in a utility role, but by 1892 Lowe had
established himself as the regular second baseman. To Boston fans he
would be lionized for his 1894 Memorial Day performance against Cincinnati at Boston's Congress Street Grounds, which had been pressed
into temporary service due to a fire at the South End Grounds a few
weeks earlier. After going zero for six in the morning game of the doubleheader, Lowe homered in four consecutive at bats in the afternoon
game, the first person ever to hit that many home runs in one contest.
The left-field fence at Congress Street Grounds was only 250 feet from
home plate, and some denigrated Lowe's feat for that reason. But no
true Boston fan did. The word got around that Lowe had dined on fish
between games of that doubleheader, and for days afterward his fans
made certain that Bobby was well stocked with fish.[12]

The third key addition was Hugh Duffy, a mill worker who had taken
up baseball as a semipro for a weekend diversion. Duffy surfaced with

the Lowell, Massachusetts, team in 1887, but he quickly signed with Chicago when the White Stockings offered him two thousand dollars. This did not impress Cap Anson, who took one look at the new arrival, just five feet seven inches tall and barely 150 pounds, and told him, "We already have a batboy."[13] He had come to Chicago with a reputation as a pitcher and shortstop, but Anson found his skills at both those positions suspect and converted him to the position at which he became famous, outfield. Once Duffy picked up a bat, all doubt about his major-league potential vanished. He hit .312 for the White Stockings in 1889 and .320 for the Chicago Players' League team to which he jumped during the 1890 war. When the Brotherhood War ended, Duffy, a native New Englander, was delighted to be purchased by the Boston team in the American Association, for which he batted .336 and drove in 110 runs. When the American Association folded following the 1891 season—a delayed casualty of the 1890 war—Selee moved quickly to get Duffy under contract. A special favorite of the Irish fans, Duffy was also adopted by the city's German contingent, thereby melding two of the city's major ethnic subgroups. To complement Duffy, Boston also signed Tommy McCarthy, a veteran outfielder who was also left teamless by the American Association's collapse, and until McCarthy's retirement in 1896, Duffy and McCarthy were jointly known around the league as the "Heavenly Twins."

Three-Time Champions

The remarkable result of all of these moves was the transformation of the Beaneaters from a fifth-place club in 1890 to a championship club in 1891 and a budding dynasty by 1892. With Nichols a dominant pitcher, with Long emerging as the game's best shortstop, and with Selee drawing the best from the returning talent, Boston beat out the White Stockings by three and one-half games in 1891. With Duffy on board for 1892, the Beaneaters became the first team in baseball history to win 100 games, claiming 102 of their 150 contests. The National League, which had expanded to twelve teams by swallowing four clubs from the dead American Association, adopted a unique "split season" that year, selecting first- and second-half champions. The Beaneaters breezed to the first-half title, saw Cy Young's Cleveland club beat them out for the second-half title, and then easily dismissed Cleveland in the postseason championship series. Only the great White Stockings teams of 1880-82 had succeeded in capturing three straight National League pennants, but Selee's club matched that achievement in 1893, winning eighty-six times with a .667 percentage that bested runner-up Pittsburg by four games.

Beaneaters fans reveled in the prospect of an unprecedented fourth straight championship under Selee for 1894. What they could not have seen coming was the rise of a new—and, many thought, corrupt—dynasty. The Orioles of 1893 had been a tame, tepid bunch, winning only sixty games; they had finished more than twenty-five games behind the Bostons. In addition, the Orioles played—at least in the eyes of Boston fans—a fundamentally disreputable game. They cut corners, cussed umpires, and obstructed runners—anything, it seemed, to win. Because the Orioles had little on-field talent in 1893, their disgusting traits were more annoyances than anything else. But then Boston fans watched in disbelief as new additions Willie Keeler and Hughie Jennings joined holdovers John McGraw and Joe Kelley in energizing the team. From eighth place in 1893, the Orioles swept over Boston's hopes for a fourth straight title in 1894, winning 89 of 128 decisions to best the Giants by three games and the Beaneaters by eight. It marked a twenty-nine-game improvement in Baltimore's record over that single season. To the Boston fans' horror, the Orioles repeated in 1895, this time with eighty-seven victories. And in 1896 Baltimore won its third straight pennant by the most convincing margin of all—with ninety victories and a .698 winning percentage. Boston lingered in fourth place, sixteen games behind Baltimore.

It was not merely that Baltimore won and Boston lost. In proper Protestant Boston, it was also the atmosphere and culture of the change. What in 1893 could be overlooked as an unpleasant annoyance perpetrated by second-raters loomed, after three headline-grabbing championships, as an ongoing desecration, of both the game and the culture. Selee's teams mirrored the city's puritanical approach to life. Boston was, after all, the city of Ralph Waldo Emerson and Oliver Wendell Holmes, the great Boston Brahmin intellectuals of the mid-nineteenth century whose writings on self-reliance, prudence, and the primacy of spiritual law came to be accepted as laying out a set of core American virtues. Baltimore was at heart a wharf city, considerably more hardscrabble than Brahmin. The Orioles' openly roughhouse tactics played right into the Bostonian stereotype of the immigrant shanty Irish Catholic forcing unwanted change on a stable nation.

These were large issues in the 1890s. More than four million immigrants entered the United States during the decade. Italians and Russians formed the largest groups of arrivals, and the nearly forty thousand Irish represented the third-largest group. The trend caused particular concern among New England's intellectual class, which saw the newcomers as threats to Protestantism, culture, language, and civil life—in other words, to the America they knew.[14]

But baseball, the most powerful recreational force in the nation, shaped life as well as it reflected life. And this was not merely true in big-league cities. When major-league mores got rough, they percolated throughout the game and society. Sandlotters, after all, loved to imitate their heroes. A player-umpire dispute arose that August between amateur teams in Newbern, Alabama. The player, Sidney Gooden, knocked down the umpire, Richard Lee Jr., during an argument. Richard Lee Sr., the ump's father, rushed in and attempted to strike Gooden with a bat. The elder Lee was arrested. As he was being removed, Gooden grabbed his own bat, came up from behind, and struck the father a fatal blow to the head. A combination riot and gunfight quickly broke out, and when it was over fifteen minutes later two men had been slain, one by the younger Lee. He fled but was hunted down with the use of dogs.

That kind of violence was an example of scenes played out regularly on major-league fields across the country. In the same way Protestant America marshaled against the societal challenges it saw as threatening, so too did the relatively Brahmin Beaneaters come to defend baseball's ramparts against the threat posed by Baltimore's more cutthroat approach. Boston was a natural for this role, both because of its image as a refined city and because of the temperament of the team's leader. "The fact that the Bostons have always been noted for their gentlemanly deportment is due, in a great measure, to the example set by Selee, who will not countenance anything that smacks of rowdyism or 'dirty ball,'" contended one of the era's leading sports publications. "Such a manager must be a keen, shrewd, aggressive, hustling and almost boisterous individual."[15] In fact, Selee was none of that; the most common description of him was as "a quiet little man with the calm, placid countenance, the unobtrusive manner and the forehead high and broad . . . strongly intellectual. He seemed as such men always do seem, quite ordinary." Players sometimes intimated that the Beaneaters "might get along just as well without him."[16] But the team's results made clear that this was not true; on the bench, his quiet somehow projected a forceful personality.

Through the three-year transformation of the National League into an organization dominated by Baltimore's fast and often thuggish style of play, Selee struggled to restore what the team's faithful still viewed as the rightful order. Notwithstanding the Orioles' ascension, any true Boston fan knew, as of the conclusion of the 1896 season, that the team's problems were not as simple as the improved level of Baltimore's play. The Beaneaters had deteriorated. Aging stalwarts of the three-year pennant run—Clarkson, Nash, McCarthy, and veteran first baseman Tommy Tucker—no longer performed to fans' expectations. Clarkson had been the first to go. Ignoring the sentiment accrued by the thirty-year-old's 287 victories, more than half of them for the Bostons, Selee traded him to Cleveland midway through the 1892 season. The deal initially alarmed the partisans; Clarkson delivered seventeen more victories for his new team by year's end. But Selee knew a fading arm when he saw it developing, and he resolved to get value while the market held. Clarkson lasted less than two seasons with the Spiders, losing more games than he won in both years. His replacement, right-hander Jack Stivetts, was already on hand, another pickup from the remnants of the folded American Association. A thirty-three-game winner with the association's St. Louis franchise the previous season, the twenty-four-year-old Stivetts assumed the second spot in the rotation behind Nichols in 1892. An imposing six feet two, Stivetts could hit as well as pitch. Robert Tiemann and Mark Rucker, authors of *Nineteenth Century Stars*, recall that on successive days in August of the 1892 season, Stivetts hit a home run to win an extra-inning game against Brooklyn and then pitched a no-hitter.[17]

Transformation

Tommy Tucker, a fan favorite since his arrival in 1890, remained with the Beaneaters into the 1897 season. He alone among the Bostons was an Oriole type of player, heady but rowdy and more than occasionally conniving. Selee could tolerate that, but he could not tolerate the way the big first baseman's bat and feet had slowed down. From a high of .330 in 1894, his batting average fell to .247 the following season. Worse, balls he was expected to pocket skipped past him unheeded. It had taken Selee an uncharacteristic three full seasons to find Tucker's replacement, even though that replacement was sitting alongside him for most of that time. Nobody envisioned Fred Tenney, a kid signed out of Brown University following his graduation in 1894, to be the answer at first base. He could hit, true enough—a .395 average during the second half of that rookie season attested to those skills. But Tenney had come to the majors as the rarest of all players—a left-handed catcher, and a poor one at that. From 1894 through 1896, Selee tried him behind the plate and occasionally in the outfield. It was not until the club broke badly in April of 1897 that Selee tried the big left-hander at the most obvious place. Initial reviews were modest at best. "Rather out of place," offered Tim Murnane after one early start there.[18] Murnane was a cogent analyst, but this time he was wrong. Fortunately for the Bostons, Selee knew it, for he rejected a proposed deal that would have sent Tenney to New York that same week. Tenney's teammates agreed. "We want to keep men of the Tenney stamp," asserted Hugh Duffy, by then the club's captain. "If he is let alone for a while he will play first base all right."[19] The Beaneaters did make a deal, though; they traded Tucker.

Like Tucker, Nash had been a star of the early 1890s pennant run. Unlike Tucker, he remained one of the best at his position, leading the league in fielding percentage in 1892, 1893, and 1894 while batting as high as .291. Selee felt Nash's skills, like Clarkson's, would soon diminish. He turned thirty in 1895, and his hands showed the effects of playing third base in the major leagues for a decade with little or nothing in the way of a glove. Selee packaged him to Philadelphia in a deal that returned Billy Hamilton, a trade perceived as a swap of soon-to-fade front-liners. Selee made the correct read. As a center fielder in Philadelphia since 1890, Hamilton, at age thirty, had batted .380, .403, and .389 while setting stolen base records. He had stolen 100 bases in 1894 and followed that up with 97 steals in 1895. The batting eye that complemented that foot speed made him the ideal lead-off batter, perhaps the game's best until Rickey Henderson. Hamilton had drawn 224 walks during those two final seasons in Philadelphia, running his on-base averages to .522 and .490. In Boston in 1896 he batted .366 at the top of the order, adding 110 more bases on balls and 97 stolen bases.

In Philadelphia, meanwhile, Nash did precisely what Selee had expected. His average fell from .290 in 1895 to .247 in 1896. He was gone from the game by 1898.

Selee could afford to lose Nash because Jimmy Collins was available. Signed out of Buffalo in the Eastern League, Collins was twenty-five when he put on a Boston uniform in 1895. Casual fans might have wondered why Collins was traded to Louisville after playing only ten games, all of them in the outfield. But the trade was a ruse; it was both a loan to the poverty-stricken Colonels and a chance for Collins to learn the intricacies of third base without requiring that Nash be benched. Per a prior understanding, he was traded back before the 1896 season, and he quickly succeeded his predecessor as the league's surest fielder.

Collins developed a particular reputation as the game's best defender against the bunt. In an era when baseballs stayed in play for innings at a time and the long ball was a rarity, the inside game—bunting and place hitting—ruled. None were better at this than the pair at the top of the champion Orioles' order, McGraw and Keeler. "I came to the conclusion that there was only one solution to this bunting game," Collins would say later in life. "A third baseman had to give himself a chance to get those fast guys."[20] So he played on the edge of the infield grass. This was revolutionary and riskier than it sounds, given the absence of good gloves. Third base was as hot a hot corner then as it is today. A fielder playing that position at the edge of the infield grass was risking both error and injury.

The test of Collins came against the Orioles themselves. They had read of Collins and openly challenged him. McGraw, leading off, dropped a nice bunt toward third. Collins raced in, picked up the ball, and threw the speedy batter out by a step. Next was Keeler. Collins got him as well. Jennings, the third hitter, bunted in the same spot, and Collins threw him out to end the inning. Leading off the second, Kelley bunted a fourth time, and for a fourth time Collins raced in, making a one-handed pickup and throwing underhand to get the runner.[21] It was said that the Orioles rarely tried to bunt on Collins again.

Not all of Selee's moves had been planned. Charlie Bennett, another fan favorite, had been a pillar behind the plate throughout the first two seasons of the club's pennant streak. At thirty-eight, his best days probably were behind him, yet he remained the regular catcher on a first-place team until a freak and horrible accident following the 1893 season. On a hunting trip, Bennett raced to catch up to a moving train in Wellsville, Kansas. He reached for the grip and slipped and fell beneath the train's wheels, which severed both of his legs. Selee turned first to Charles Ganzel, another veteran who had shared duties with Bennett through that pennant streak. But Ganzel had never in his career been more than a part-timer, and at age thirty-two he was not the man to rally the pitching crew. So after the 1895 season, Selee bought Marty Bergen from Lewiston, Maine, of the Eastern League. The Pirates, the first to recognize Bergen's talent when he was a nineteen-year-old playing for Wilkes-Barre, had sent him to Lewiston with the hope of hiding him while he matured. But "farming" players, although it was commonly done, was technically illegal in the 1890s, making Bergen's Pittsburg contract unenforceable. When the Beaneaters offered one thousand dollars to Lewiston management for the catcher, Bergen went to Boston.

The maturation that Pittsburg had sought was partly physical but also emotional. Even in Lewiston, and certainly by the time of his arrival in Boston, Bergen was widely viewed as an erratic figure. Not even his marriage with the former Hattie Gaines of Lewiston had the stabilizing effect that matrimony often has on a young character. Bergen's problems were not like the usual acts of poor judgment that typically get youngsters into trouble. He was described as having "reticent and moody spells."[22] Today his behavior, which included unpredictable and often threatening outbursts in response to imagined slights, might be diagnosed as schizophrenic, but in 1897 no such diagnosis existed. Certainly his presence prompted strange and mixed reactions. "He was perhaps the best baseball catcher I ever saw," Hugh Duffy would say later.[23] Yet, added teammate Ted Lewis, "I have always been afraid of him."[24]

The one thing that players and Rooters alike agreed on was that Bergen could both catch and throw. He established that reputation as a rookie in 1896. He quickly became the regular, with Ganzel the backup again. With Bergen at the backstop, Selee's remaking of the Bostons was nearly complete. The infield of Tenney, Lowe, Long, and Collins was plainly the game's best. Nichols and Stivetts led a staff that included blossoming left-hander Fred Klobedanz and brilliant rookie right-hander Ted Lewis.

If ever a player did not seem to fit with the rough-and-tumble nature of the game that was popular in the 1890s, it was Ted Lewis. A twenty-three-year-old honors graduate of Williams College, he signed a major-league contract with the Beaneaters only after adding a stipulation that he would not be asked to pitch on Sundays. For that action he became known almost immediately as "Parson" Lewis. Teammates and fans alike delighted in relating the story of how Lewis had met his wife. While pitching summer ball one day in Richfield Springs, New York, he had promised a friend that he would usher the woman, whose name was Margaret, to her seat. There were only two problems with that commitment. The first was that Lewis was scheduled to pitch that particular game. The second was that Margaret arrived late. In fact, Lewis was already facing the first batter when she showed up. Seeing her from the mound, Lewis gallantly called time-out, dropped the ball, walked off the mound, and escorted her to her seat, as he had promised to do. Then he resumed pitching.[25]

The final piece of the puzzle for Selee arrived at training camp in 1897 in the person of rookie outfielder Chick Stahl. He filled the roster spot held by the recently retired McCarthy. The product of a family of twenty-three, Stahl arrived without much of a reputation but quickly won the right-field job. He batted .354 to anchor the middle of the batting order along with Duffy. With that lineup, Selee believed he could at least challenge the Baltimore champions and restore Boston's primacy. Soon the fans began to believe it as well. They came in increasing numbers to the South End Grounds, the regulars soon congealing into a familiar throng gathered behind the home bench. By July the throng had acquired a public identity: the Boston Rooters. They took outward pride in the fact that the record for most pennants won by any city—twelve—belonged to the "hub of the universe." That counted the six National League standards as well as four captured in the National Association, plus the 1890 Players' League title and the 1891 American Association championship during years in which those were considered major leagues. As they boarded that train at the Park Square Station on September 23, the Rooters' every intention was to see their heroes extend that record and at the same time give the Orioles a lesson in the merits of clean baseball.

3. Spring Thunderbolts

To understand the dispute between Amos Rusie and Andrew Freedman, it is necessary only to understand the difference between Indiana and Tammany Hall. Rusie was thoroughly a Hoosier—a teen out of the hamlet of Mooresville who journeyed the thirty-five-mile distance to Indianapolis to make his big-league debut during the city's final major season in 1889. He stood a tall six feet one and a powerfully built 200 pounds, and the 12-10 record he compiled on a team that won only fifty-nine games earned him plenty of notice. That and his fastball. Virtually from the start, he was "the Hoosier Thunderbolt."

Acquired by the Giants in 1890, the nineteen-year-old dominated the National League's best hitters, working 549 innings that first season. Until the rules were modified in 1893, pitchers had to deliver the ball from within a box that was fifty feet from the plate. Although pitching was easier from fifty feet, 550 innings nevertheless is a lot of work—in fact it was about half of the team's full season.

Rusie lost thirty-four of his sixty-three decisions that season, a statistic that says more about the depleted state of the New York offense than it does about Rusie. After all, he delivered a 2.56 earned run average that was fourth best in the league, and he led in strikeouts with 341. In 1891, when the Brotherhood War ended and New York re-signed several of its former stars, Rusie won thirty-three times in fifty-seven starts, again topping five hundred innings and again leading in strike-

175.
Amos Rusie.

Fig. 6. Amos Rusie, the Hoosier Thunderbolt, whose 1896 season-long holdout prompted league owners to band against Giants owner Andrew Freedman. (National Baseball Hall of Fame Library, Cooperstown NY.)

outs. It was his first of four consecutive thirty-victory seasons. By Memorial Day of 1895, "the Hoosier Thunderbolt" had already won more than 175 games, and he was only then celebrating his twenty-fourth birthday.

He had also learned much about the unpleasant ways and means of the business side of baseball. The reserve clause had been one of the issues precipitating the Brotherhood War. With the war's end, the Players' League evaporated, and when the American Association also collapsed one season later, the cumulative effect was to glut the market with 160 more major-league veterans than there were jobs. National League club owners reacted predictably: they slashed payrolls.

Fig. 7. National League club owners and officials gather in February of 1897 for a conference on the Rusie situation. Among those pictured are league president Nick Young (seated, center) and Chris Von der Ahe, Ned Hanlon, Frank DeHaas Robison, and Harry Von der Horst (standing, second through fifth from left). (McGreevey Collection, Boston Public Library, Print Department.)

John B. Day, owner of the New York Giants, delivered the news to Rusie in the middle of his thirty-two-victory 1892 season. When Rusie threatened a work stoppage, Day backed down, but only temporarily. At season's end, he released Rusie—presumably secure in the knowledge that none of the league's other eleven owners would sign him—and then handed the pitcher an ultimatum. He could pitch for the Giants at a lower salary for 1893 or he could not pitch at all. Rusie signed and won thirty-three more games.

Tammany's Team

But Day's baseball finances were perennially shaky, and he began to look around for partners. In New York in the latter half of the nineteenth century, financial partners could be found easily, especially if you were willing to compromise your control. In January of 1895, control of the Giants was passed to Andrew Freedman, a thirty-four-year-old product of Tammany Hall, the Richard Croker–led Democratic machine that dictated all issues of importance in New York

City. Freedman's ruthless success in real estate had been predicated on the concept of "no questions asked." As a club owner, he was a reviled figure, his tenure marked by decisions as self-aggrandizing as they were vindictive.

Freedman's first action was to fire the team's manager, John M. Ward. Behind Ward, the Giants had finished second to the Orioles in 1894 and had beaten them in the Temple Cup series. But Freedman believed in sycophantism, and Ward was decidedly no sycophant. He had been one of the central figures in the organization of the Brotherhood—the short-lived union—in 1887, and in the subsequent Brotherhood War of 1890. Three men managed the Giants in Ward's stead during that 1895 season, including Dirty Jack Doyle and Harvey Watkins, whose qualifications included time in the business office of P. T. Barnum's circus.[1] Under Freedman's operation, the Giants fell from second place in 1894 to ninth place in 1895.

Given Rusie's reputation for dickering over money, a collision between the club's new owner and its biggest star was inevitable. It flared up within weeks of the purchase. Coming off his fourth straight thirty-victory season, Rusie demanded five thousand dollars for 1895. Just ten days before the team ship was due to set sail for spring training in Florida, Freedman sent George Davis, the team's shortstop and managerial designee, to, as the *New York Times* put it, "announce the club's terms." The offer, although undisclosed, was described as "more than he got last year and larger . . . than any League pitcher will receive."[2]

Rusie did join the Giants, making forty-seven starts and pitching 393 innings. But he won only twenty-three decisions—the same number he lost. Declaring that Rusie's subpar performance had derived from slack effort, and particularly asserting that the pitcher had been drunk during an appearance in Baltimore, Freedman levied two hundred dollars in fines at season's end, deducting the amount from Rusie's final paycheck. Rusie took the fine as a backdoor salary cut and refused to report in 1896 unless it was rescinded. In a public relations contest between the heroic pitcher and the syndicate-controlled owner, public sympathy was one-sided. "Every independent, fair-thinking man is with Rusie in his stand," reported the *Sporting News*.[3] Remarked O. P. Caylor of the *New York Herald*, "The Giants without Rusie would be like Hamlet without the Melancholy Dane."[4]

The pitcher accompanied his refusal to play with an appeal of the fine to the league's board of directors. In June of 1896 the board upheld the fine. But they also negotiated among themselves to try to find a way out of what they saw as a looming crisis. They had plenty of reasons to do so. First, the nation was emerging from one of the deepest economic troughs in its history, the fiscal storm that would become known as the "panic of 1896." In that year alone, the value of a dollar had fallen nearly 4 percent. Owners knew that spending on luxury items fell in troubled financial times, and as 1897 dawned, baseball was by any definition a luxury item. Second, Rusie was probably the biggest draw of his day, worth real money any time the Giants came to town. Third, they believed that Rusie, having sat out the entire season, was likely to file a suit challenging the Giants' right to prevent him from declaring himself a free agent and signing with another team—in other words, a suit that would invalidate the reserve clause. In January 1897 Rusie lived up to their expectations and filed the suit.[5]

Desiring to put the entire issue behind them, magnates pleaded with Freedman to get his star under contract. Freedman would not consider anything short of Rusie's capitulation.

Bucking One's Head

Reports of a settlement first surfaced on April 12, and the deal was to be finalized at a secret meeting of league officials the following day. J. Earl Wagner, president of the Washington team, confirmed plans for the meeting, saying that "the pecuniary advantages to say nothing of the desire of the public" impelled a settlement.[6] But in the face of Freedman's opposition to what he saw as a capitulation, the meeting went nowhere. Two days later, with Rusie's lawsuit as a backdrop, club owners convened another special meeting. They talked for six hours, proposing to throw five thousand dollars into a kitty to pay Rusie for his lost fine and his legal expenses if he would drop his suit and come back to the Giants. "It was pointed out to the New York magnate that the move would stimulate base ball all over the country," newspapers reported.[7] Freedman remained adamant. "I have offered Rusie $2,400, and unless he signs and gets down to business he will not play ball at all," Freedman told the newspapers. "Nor will I revoke the fine."[8]

"There is such a thing as bucking one's head against a stone wall," lamented Dodgers owner Charles Byrne in a pointed analogy to negotiating with Freedman. "Now," added Byrne, as the session adjourned for the night, "the question comes whether one member of the company of twelve is to override the wishes of the majority."[9]

For his part, Freedman declared the whole thing a team issue outside the league's purview. "To compromise would be to throw discipline to the winds," he told the *New York Journal*. "Without discipline, no ball club can succeed."[10]

Others, however, saw the situation differently. "The New Yorks cannot get along without Rusie," reported the *New York Times*, quoting "an old follower of the game." The same source reported to "have it on the best authority that Rusie can get along if he never plays here again." Therefore, the source predicted, "in a few days you will hear of Rusie surrendering; that's the way club officials put it nowadays when they try to make the public believe that they have brought a stubborn player into line. Mark the prediction."[11]

The "old follower" pretty much got it right. Essentially ignoring Freedman, club owners went directly to Rusie with their five-thousand-dollar offer; he accepted and was in uniform by late April, debuting against Washington at the Polo Grounds before an adoring crowd of thirteen thousand. They cheered loudly when he struck out the first batter he faced and even louder when he completed the 8–3 victory over the Senators.

Albert Spalding, the sporting goods titan and at the time a prominent investor in the Chicago White Stockings team, aligned himself with Freedman's foes, in the process coining a term for the era. What Spalding saw, he related in his autobiography, was "a certain clique [coming] into the league for purposes of pelf . . . absolutely devoid of sentiment, caring nothing for the integrity or perpetuity of the game beyond the limits of their individual control thereof. With these men it was simply a mercenary question of dollars and cents." Concluded Spalding, "I do not know how better to characterize the monstrous evil which at this time threatened the life of Base Ball than to denominate it 'Freedmanism.'"[12]

Rusie's return to the Giants invigorated the team's status among contenders for the 1897 championship, although the three-time defending champion Orioles remained heavy favorites. The Beaneaters? To knowledgeable fans, any team with Kid Nichols, Billy Hamilton, Herman Long, and Hugh Duffy merited consideration. At the same time, Frank Selee had plenty of issues to sort out as he took his team to spring training that March. His club was now three years removed from its most recent championship. Selee had not yet effectively replaced slugging outfielder Tommy McCarthy, who was traded following the 1895 season and had since retired. Tommy Tucker, the incumbent at first base since 1890, had as many detractors—who found him slow afoot and at bat—as backers. And who, other than the reliable Jack Stivetts, would pitch behind Nichols? Fred Klobedanz was barely tested; as a rookie in 1896, the left-hander had started only nine games. Jim Sullivan was back, but what of it? He had gone only 11-12 in his twenty-six starts and was a mere one game above .500 for his career in Boston.

Not that Selee was without options. Fred Tenney, who until 1896 was a utility figure for the Beaneaters, opened eyes when he batted .336, a persuasive argument for playing time. But Tenney had been brought up as a catcher. Selee switched him to the outfield after one season, more or less as an act of mercy. He had not distinguished himself in right field either. That opened the door for a kid named Chick Stahl, who came to the majors with a reputation as a dangerous batter. For mound depth, Selee believed that the college pitcher Ted Lewis might serve. Spring training would be the test of all of the team.

Spring workouts in the 1890s were not like the well-publicized and well-attended series of exhibition games we are familiar with today. Teams rarely tried to schedule anything resembling a full series of games. At a time when many ballplayers worked off-season jobs to supplement their baseball incomes, and those who did not have jobs often laid around, spring training was much more of a conditioning exercise combined with strategy-based workouts. So much a factor was conditioning that some teams felt the need to work out near a spa or therapeutic resort simply to boil the off-season's liquors out of their players. Cap Anson's Chicago Colts were frequent guests at Hot Springs, Arkansas, for precisely that purpose.

Teams could afford to focus more on conditioning and strategy because they had far less need to use the spring to pare down their rosters. Clubs that normally played the regular season with fewer than twenty players on their entire payroll might bring one or two prospects to camp with them, but no more. If you went south, the assumption was that you had already made the team.

The *Nacoochee* to Savannah

Even as late as 1897, the aftereffects of the Civil War were still apparent in train service. As a consequence, the Beaneaters, among other teams, opted for a steamship as their vehicle of choice to travel to Savannah, Georgia, for the opening of their camp. It was a slow-gathering club that arrived at the wharf on March 17 to board the *Nacoochee* for the four-day journey.[13] Their arrival was slow in more ways than one, for some had not yet returned signed contracts. Billy Hamilton, Fred Tenney, Jimmy Collins, and Ted Lewis all tarried past the March 1 signing date. Tenney and Lewis had since clarified their situations, but Hamilton and Collins both reported aboard with unsigned contracts in their pockets. Hamilton, although a league veteran of several springs, had another reason to be hesitant about the trip: he hated open water. "It wouldn't have taken much to change Billy's mind about the method of travel," Tim Murnane reported in the *Boston Globe*.[14] Onboard, the outfielder was delighted to reestablish acquaintances with his friend Stivetts, who had seen fit to bring along several seasickness curatives. Hamilton must have stayed close to Stivetts because he was one of the few Beaneaters who made the voyage in good health. Duffy, Collins, and Tucker reportedly also flourished, but the others—including Stivetts—suffered from seasickness.

The timing of the departure was ironic in one respect, coming as it did on the day after Bob Fitzsimmons's surprise knockout of James J. Corbett to take the world heavyweight championship. Boston fans might have seen the result as a portent, since they too hoped to take a title away from a Corbett—Jim's young brother, Joe, who pitched for Baltimore.

For a time it appeared that Lewis, the religious rookie, would miss the boat entirely. But having agreed to Selee's terms only days before, he showed up with the last of the crew just as the ship was preparing to depart. There he joined the players at the rail, waving goodbye to his new wife in a scene familiar both then and today.

Life on a spring training ship had its pleasant moments, but on the whole the accommodations were spartan. The team installed two punching bags on board to allow players to get in a workout. But Tucker broke through one of them with what the *Boston Journal* described as "a terrific right." Marty Bergen supposedly put in ten miles of roadwork around the deck, much of it while carrying an umbrella through the fog and rain that dominated the first couple of days.[15] But that was about the extent of opportunities for physical activity.

The Beaneaters stepped off the *Nacoochee* onto the dry land of Savannah on the afternoon of the March 21—greeted by Herman Long, Doc Yeager, and Chick Stahl, who had made separate travel arrangements—and quickly learned several more lessons about the training regime circa 1897. The practice field, although sodded, remained rough and uneven. It was also a sandy surface, and although that should have come as no surprise in the coastal city of Savannah, it was different from anything they would see once league play commenced.

Their playing schedule also took a hit. Ned Hanlon, whose Orioles were training in Macon, Georgia, wired to decline Selee's invitation to make the trip to Savannah for exhibition games. Selee would have to fill in with games against local teams.

Then there was the matter of the hotel itself. In those days (and for many years thereafter), ball clubs did not necessarily lodge in the city's finest hostelries. And even if they did, it would not guarantee much in Savannah. Club management had made arrangements, essentially sight unseen, to put the team up at a place called the DeSoto. There they were assigned rooms in the rear, where they found themselves susceptible to chilling winds that blew through the lightly sealed windows, creating a more or less constant draft. That would be bad enough for any visitor, but it was worse for athletes. Training fields did not have amenities such as locker rooms or showers in those days, and even some of the finer hotels had only one bathroom per floor.[16]

A Fleabag Lifestyle

The training routine called for the players to rise by 7:30 a.m., eat breakfast, don their uniforms, and begin a run from the hotel to the field by 9:30. Inevitably, the local boys would tag along, each trying to be the one kid who could beat a big-league ballplayer across the roughly one-mile distance. That was a tall order against Boston, which featured not only five-time stolen-base-champion Hamilton but also Long, Collins, and Duffy—each known for his speed—as well as brash newcomers Tenney and Stahl. A two-hour workout followed, sometimes featuring a series of sixty-yard dashes, which Hamilton dominated. Then it was back on the run to their hotel to change out of their uniforms for a rubdown and lunch, followed by another two-hour afternoon workout. After three or four days of changing sweaty clothes in drafty rooms, chills, body aches, and severe colds were common. Sullivan was laid up for several days, and Selee threatened to move the club if better accommodations—rooms in the front, away from the drafts—could not be obtained. They could not. Ball clubs were far less desirable tenants as a class in those days, and the DeSoto had sold its best rooms to its more respected customers. Anyway, Selee's threat was always hollow, for there were no better places available in Savannah. So the Beaneaters simply suffered.

None had it worse than Sullivan, who needed a good showing at camp to prove to Selee that he was reliable. To that end, he had been happy to get the start in the spring's first exhibition game against a local club that would be supplemented by the pitching of Nichols and Stivetts. Loaning the local nine one or two of your best pitchers was a common practice in those days; how else were your hitters supposed to see big-league-quality pitching? Although he gave up a home run to one of the local punks, Sullivan looked good in his four innings before he was relieved by Ted Lewis. Even better, Stahl's surprising work with the bat helped the Beaneaters defeat Nichols, Stivetts, and the locals 6–4. Everything had been very upbeat.

But that was two days before the cold drafts did their work. Sullivan had not practiced with the team since and went to bed knowing it would be several frustrating days until he would play again.[17]

Lewis was the next to be sidelined. Following a two-hour morning workout, the rookie pitched seven innings for Savannah in the second exhibition game. They were impressive innings, helping the amateur team edge out the Bostons—who had Nichols, Stivetts, and Klobedanz pitching for them—by a run, 4–3. But when Lewis left in favor of one of the locals, he too reported soreness. Nichols, who had pitched three innings, also complained. Selee wondered whether the two games in four days had been too much for his unconditioned and poorly domiciled staff.

Happily, two days of poor weather intervened, postponing another scheduled exhibition and forcing the workouts inside, where they assumed a more relaxed, carnival-like atmosphere. One workout consisted of indoor baseball, which was little more than a frolic, with pitchers umpiring, infielders pitching, and the whole thing halted after six innings due to "darkness."[18] The following day they repaired to the gymnasium of the local Catholic library school, where handball and more indoor baseball dominated the agenda. By the third day of April, both the weather and the pitchers' arms had improved sufficiently that the Beaneaters met Savannah in the deciding game of their three-game series. Lewis, Sullivan, and Nichols all pitched. But the real star was Stahl, the rookie outfielder. "It looks as if Selee has struck a kingpin," reported Tim Murnane in the *Boston Globe*. "[Stahl] hit the ball every time he came up today and got three singles and a double."[19]

By then the Beaneaters were ready to abandon Savannah and begin the long journey northward that was a feature of training trips in those days. It would begin with an extended stop in Charleston for more practice and two games against another local club. Selee pronounced himself satisfied that "the right policy is being pursued in starting in deliberately and carefully so that no one would be crippled." He said the sixteen players under contract collectively had the ability "to make our opponents play ball from start to finish." He also announced a set of team rules for the season: "Rise at 8:30 a.m., in bed by 11:30, and daily 11 a.m. meetings on the road 'to talk over strategy.'" Then he imposed one more rule, which he declared would be "strictly enforced": no drinking before games.[20]

The first portion of the northward barnstorming tour showed off the major-leaguers' batting and fielding skills. Long and Collins dazzled a crowd of several hundred with their glove work in the first game at Charleston. The following day's feature, which was called after five innings so the team could catch a train for Greensboro, North Carolina, was less formal, with Duffy working two innings on the mound and Selee umpiring. In Greensboro on April 7, Nichols and Stivetts challenged the local club, and the result was predictable: a 17–2 rout. Hamilton, Long, and Klobedanz all homered off the amateurs. From there the overnight train took them to Newport News, Virginia, where Hamilton continued to bash the ball and Duffy made two dashing catches in left. Rain washed out a planned game the next day at Norfolk. Then in Richmond on April 10 the Beaneaters easily beat a local professional team 10–1 on a field of ankle-deep mud. Again, the succession of games took a toll on a team that was still rounding into form. An ailing Sullivan was ordered back to Boston in hopes that he would be ready for the season opener. Selee at first ordered Klobedanz back as well, but he rescinded that decision at the pitcher's pleading and allowed him to continue with the team.[21]

On April 12, Boston beat Princeton College by only a run in a performance panned by the local press. Two days later, Nichols, Klobedanz, and Stivetts stopped Wesleyan College on their home field in Middleton, Connecticut. By then Collins, the last of the holdouts, had signed his contract, and Lewis had shown that his arm could be counted on. The final training games included a morning-afternoon doubleheader in Connecticut—the first game in Winstead and the second in Torrington. Other than Sullivan, the team looked ready for the season. The *Boston Journal* pronounced Selee's club "fine as silk." The newspaper asked league managers for their predictions, and Selee selected "Boston or Baltimore." Hanlon refused to pick a winner but strongly suggested that he believed his team would prevail. "Stenzel will greatly add to our batting strength, as well as McGraw, who is in fine condition and fielding better than he ever did," Ned told the *Journal*, adding, "I think we ought to win." Among managers who expressed an opinion, more picked the Orioles, although the Beaneaters and Cleveland also had support.[22]

Patriots' Day

The fans certainly thought Boston was ready to contend. A crowd of twelve thousand made the visit out to the South End Grounds for the opener against the Phillies, a game scheduled three days before any others in deference to the observance of Patriots' Day in Boston. Philadelphia lacked much in the way of pitching, but its tandem of the great Ed Delahanty, a two-time .400 batter, and the phenom Napoleon Lajoie provided plenty of punch.

South End Grounds was considered one of the classic parks of its day, largely because of two factors: the site's many years of use as a ball field and the fact that it hosted a perennially good team. The facility itself was not all that old; it had been raised in two months after a fire destroyed its predecessor in the middle of a game on May 15, 1894. Like all parks in those days, South End and its predecessor—along with much of the rest of Boston—had been constructed of wood. In addition, ambient combustible material—hay and straw used as feed and oil used for lamps—was underfoot everywhere. With several thousand people together in such a confined space, and given the contemporary popularity of cigars, fire was a distinct possibility. Nobody knows why flames broke out in the original South End Grounds during the third inning of the game with the Orioles that day, but it raced through the susceptible facility, leaving patrons and grounds crewmen alike barely enough time to escape.

The reconstructed ballpark featured twin spires atop the grandstand, suggestive of the Churchill Downs racetrack, except that the grandstand was smaller. In fact, most everything about the South End Grounds was smaller, beginning with the number of seats. Team owners had made the serious mistake of underinsuring the original property, so when it succumbed to flames they could not afford to rebuild it fully. As a result, even though the structure itself was new, even the most loyal Rooters grumbled about the cramped quarters that did not allow their heroes to properly show off their skills. It was only 250 feet to the foul pole in left field and 255 to the one in right field, and the railroad tracks that impinged on the park on two sides eliminated almost all of the foul territory down the lines. Worse, passing trains could be counted on to periodically rain smoke and cinders down on the third base patrons and on the field itself. If the wind was right and the traffic heavy, games were halted in order to allow the haze generated by the trains to clear.

Management tried to make up for the kids' ball dimensions down the lines by extending the fence between left center and right center to 440 feet or more in an extreme bathtub shape. For the owners, that had a side benefit. On days when the demand for seats exceeded supply, the excess crowd could be penned behind ropes strung in deep center field. On such occasions, a special ground rule was imposed; anything into the crowd was two bases. Still, for a renowned ballpark, the place had an antiquated feel to it. The *Sporting News* exclaimed, "A dirtier ground does not exist."[23]

The outfield had plenty of room for spectators, at least in the center. In those days, of course, the dimensions were largely irrelevant to Boston batters, who rarely came to the plate with the fences in mind. In 1896 Herman Long had led the team in home runs with six, a feat attributable more to his speed than his muscle. The entire team had hit just thirty-six home runs, and even that meager total was the most of any team in the league's first division.

As everyone assumed he would, Selee gave the ball to Nichols for the season opener. Kid took the mound under sunny skies but unusually strong winds that complicated the fielders' lives. Although not at the top of his game, Nichols was more than respectable for most of the afternoon, allowing one run in the fifth inning when Billy Nash slapped a hit-and-run single to right that sent rookie Sam Gillen around to third. Al Orth, a light-hitting second-year pitcher whose abilities would be summed up in the nickname "the Curveless Wonder," nibbled at a careless Nichols fastball and plopped it inside the left-field foul line to produce the first run. With two on and two out in the ninth, the score was 3–0 as Nichols looked in at the dangerous Lajoie. In the grandstand there were murmurs about the strapping second-year player who had made his mark as a rookie in 1896. At six feet one and 195 pounds, and with a lush head of black hair, the twenty-two-year-old native of Woonsocket, Rhode Island, perfectly fit the description "tall, dark, and handsome." He also could hit, as his .326 rookie average showed. How had Boston let a prime prospect from New England get all the way to Philadelphia? fans asked one another without bothering to speculate on an answer.

Lajoie may have been a visiting neighbor, but baseball was no gentleman's game, and this was no spot for pleasantries. Nichols's first pitch, a fastball, came buzzing directly toward the big Rhode Islander's head. He turned out of its path. A second fastball followed, lower and not as close. Lajoie swung and the ball flew over the left-field fence far enough from the pole that no doubt would be cast on its legitimacy. The 3–0 lead was now 6–0.[24]

Between that hit and Orth's work on the mound, the festivities appeared to have been thoroughly spoiled as the Beaneaters came to bat for the final time. The Philadelphia pitcher had not allowed a hit until Bobby Lowe's with two out in the fifth, and no Boston base runner had reached second until Hamilton did so in the eighth. Worse, after Nichols led off the ninth inning with a walk and Hamilton was retired, pinch runner Stahl tried to make third on Tenney's single to right. The throw easily beat him, but the rookie kicked at Nash's glove and dislodged it. For one of the few times that afternoon, you could hear noise at the South End Grounds. Stahl scored seconds later on Long's ground out. At least the Bostons had avoided the embarrassment of a shutout.

Duffy reached first base on a weak fly to short center that scored Tenney; then Collins lined a solid base hit. Now the Boston partisans were on their feet. Lowe also singled, loading the bases. Suddenly, as Tucker came to the plate, they had reason to hope; a home run, however unlikely, would tie the game.

The first pitch was a fastball, as Tucker expected it to be, and he was ready, sending it for the distant reaches of right field. The ball hit the board fence about two feet from the top, clearing the bases and putting Tucker safely at second. Even so, it was a piece of bad luck, for the fence had been raised several feet in that spot during the off-season; in previous years the same ball would have been a home run. But that was as close as the home club would come on this day, for the next batter, veteran catcher Charles Ganzel, was retired on an infield grounder.

For Selee the failure to rally from six runs behind in the final inning was not the toughest part of the defeat. Such a rally would not happen often, and he believed it would not be needed often either. Anyway, Ganzel was about the last regular he would want up in such a situation; he had only started because Bergen's hand was sore. No, the tough part was that the schedule called for that league opener to be followed by two days of official idleness before league play resumed. And when it did, the resumption would take place at Baltimore's Union Park, one of the toughest places for a visitor to play ball.

Until then, all the Beaneaters could do was run through a couple of exhibition games against local teams on the unlikely chance that such action would prepare them to meet the Orioles. That was the league-wide tune-up plan. The Giants, for example, took on the town team of Elizabeth, New Jersey, and got whatever practice a team acquires from winning 40–1.

Neither of the Beaneaters' final exhibition games appeared to have helped them. After disposing of the Taunton team with a seven-run first, Boston looked lethargic in a 9–6 loss to Pawtucket. Selee knew that any club incapable of handling Pawtucket would be in for a tough time at Baltimore.

4. Parade of Champions

The city of Baltimore knew how to welcome a champion. The opening of the 1897 season marked the third straight year a championship banner would be raised over Union Park following much pomp and circumstance and more than a little levity.

"A trombone player has written an Oriole march and dedicated it to the team," observed Albert Mott, a well-known bicycling official and rabid baseball fan who doubled as *Sporting Life*'s Baltimore correspondent. Mott then turned that bit of news into a spring training weather report. "Do you know what an Oriole march is? Well, it's wet, that's what it is," he joked.[1]

The city appointed an official committee to organize the opening-day events, and the committee made sure that every business, ward, and parish would have a chance to be involved. They even extended a personal invitation to President McKinley, who had promised to try to make it if the demands of his position permitted him to do so. They did not. But state and local business virtually ground to a halt for the event. The *Baltimore Sun* reported that "all the state and city officials, 1,000 bankers and merchants, and 500 priests and clergymen of all denominations will be on hand."[2] Detailed plans were drawn for a parade in precisely the following order: "Police escort, full fifth regiment band and drum corps, committee in carriages, four-horse victoria in which

Fig. 8. The 1897 Boston Beaneaters. *Front*: Jimmy Collins, Chick Stahl, Bobby Lowe. *Middle*: Herman Long, Kid Nichols, Doc Yeager, Frank Selee (manager), Hugh Duffy (captain), Fred Tenney, Billy Hamilton. *Back*: Jim Sullivan, Jake Stivetts, Bob Allen, Charles Ganzel, Fred Klobedanz, Ted Lewis, Fred Lake. (National Baseball Hall of Fame Library, Cooperstown NY.)

President-manager Hanlon and treasurer Von der Horst will be seated; five carriages containing the three-time champions; float decorated in red, white, blue, orange and black colors; with the 1896 pennant at the front, those of 1894 and 1895 at the rear, and the Temple Cup in the center; carriage containing the Boston management; five carriages with Boston players, newspaper men and citizens escort."[3]

The parade route taxed the diligence of the celebrants. Beginning at the Eutaw House at 1:15 p.m., it wove through crowds five and six deep downtown, then uphill about a mile toward the city's George Washington monument, circling the monument itself before proceeding to Huntington Avenue, a distance of about two and one-half miles.

Once at the park, the parade participants left their carriages, formed four lines, and strode through the gates to march music and the cheers of thousands more of the team's fans. "An inspiring sight . . . the parade

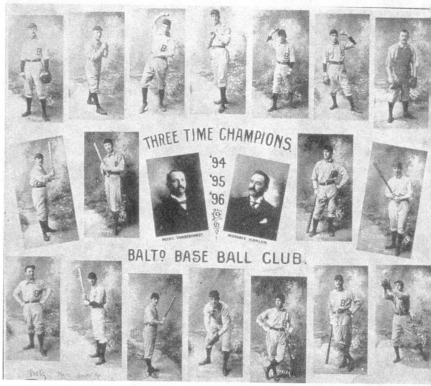

THREE TIME CHAMPIONS
'94
'95
'96

BALTⱰ BASE BALL CLUB.

9. The 1897 Baltimore Orioles. *Top*: Boileryard Clarke, Doc Amole, Bill Hoffer, Joe Corbett, Arlie Pond, Jeremiah Nops, Wilbert Robinson. *Middle*: Heinie Reitz, Hughie Jennings, Harry Von der Horst (president), Ned Hanlon (manager), Joe Kelley, Jack Doyle. *Bottom*: Joe Quinn, Tom O'Brien, John McGraw, Hank Bowerman, Willie Keeler, Al Maul, Jake Stenzel. (Transcendental Graphics, Boulder co.)

of champions in their new uniforms, the stirring music of a fine band, the display of the Temple Cup and of the three pennants in miniature," remarked the *Boston Herald*'s J. C. Morse in *Sporting Life*.[4]

If that seems like a garish way to celebrate the start of a baseball season, it is nevertheless consistent with the celebration of baseball in Baltimore in the mid-1890s. In fact, it was not sufficiently garish. Once at the ballpark, the parade order was reassembled for a march to the center of the playing field, where the three pennants were all unfurled and then raised on three flagstaffs set in a corner of the grounds.

The three-time champions had emerged from their spring workouts as proud and confident as always. Even before practices began, John

McGraw confessed to a reporter, "I just don't see how we can lose."[5] Others did have a theory about how Baltimore could lose, and it hinged on rumors concerning the health of the team's star shortstop, Hughie Jennings. During the winter, it was said, he had injured his arm. At the team's Macon, Georgia, training site, nobody knew about the injury because they had not seen Jennings. Ned Hanlon had granted the shortstop permission to report late in order to coach the baseball team at the University of Georgia, an interest that developed from his work with McGraw at St. Bonaventure College. So except for one or two exhibitions in which the Orioles played Jennings's college team, Jennings wasn't even with the team until April 1, when they prepared to break for their northern journey. Instead, Hanlon worked his infield sub, Joe Quinn, at short.

No Competition

Hanlon had had more immediate concerns in preparing his team—specifically, the weather. He had made it a point of taking the Orioles south for the heat and isolation, but that also meant putting up with the spring rains in Georgia. The rain that canceled workouts and forced them inside was one reason he had dismissed Selee's proposal for a series . . . that and the fact that he saw no value in putting his team's progress or lack of it on view for his rival. The truth was that the Orioles were already behind Hanlon's demanding schedule.

Much of what they had done in Macon had amounted to running in mud. Belying his bulk, Wilbert Robinson was the most fanatical at this, routinely running the mile between the team's hotel and the field, then taking another mile or so run around the track, and then running back to the hotel, both in the morning and in the afternoon.[6] Others tried innovative variations on the theme. McGraw brought his bicycle with him and often used it to cycle the distances. The team's star lead-off hitter spent most of his free time in the batting cage, where he worked to perfect both his bunting stroke and his swing.

The work showed during a late March game in Columbus, Georgia, against a local team. McGraw batted five times, collecting two singles, a double, and a triple, and spraying those hits to all fields, apparently on demand. Indeed, for McGraw and all of the Orioles, the roughest part about the two-day Columbus trip had been the accommodations. They checked in at their hotel only to learn that the entire team had been assigned to a single room.[7] It took lobbying on the scale the team would normally use against an umpire to free up enough accommodations for everyone to get a decent night's rest. The next day one of the town's leading citizens, owner of the local electric car line, made up for the previous lack of hospitality by treating the players to tours of the city.

When Jennings rejoined the team, he sported a new red mustache that matched his hair. He denied any lingering arm problem, although his language suggested that there had been—and could still be—something to the story. "My wing is all right and I can do my own backing up," he told teammates.[8]

From Georgia the club had tried to play its way through North Carolina and Virginia, splitting into two camps. One was led by Hanlon, the other by Joe Kelley. But rain often interfered. Five games were scheduled for the first week of April, but only one was played, and that was by Kelley's group in Charlotte. There the Orioles easily beat a local team, scoring 24 runs. A few days later they put up 22 runs against a Newport News team. Their averages looked fat: Heinie Reitz was batting .667; Hughie Jennings and Joe Kelley were above .500; and Willie Keeler, Wilbert Robinson, and Jake Stenzel were above .400. But the players felt uneasy. They weren't getting in enough games, and they certainly hadn't felt challenged by the low-level competition they were facing.[9] By the time they arrived in Baltimore for a week's worth of exhibitions before the opening of the regular season, hardly any team had played them within five runs.

Hanlon, for one, felt they had been challenged enough. "The trip was more than usually enjoyable," he told the Baltimore fans. He pronounced the team, including Jennings, "in fine condition."[10] Their final tune-ups had included a game against Princeton's Ivy League champions. In those days the champion of the Ivy League was commonly considered the superior team in college athletics, so the match-up was billed as pitting the best professional club against the best amateur one. The game itself was no contest, Baltimore winning 10–1 in front of its home fans. But that game and two others on the home grounds against Toronto's minor-league team gave Jennings the opportunity to put to rest local concerns about his health. New rumors had refreshed those concerns. A report out of Washington said a Hanlon emissary had put out feelers regarding the availability of Senators shortstop Zeke Wrigley. Hanlon vociferously denied them. "There is not a word of truth to it," he said. "I don't know (the agent) or Zeke Wrigley, and I don't want to."[11] It's probable that the Senators, who had a first-rate young shortstop in Gene DeMontreville, had started the rumor as a means of creating demand for Wrigley. Any player Hanlon valued would be worth more on the trade or sale market. In any event, Jennings stayed in the lineup at shortstop, and Wrigley played out the season in Washington as a utility hand.

In the final days of training, the Orioles were forced to confront one other rumor—that they were negotiating the trade of Jack Doyle to Brooklyn. This one had more staying power, and not merely because Brooklyn coveted him. As a Giant in 1894, Doyle had welshed on his deal with Keeler to split their Temple Cup shares fifty-fifty, keeping the full amount of New York's share for himself. The bad blood that he had created had never fully healed. That act, combined with Dirty Jack's penchant for profanely riding teammates as hard as opponents (although he was far from alone among the Orioles in this behavior), made him one of the most widely hated players in the league.[12] Even so, Hanlon was able to look past the disruption Doyle presented in the clubhouse, which was naturally turbulent anyway, to his unquestioned ability. The Orioles had won with Doyle in 1896, and Hanlon felt they could do so again in 1897.

Unionization's Brief Rebirth

The club Selee brought to Baltimore was unsure of itself. At thirty-three, Tommy Tucker had slowed visibly. The manager wanted to give Chick Stahl a chance to show what he could do, but Fred Tenney was playing too well in right to be removed. It was now clear that Marty Bergen's sore finger would have him out for several days at the minimum. Then there was the pitching staff. Jim Sullivan's arm had not responded, leaving only Kid Nichols, Jack Stivetts, Fred Klobedanz, and the untried rookie Ted Lewis. The situation worried Selee enough that he allowed Herman Long to work out as a pitcher in practice, although putting the league's best shortstop on the mound was a move that even Selee would consider only as an emergency measure.

At least there was one issue that the Boston manager didn't have to worry about with his players: unionization. A rebirth of the Brotherhood movement, which had swept the league a decade earlier and led to the ruinous war in 1890, had emerged in several cities. Boston players acknowledged hearing the talk but seemed less immersed in it than others. Long, who had come to the National League during the Brotherhood War, called the whole issue exaggerated. He did not dismiss the movement, however, telling J. C. Morse that interest in a "beneficial and protective order" lingered.[13]

The $2,400 salary cap, a residue of the postwar years, remained a sore point among players, especially the game's stars. Probably the chief agitator was Chicago Colts pitcher Clark Griffith, one of the few nonveterans of 1890 to emerge in the wake of the market consolidation in 1891. Griffith hadn't fully blossomed until 1894, when he won twenty-one games for Cap Anson's club, but by the start of 1897 his record showed seventy victories and only thirty-nine defeats for Chicago.

Griffith viewed his complaint with missionary zeal, playing without a contract in April and reportedly demanding a raise to $2,500. The Colts' owner, James Hart, was unsympathetic. "I voluntarily told him there would be a difference of $400 between his salary this year and last," Hart told the press. "Strange to say he was not satisfied. Can't you make it $500," he reported Griffith as saying, and added, "I told him not to make such a demand; that it was unreasonable and would not be listened to."[14]

After being rejected by Hart, Griffith set about to strengthen his coterie of complainers. At least half the members of his own Colts team quickly signed on, and they took the cause on the road with them to St. Louis and Cincinnati. "We are getting tired of earning more and more every season for the magnates and getting none of it," Griffith told reporters in Cincinnati.[15] Out of St. Louis emerged reports that at season's end the players planned to challenge the legality of the reserve clause—the contractual stipulation that bound players to teams indefinitely—as well as the salary scale and the fining system. Griffith recalled a promise made by the owners following the Brotherhood War's settlement to the effect that the $2,400 salary cap was only a temporary measure to be lifted once that war's debts were retired. "That debt was wiped out in the fall of 1895," Griffith asserted, citing as evidence the discontinuance of a 10 percent assessment against team profits. "Did we fare any better in 1896? Are we faring better in 1897? If possible we are faring worse," he argued.[16]

In Baltimore the Orioles met, and Kelley and Jennings confirmed that all had informally agreed to join the movement. Jennings explained why. "Just look at how ballplayers are treated now," he complained. "Why should they not organize?"[17]

Although Anson did not try to publicly quash the incipient insurrection among his Chicago team, he made it clear that he was not in sympathy with it. "Griffith . . . has some willing lieutenants," he conceded. But, he added, "the League has spotters everywhere, and . . . I am sure it will be unpleasant for the player who became too zealous in his reform movement." In an era known for its often-violent labor unrest—the Haymarket riots and the Pullman strike were both fresh in memory—Anson's remark was ominous. He termed the Brotherhood "still enough of a recent disaster" to quell any serious talk of insurrection.[18] That was also the view of the major sports publica-

tions. "Did it ever occur to the Chicago player philanthropist that in
the event of the consummation of his ideas and their legitimate frui-
tion in a strike, the history of the Players League war would repeat itself?" asked *Sporting Life*.[19]

Swept from Baltimore

Fortunately for the league's peace, if not for the players, the April strike
talk turned out to be a tempest, dying out either because of the pennant race itself or, as Anson had suggested, because of the players' dis-
interest in revisiting 1890. Regardless, Selee now was able to focus on
his slim pitching staff, a problem that worsened almost immediately.
In front of the rabid capacity crowd of 13,500 Baltimoreans, Stivetts
pitched the first five innings, complained of a sore arm, and was pulled
in favor of Klobedanz with one runner on base and one out in the
sixth, the Beaneaters leading 5–4. Orioles baseball almost immediately took over.

The second batter, Jennings, leaned into a fastball and was hit. Then
as now, a rule was in effect denying first base to a hit batter if he deliberately tried to be hit, but Jennings was a master at avoiding detection.
It was the first of forty-six times he would gain first base in this fashion during the season. The Beaneaters squawked loudly to the game's
only umpire, Tom Lynch, protesting that Jennings had been up to one
of Baltimore's usual tricks. But Lynch stood firm. He was one of the
few veteran umps in the National League in 1897 and also one of the
few who were not easily intimidated. At a time when an umpire's career was often measured in days or weeks, Lynch had umpired professionally for eight seasons, and it is no exaggeration to say he was the
most respected official on the National League staff. He earned that respect through the firmness and certainty of his calls. The best "kickers"
could argue, cuss, and browbeat a reversal out of some of the stiffs the
league allowed to arbitrate, but even the orneriest players knew there
was no point in trying to push Tom Lynch. All it would get you was a
fine and possibly an ejection.

Klobedanz followed the rhubarb by walking Kelley on four bad pitches, loading the bases for Doyle. The Oriole first baseman had already hit safely three times against Stivetts, and he shot Klobedanz's first pitch over Billy Hamilton's head in center for two easy bases. The three resulting runs gave the Orioles a 7–5 advantage, and from there Baltimore pulled away to a comfortable 10–5 victory.

But if Orioles fans read the score as a portent, they were focusing on the wrong detail. As it turned out, the most significant play of the game was the one in the very first inning in which McGraw suffered a sprained ankle. The seriousness of the sprain was not immediately clear, but the injury would sideline him for several weeks. It was also the start of a trend among the Orioles, who from that day forward rarely put their starting lineup on the field intact and healthy.

If Selee had any reason to cheer as he rose for Friday's second game of the series, it stemmed from the realization that Kid Nichols was taking the mound against Arlie Pond, the Johns Hopkins University medical student. Entering the eighth inning, Nichols's work had been good for a 5–4 lead in a game that lived up to all expectations, in both quality and roughness of play. Boston runners especially complained that Doyle, Jennings, and McGraw's substitute, Quinn, were taking advantage of Lynch's inability to follow the ball and the base-path action at the same time. This sort of beef was, of course, nothing new in Baltimore, and the home fans loudly dismissed it, as did Lynch, who adhered to the dictum that an umpire can't call what he doesn't see.

In the eighth inning, Baltimore's precision overcame Nichols's skills. Keeler led off and spun one past Bobby Lowe into right field. With Jennings at bat, the assumption was that the Orioles would try their specialty, the hit and run. They had already tried it several times, including once in the sixth inning, when Tenney's superb throw on Jennings's hit to right field cut down Keeler as he tried to take third base. This time Jennings rapped it on the ground past Tucker, allowing Keeler to reach third easily and touching off a verbal storm in the grandstands. Now the Orioles' options were essentially limitless. With the

tying and lead runs at third and first and Kelley due up, they could re-
prise the hit and run, try a double steal, squeeze, put on the Baltimore
Chop, or—perhaps the least likely scenario—simply let their cleanup
hitter swing away. The Boston infielders drew in, assuming some sort
of trickery was afoot.

The trickery turned out to be Jennings breaking for second on a double steal. Doc Yeager fired to get him, but the throw eluded Long, and
Keeler trotted home with the tying run. Now Kelley chopped one to
Jimmy Collins, who in his haste failed to handle the ball. Doyle went
down on an infield bouncer, but outfielder Jake Stenzel and catcher
Boileryard Clarke both touched Nichols for hits, allowing Jennings
and Kelley to score. The final score was 7–5.[20]

Selee retreated to the Eutaw House in a state of concern, if not panic.
Not only was his team 0-3, but Stivetts's injury reduced his pitching
options to just three—Nichols, Klobedanz, and Lewis. "I don't think
Stivetts will do much more pitching for the Boston team," he told Tim
Murnane that night. "He is growing rather stiff."[21] In time, that medical opinion would prove to be unduly pessimistic, but there was no
doubt that the Beaneaters needed one or two more arms. Selee sent out
an emergency call to John "Sadie" McMahon, a twenty-nine-year-old
right-hander who had left the Orioles the previous winter in a dispute
over salary, after winning eleven games. From his Wilmington, Del-
aware, home, McMahon wired his reply; he was interested in pitching again, but not on Boston's terms.[22] Eventually he would sign with
the Dodgers, appear in nine games, lose six of them, and record a 5.86
earned run average that was easily the worst of his nine-season career.
It sent him into retirement for good.

Few other options were available. Selee had run off one possibility,
Cozy Dolan, during spring workouts, refusing to either pitch him or
release him. Dolan had been unimpressive in auditions with the Beaneaters in 1895 and again in 1896. Hanlon offered to sell Selee an arm
from his more plush stable of eight pitchers, but that possibility never
got beyond the initial stages, largely because, as Murnane put it, "any-

thing Hanlon is willing to sell Selee is not anxious to buy."[23] That left Selee ticking off the possibilities at the minor-league level. He had seen one or two kids during the Pawtucket exhibition a few days earlier; perhaps one of them would help. Observed Murnane, "If anything should ever happen to Nichols, what would become of Boston?"[24]

Pitching was not Selee's only problem. Hugh Duffy had been miserable most of the spring and looked slow through the first three games as well. Selee suggested a fill-in be used for him. Duffy, a two-time batting champ who had not hit below .300 in nearly a decade, took that as a hint that he was no longer needed and bluntly invited Selee to trade him. Selee just as bluntly told Duffy that anybody who could bat .440, as Hugh had done a mere three seasons before, wasn't going anywhere and that his challenge was to find a way to break out of his slump.[25]

There the matter lay as the final game of the Baltimore series opened. A crowd of 5,500 watched Joe Corbett announce his presence in the rotation by striking out Hamilton and Tenney and dominating the game from that point on. Among the Beaneaters, only Duffy and Lowe hit against Corbett solidly, and the visitors' only run was scored after the outcome had been decided.

Boston's problems involved virtually every facet of play, mental as well as physical. In center field, Hamilton botched a line drive, allowing two runs to score, and at first, Tucker failed to reach two grounders that Selee believed a competent first baseman should have put away. At least Selee had lit a fire under Duffy; after their exchange, the outfielder raised his average to .430 by the conclusion of the series.

Coaching breakdowns led the list of mental miscues. The Beaneaters had failed to school themselves sufficiently in a new rule limiting teams to one coach on the field while there were runners on the bases. The rule had been enacted before the season began because coaches were widely used as agitators, either to rile the opposition or to bait crowds into trying to intimidate umpires.[26] Like a lot of things, that kind of coaching was considered a particular specialty of the Orioles, whose savviest veterans (and best kickers) shared time on the coaching lines.

But the Beaneaters' lone coach too often was not in the best position to help Boston runners. With Tenney performing the coaching duties during one of the Baltimore games, Tucker reached second base and Yeager's firm single to center seemed sure to score him. But Tenney failed to move from first to third (as most coaches were expected to do with a runner at second), so Tucker had to slow as he rounded the base and look over his shoulder to determine whether he could score. By the time he did that, the answer had changed from yes to no. He held up and never reached home plate. "The Orioles never committed such blunders," Tim Murnane remarked. "'Tis these little things that make a phenomenal aggregation of the Baltimore players, and make a great lot of players like the Bostons rather tame by comparison."[27]

As had been the case on Friday, Quinn, Jennings, and Doyle made things rough for those few Boston base runners who were able to hit against Corbett. (Quinn, who must have had an unusual pang of conscience for an Oriole, actually went to Eutaw House after the game in a futile attempt to make amends with the Boston players. Hamilton rejected his peace overture in what Murnane described as "rich style."[28]) As the base runner, Doyle also intimidated Lowe into fumbling a double-play ball at second. But none of that truly factored into the 7–1 outcome. The superiority of Baltimore's pitching was the real issue.

Besides, Boston fans were hardly the only ones complaining about the coaching limitations. Elmer Bates, *Sporting Life*'s correspondent in Cleveland, saw those limitations as a prissy concession to propriety that was unworthy of a manly game. "So far as this city is concerned a return to the old coaching rule [of] two men up with a man on base will be heartily welcomed," Bates wrote. "Baltimore, Pittsburg and Cincinnati may enjoy croquet and lawn tennis methods applied to base ball, but the old way is good enough for Cleveland."[29]

The Freeloading Neighbors

When the Beaneaters left Baltimore, Brooklyn came in and handed the Orioles their first defeat of the season. As was often the case with 3:30 p.m. starting times, darkness played a role in game conditions, as did well-used baseballs. The Orioles had forged a 3–3 tie in the sixth inning when Kelley's second hit of the game, a double, drove home Quinn and Jennings. From then through the ninth inning, both Baltimore's Bill Hoffer and Brooklyn's Harley Payne held their opponents scoreless. It was after 5:30 p.m. and getting dark when the tenth inning began, but neither captain petitioned umpire Bob Emslie to call the game short of a decision. All it took was a bad-hop grounder that baffled third baseman Quinn, plus a sacrifice, to put the lead run in scoring position for Billy Shindle, who drove it home with a line double. With his team now trailing 4–3, Doyle went after Emslie, lobbying the ump that it was too dark and too dangerous to continue play. Had Emslie bought the argument, the score would have reverted to its 3–3 standing after nine innings. But Emslie wasn't buying. He forced the Orioles to bat in the bottom of the tenth, and given the condition both of the sky and the ball, they essentially had no chance. Clarke, first up, had the best rip, but Shindle got in the way of his one-hopper to third and threw him out. Hoffer went down flailing at the air, and Quinn managed nothing more than a game-ending pop-up.[30]

Robinson reported to the park for the series' second game with a sore arm, a condition possibly aggravated by the cold and windy conditions. His bat still worked, though. The catcher's three hits included a single, following a double steal by Stenzel and Reitz, that put two runs across and gave the Orioles the 12–8 win.

Although Von der Horst was thrilled with the results of the first series, one serious concern surfaced during the games. Orioles fans who were disinterested in paying the fifty-cent grandstand admission fee had taken to climbing the rooftops across the street from the park for an unimpeded view of the games. In some cases, property owners had begun to rent out the space. Recognizing a costly trend when he saw one, Von der Horst tried erecting screens to block the view from the street. But the screens were awkward to move and ineffective. So before the second game of the Brooklyn series, Von der Horst talked the commissioner of the city's building inspection office into issuing an order. It prohibited homeowners along Barclay and Twenty-fourth Streets—essentially beyond the left-field and right-field bleachers—from allowing people to climb onto the roofs. The stated rationale was the danger of a serious accident, possibly even a collapse, from the weight of people on the roof supports.[31] The prohibition worked, if only briefly.

Those inside the park had plenty to watch, and a normal amount to beef about, during the Brooklyn finale. Emslie's ball and strike calls set Boileryard Clarke off time and time again, a fact that fans naturally ascribed to the umpire's inadequacies. "Clarke is fair-minded and impartial and a fine judge of balls and strikes," the *Baltimore Sun* said, with no suggestion of sarcasm.[32] But the Orioles were experienced enough to not let a little thing like complaints about umpires distract them. In the fifth inning, Keeler's somersault catch of a low liner brought the 3,500 fans to their feet. Stenzel contributed four hits, as did Clarke, and Keeler had three hits and a walk. That walk, coming with two out in the fourth, touched off a four-run inning that was classic Orioles baseball. Doyle followed it with a hit-and-run single that sent Keeler to third, and then Doyle stole second, drawing a wild throw that let Keeler score. In quick succession, Stenzel, Reitz, Clarke, and Corbett strung singles, the last three also of the hit-and-run variety. The net was four runs.[33]

The Giants came in next. Partly because New York's style of play mimicked Baltimore's, New York was a favorite rival. Now with Amos Rusie back from his 1896 absence, the rivalry promised to be even hotter. Bleacher fans greeted team captain "Scrappy" Bill Joyce and his club with sarcastic choruses of "The Sidewalks of New York" and "On the Bowery" between derisive characterizations of most of the Giants players.[34] The game, pitting Orioles pitcher Jerry Nops against flighty left-hander Ed Doheny, was a 1–1 tie until the fourth inning, when the Orioles' aggressive play unnerved the visitors. Stenzel started it with a double, broke for third, and scored when Giants catcher Parke Wilson's hurried throw sailed into left field. Reitz walked and tried a steal of second. Wilson again threw wildly, so Reitz took off for third. When outfielder George VanHaltren followed with a wild throw of his own, Reitz continued around to score. The Orioles were capable of making even good clubs look like sandlotters, and when they sensed weakness, they attacked harder. Another walk, a single, and a passed ball put runners on second and third for Keeler, who drove the ball over VanHaltren's head and off the top of the fence in center for three bases, allowing two more runs to score. When Kelley walked, the Orioles tried another double steal, but this time shortstop George Davis cut off Wilson's throw to second and returned it home in time to cut down Keeler's scoring effort.[35]

There was no stopping Willie Keeler during Friday's second game. Facing Mike Sullivan, a late substitute for Rusie, he hit safely all four times up, scored three times, stole three bases, and helped work two successful hit and runs. Almost single-handedly the little outfielder had been responsible for those three runs. In the first inning he bunted safely, took second on Sullivan's bad throw, and then raced all the way around to score on a wild pitch. In the fourth he beat out a grounder to first, lit out for second, and continued to third when Kelley found the hole that had been opened on the left side. Then he daringly scored on a fly to shallow left field. In the sixth inning he again bunted safely, reached third on a hit and run with Jennings working the bat, and scored on Doyle's fly to center. It was the kind of breathtaking ball that Orioles partisans had come to expect, and it helped the champions win 5–3, their seventh victory in eight tries. In addition to Keeler's brilliance, the game featured another of the disputes for which Union Park had become famous. In the sixth inning, Jennings barreled home from second on Stenzel's infield single, only to be thumbed out by Lynch. The shortstop and the 3,700 in attendance thought he was safe, and they let Lynch know about it in colorful terms.[36] Despite the call, Baltimore's record now stood at 7-1. Only the surprising form showed by Philadelphia, Cincinnati, and Louisville—each also with just one loss—had kept the Orioles from opening a large early lead.

Joyce may have planned to save Rusie for the expected big Saturday crowd; if so, that idea fizzled when rain washed out the contest. The only benefit was an extra day for the players to prepare for their first and longest road excursion of the season. Beginning on Monday, May 3, in Brooklyn, the road trip would take them to nine of the circuit's eleven other cities and deny their fans another chance to visit Union Park for more than a month. One thing was certain: Hanlon would send a formidable offensive lineup on the road. In their first eight games at home, the champions had hit a collective .325 and averaged nine runs per game. Among the regulars, Keeler—who had hit safely in all eight games—was above .500 and Kelley was above .400.

Decapitations at First

Selee used the journey to Philadelphia following the Orioles series to try to repair some of his team's problems. Tucker, who was off to a .200 start at the plate and whose painful awkwardness had contributed to three errors at first base (not to mention that he missed several balls Selee felt he should have reached), was benched. Stahl, who was more aggressive and had a better arm than Tenney, was given the right-field job. Tenney was brought in to see whether he could handle first base. He had flunked badly in a trial at that position during the spring training games of 1896, but he was off to a .353 start and was one of the few Beaneaters hitting the ball. "I doubt if Tenney will field as well as Tucker," Tim Murnane wrote the next day in one of his least prescient observations.[37] The veteran reporter concluded that the team would be better off because, as he wrote, "what [Tenney] loses on first base young Stahl will make up for in right field because [he is] plucky in going after those low liners that [Tenney] usually took on the first bound."[38]

Selee had to find out whether Stahl could hit major-league pitching, because other parts of the Boston lineup were soft. Hamilton, the speedy lead-off hitter, had gotten just three hits in his first seventeen shots against the Phillies and Orioles. The vaunted left side of the infield was going about as badly. Collins finished the first week batting .200, while Long had more errors afield (six) than hits (four in eighteen at bats).

Stahl announced himself with three solid hits the next afternoon at Philadelphia's Huntingdon Street Grounds, including a run-producing double in the second and a key base hit that spurred a ninth-inning rally. Those more than offset his only fielding attempt, an amateurish effort on a fly ball that he lost in the sun. Tenney played an uneventful first inning, and Murnane's assessment was unflattering. "He had a lot of trouble trying to keep one foot on the base, often dancing around like a decapitated hen."[39] Vivid imagery indeed.

The game, played in front of a crowd of about 6,500, which was strong for a Monday in Philadelphia, could easily have been Boston's fifth consecutive loss. But after entering the ninth inning trailing by three runs, the Beaneaters rallied for a tie before the game was halted by darkness. The rally involved overcoming more than the three-run deficit, for the home team stalled its way through the top of the ninth in the hope that Tim Hurst, a veteran umpire and also one of the game's feistiest, would call it off because of darkness. Hurst, the only umpire harder to intimidate than Lynch, flatly refused.

That left it up to the play on the field to decide the game. Stahl's third hit, coming with one out and runners at first and second, drove Long home with the first run. Lowe fanned, putting the Phillies within one out of the victory, when base runners Duffy and Stahl combined on a double steal. That strategy paid off when the next batter, Collins, slapped a game-tying single to right. Collins followed with a steal of second, inviting the Phillies to intentionally walk pinch hitter Klobedanz, who was recognized for his skill with the bat. Phillies pitcher Jack Taylor had a better idea; he drilled Klobedanz squarely in the shoulder. With no other options, Selee had to let his light-hitting substitute, Doc Yeager, take his scheduled turn in the box. Yeager grounded out feebly, and by then it was so dark that even Hurst had to agree to call the game in an 8–8 tie. But that was better than the next day's contest, when Kid Nichols lost for the third straight time, 10–8. Boston again staged a ninth-inning rally, this time scoring four runs, but the Beaneaters were so far behind that it made no difference. The only consolation was the effortless inning Sullivan worked in relief of Nichols in the top of the ninth. (Home teams had the right to select whether to bat first or last, and several often chose to hit first. At a time when a baseball might remain in play for four or five innings, some clubs considered it more of an advantage to get the first cuts at a ball that had not yet been beaten around than to have the final at bat.) The proud Beaneaters not only were winless, they were by themselves in twelfth place.

The season-opening losing streak ended with Wednesday's wrap-up game in Philadelphia, when Collins's brilliant fifth-inning handling of a bases-loaded grounder offset what otherwise would have been fatal damage caused by Stahl's loss of a fly ball in the sun. Long contributed three hits. The enthusiasm lasted less than one day. On Thursday, before 2,500 fans in Washington, errors by Collins and Long undermined Lewis's pitching and gave the Senators four second-inning gift runs in a 5–3 decision. "Put that mob in cotton and ship them to Oshkosh," a fan wired Selee at the hotel.[40] A more productive suggestion came from Washington manager Gus Schmelz, who expressed interest in Tucker. Selee didn't want what Schmelz was offering—first baseman Ed Cartwright—figuring that Tenney was the solution at that position. But if Schmelz wanted Tucker, Selee would be glad to talk, especially if Washington was willing to discuss its pitching staff.

For the second time in the season's first two weeks, coaching errors undermined a potential victory against the Senators on Friday. The gaffe occurred in the third inning, after Hamilton reached second base. The next batter, Long, slapped one off shortstop Gene DeMontreville's body and into center field. But with the only Beaneaters coach again wasted along the first base line, Hamilton reprised the problem of a few days before, stopping to look back and then holding up, never to cross the plate. The game was called in a 3–3 tie after ten innings. The next day's rainout at least had the virtue of allowing the Beaneaters to take an early train home.

Selee joined them only as far as New York, stopping there to see whether he could pry a pitcher away from Freedman. The Giants owner's asking price was steep: Tenney. Don't do it, team captain Hugh Duffy protested: "If he is let alone for a while he will play first base all right."[41] Duffy was concerned too that the pitcher most likely to be pried out of New York was left-hander Doheny, whose reputation for strange, surly behavior exceeded even that of Boston's own Bergen. "We don't want that fellow," the captain pointedly told Selee.[42]

Wisely, as it turned out, Selee listened to his captain. He did not trade Tenney, did not acquire Doheny or any other pitcher, and left well enough alone. Selee may not have sensed it—Boston fans probably would not have believed it—but their 1-6, last-place team had already weathered its longest losing streak of the season.

National League Standings (Evening of May 1)

TEAM	WINS	LOSSES	PERCENTAGE	GAMES BEHIND
Philadelphia	8	1	.889	—
Baltimore	7	1	.875	½
Cincinnati	6	1	.857	1
Louisville	5	1	.833	1½
Pittsburg	3	2	.600	3
Washington	2	4	.333	4½
Brooklyn	3	6	.333	5
St. Louis	2	5	.286	5
New York	2	5	.285	5
Cleveland	2	5	.286	5
Chicago	2	6	.250	5½
Boston	1	6	.143	6

5. Suspected Criminals

The simplest way to illustrate the lot of the major-league umpire in 1897 is with a couple of figures. The single umpire system was generally in use, meaning that in the twelve-team league, six umpires would be working at any given time. Allowing for vacations, illnesses, travel complications, and the occasional desire to use two umpires in a big series, a staff of eight or thereabouts should have been adequate to the task. Yet during the 1897 season, forty-three different men umpired at least one official National League game.[1]

Baseball cannibalized its umpires throughout the mid-1890s. Players made war on them, fans assaulted them, and league officials gave little more than lip service to their support or protection. In 1895 the umpiring staff contained only three men who had umpired fifty major-league games during the previous season.[2]

Little wonder then that in June the *Sporting News* took to open ridicule of the league's umpiring corps. It repeated the definitions of an umpire that it claimed were making the rounds: a suspected criminal; an open enemy of society; an individual who has no right to live; an outlaw; a notorious robber; a convicted assassin. The verb *to lynch*, it announced, was derived from a member of this species (referring to umpire Tom Lynch).[3]

Players and fans had complained about bad calls since the game was invented. But the emergence of the Orioles in 1894, with their empha-

Fig. 10. The pugnacious Tim Hurst, who maintained his reputation as an umpiring force despite being arrested in both Cleveland and Cincinnati during the 1897 season. (Transcendental Graphics, Boulder co.)

sis on winning through intimidation, intensified the problem. As early as 1894 a Brooklyn reporter offered the following judgment regarding what he had seen on the field of play:

> [Umpire McQuade] tried his utmost to rob Brooklyn out of a well-earned victory in the first game by a number of weird decisions that call forth the derision of every spectator present. He gave Stivetts a base on balls in the fifth inning when the batter had struck out, giving Boston a run. In the ninth he called a hit by McCarthy which was foul by two feet fair, and it was only by the sharpest kind of work that Brooklyn managed to prevent Bos-

Fig. 11. Jack Sheridan, whose umpiring career ended abruptly in the summer of 1897 when he could not take the on-field abuse. (National Baseball Hall of Fame Library, Cooperstown NY.)

ton from tying the score. Later Stivetts acknowledged that he had been struck out, while Staley and one or two other Boston players declared that McCarthy's hit was foul.[4]

The umpires' difficulties were compounded by league president Nick Young's tendency to blame them. Himself a former umpire, Young scolded them in 1895 for lenience. "You must be master of the situation, or the players will boss you all over the lot," he told them. "If you are run out, it will be for lack of nerve to enforce the rules."[5]

If umpire backbone was a problem, turnover—and its twin issue, reliability—also contributed. With travel difficult and time-consuming, the custom in the event that an umpire was not in attendance was for the contesting teams to agree on an umpire. This might be a for-

Fig. 12. Thomas Lynch, the urbane umpire who refused to work doubleheaders and later rose to the presidency of the National League. (National Baseball Hall of Fame Library, Cooperstown NY.)

mer player or fan called down from the stands. But the most common solution was for the teams to appoint players to umpire. One team's selection would take the balls and strikes, the other's selection would call the bases. This practice invigorated games in nine of the twelve league cities in 1897—all but Boston, Baltimore, and Brooklyn. But it was especially prevalent among the lower-standing teams and those in the more remote western cities. More than one-quarter of the entire St. Louis home schedule was presided over by umpires who worked fewer than ten games all season. The Louisville Colonels played fourteen home games that were officiated by nonprofessionals, including six by Louisville players. Naturally, the use of players as umpires raised questions of impartiality. Dick Butler, a rookie Louisville backup catcher, worked five games, and the Colonels won four of them. Pitcher Bert Cunningham officiated on four occasions, and Louisville lost only one of the games. Considering that Louisville won only 40 percent of its games all season, those nine wins in ten games amounted to a fortuitous coincidence.[6]

The Regulars

Young hired a staff of seven umpires for the season's start: Robert Emslie, Tim Hurst, Thomas Lynch, Sandy McDermott, James Mc-Donald, Hank O'Day, and Jack Sheridan. As a group, they lacked the experience to handle the type of rough-and-tumble game that was in vogue then. Only Lynch (eight years) and Emslie and Hurst (six years each) had more than a journeyman's big-league experience. Sheridan had officiated for two seasons, McDonald and O'Day had one season each, and McDermott was a newcomer.

For the first third of the season, those seven umpires at least showed up for work. That work, by the way, tended to be in limited locales. Lynch, for example, umpired eighty-two games in the league's six eastern cities but just thirty-one in the six western cities (all when there were no games being played in the eastern cities). Emslie worked just one game between two western teams, and that was a Sunday visit by the Reds to Louisville that was sandwiched between series in which the Colonels hosted the Giants and the Phillies. Of the 129 games that Emslie umpired in 1897, only 37 were held in locations west of the Allegheny Mountains.[7]

Allowing umpires to work in selected areas may have saved money, but it also bred animosities. By the latter part of June, the more than occasional arguments, which often led to physical confrontations, took their toll. The rookie McDermott had essentially been based in Louisville; his fifty-one assignments included seventeen of the Colonels' thirty scheduled home games between the start of the season and July 1. Whether the "kicking" got to him or there were other factors is not a matter of public record, but on July 26 he walked off the job, never to return. Five days later, Sheridan quit too. He gave no public explanation, although Lynch let one slip in August. "The players simply broke Jack's heart," he told reporters.[8]

With a third of the season to go, the league umpiring staff was down to five persons charged with handling six games a day across half the nation. To survive as an umpire in that atmosphere took a tough-minded, stubborn individual. The three veterans—Emslie, Lynch, and Hurst— were prototypes in that respect. Lynch, whom the *Sporting News* mocked in its definition of the umpiring corps, was the most cerebral. Possessed of the debonair look of a businessman, he was a proper New Englander who did his best to elevate the profession. Sometimes he carried that to an extreme, such as on the occasions when he refused to work the second games of doubleheaders, asserting that he had already done what he had been paid for and that any further labor would be professionally demeaning. Lynch also took bullying as an intolerable affront, and he was known to walk off the field in the middle of a game when he felt that aspersions against him had exceeded the bounds of propriety.

Once, at New York's Polo Grounds, Lynch stopped a fight by fining the participating players one hundred dollars each. That prompted Giants owner Andrew Freedman to call Lynch a robber and several other names that have not survived in print. Such occasions, Lynch later admitted, would cause him to have to take in-season "vacations," one of which lasted for two weeks, from mid-July into August of 1897.[9]

By the time he retired during the 1902 season, Lynch had worked more games than anyone else—more than 1,200—and was regarded throughout the game as "the King of Umpires." Proof that he had emerged with his reputation intact came less than a decade later when he became the second former umpire (after Young) to rise to the position of president of the league.

Hurst was similar to Lynch only in his dedication to the game and the job. Where Lynch was debonair, Hurst was uncouth; where Lynch governed by force of intellect and personality, Hurst governed by force alone. He was purported to have had more physical clashes with ball-players than any other umpire.

A product of the Pennsylvania state leagues, with a bit of minor-league managing experience, Hurst was a short, wiry figure. "To face a crowd of 2,000 and call 'play ball' requires some grit," he explained.[10] After his umpiring days ended—the result of a 1909 incident in which he spat on the Athletics' Eddie Collins—Hurst elaborated on his dictatorial approach. "Every umpire makes mistakes," he said. "I remember that I even made a mistake at one time. At least I thought it was a mistake. I called a strike when no more than the seam of the ball was over the edge of the plate." Added Hurst, "I have been accused of making other mistakes, but that is unjust."[11]

Like Lynch, Hurst had plenty of run-ins with Freedman. In fact, between August 4, 1896, and September 20, 1897, Hurst umpired 159 games, not a single one of them at the Polo Grounds. He claimed Freedman had interceded with the league office to essentially bar him from the place.

Emslie's background was as a pitcher in the American Association, and he had retired following the 1885 season to take up umpiring. Like the other two veterans, Emslie had been tested and had proved he could withstand the abuse. No incident stuck in his memory more than his obviously missed call that settled a game between the Orioles and the Reds in Cincinnati on May 9, 1896. Emslie had Hughie Jennings to thank for that predicament. The Oriole shortstop was on second base in the tenth inning of a 5–5 tie when a ground ball rolled to Bid McPhee, Cincinnati's reliable second baseman. Representing the winning run, Jennings tore out for third. McPhee's throw would have been in time to retire Jennings, so the Oriole shouldered Reds third baseman Charlie Irwin and knocked him down, then continued around to score. It was a clear case of interference, and when Emslie made no call, the home partisans stormed the field after him. It took a police escort to get him off the field. But Emslie did not scare easily; he lasted as a big-league umpire until the early 1920s.[12]

The advantages of using two umpires were evident well before 1897, but the chief drawback obviously was expense. For more important games, the league often would assign two umpires, but those games were rare exceptions. There was frequent agitation to adopt the two-umpire system league-wide, an agitation led by noted sports writer Henry Chadwick in the *Sporting News*. "I cannot conceive why it is the league president cannot see how necessary it is that the double umpire system should be made the rule of the league," he asserted. "You reduce the chances for offensive kicking to a very great extent, and the more you lessen the kicking the greater your grandstand patronage will be; and in these days of Tebeauism the loss of that patronage is to be counted by thousands of dollars."[13]

Any umpire in any league city could count on working in a challenging environment. Writing in *Sporting Life* in May of 1897, Orioles correspondent Albert Mott reported on the following "dialogue" during an Orioles-Beaneaters series. Although the language is applied facetiously, it illustrates both the conditions that men such as Lynch, Hurst, and Emslie had to deal with and the tolerant view that many storytellers had of such incidents.

> Umpire Lynch, Duffy and Jennings and Tenney and Doyle gathered around second base at one time in the game. One could hear Tenney say, "You tried to block me off," and Jennings' reply, "I beg your pardon, but I didn't." Then Duffy would remark, "I beg your pardon, but I saw you." Then Jack Doyle sauntered down and said to Tenney, "I beg your pardon, but you are too big a man to light into Jennings that way this early in the season." Then Mr. Lynch remarked, "There, that's enough, now get back in the game," and it was all over. Did you ever hear anything so disgusting?[14]

The Privilege of Rank

As two of the league's premier franchises, the Beaneaters and the Orioles seemed to draw the more proven officials to their games. Lynch,

Hurst, and Emslie worked fifty-five of the sixty-six games played in Boston and thirty-nine of the sixty-six in Baltimore. It was Emslie who was assigned to call the Beaneaters' early May series against the Phillies in Boston, and not surprisingly, he got a roasting in the press for his work. "Umpire Emslie handled the game in good shape, but allowed the visitors to have two coaches up most of the time," Tim Murnane complained in the *Boston Globe*. "Why not live up to the rules?" Then, having conceded the propriety of Emslie's work at calling the game, Murnane retracted even that concession. "Emslie was off on strikes, giving [Phillies pitcher] Fifield all the best of it, while [Klobedanz] got the small end. Emslie did the best he could," Murnane concluded, "but facts are facts."[15]

Based solely on that description, one would assume that the Beaneaters had taken another soaking at the hands of the visitors, abetted by sloppy umpiring. In fact, Fred Klobedanz struck out ten batters, Chick Stahl delivered a couple of key hits, and Boston pulled away to a 5–2 victory. Ted Lewis was penetrable the next day, but Fred Tenney saved a run with a leaping, one-handed catch of the pitcher's high throw, and Stahl produced another key hit during a four-run seventh inning that gave Boston their 7–5 victory. Washington came in for the first of three games on Thursday, but Kid Nichols's return to form after a ten-day rest, coupled with three hits by Bobby Lowe, resulted in a 5–1 decision, the club's third straight.

The game produced two scary moments. In the second inning, Jimmy Collins pursued a foul fly by the low fence beyond third. The ball fell safely in the seats, but Collins's nose collided with the head of one of the patrons, and a fracture was feared. After a delay, Collins continued.

Then, with two out in the ninth, two singles—sandwiched around Herman Long's muff of a ground ball—filled the bases for third baseman Charley Reilly. Although not much of a power threat—he had hit just fifteen home runs in his previous seven seasons—Reilly's presence raised temperatures in the South End grandstands. It was, after all, the ninth inning, and he was the tying run. But Nichols threw him three pitches, and Reilly flailed at all three.

Nichols's performance, coming atop the work of Lewis and Klobedanz, along with signs that Jack Stivetts and Jim Sullivan might be returning to form, silenced serious concern about the depth of the staff. Murnane reported discussions of a deal that would have sent Tenney to the Giants for Willie "Dad" Clarke, New York's number three starter during the previous two years. But Sullivan's return the next day in a five-hit shutout of the Senators, coupled with Tenney's fielding, made him look less and less tradable. When Freedman demanded three thousand dollars in addition to the first baseman, further consideration of any deal ended.[16] Instead, Freedman traded Willie Clarke to Louisville, where he worked only fifty-five innings and won just two games before being sidelined with a sore arm. It was one of several great trades that Frank Selee did not make.

The Sullivan victory, which took place in bitterly cold conditions, was marred by a run-in between the Senators and Hurst. The problem arose in the bottom of the second inning, after the umpire called Doc Yeager safe at first, contending that the throw had pulled first baseman Ed Cartwright's foot off the base. The Senators infielders surrounded Hurst in argument, prompting the pugnacious umpire to, as Murnane described it, "touch catcher [Deacon] McGuire playfully under the chin."[17] McGuire did not think it was so playful; he swung at Hurst. The fact that McGuire was not even ejected, much less fined, for what easily could have been viewed as battery speaks to the way the game was played in those days.

Washington won the final game of the series, a 10–9 decision in which Klobedanz allowed nine walks and hit two batters in less than six innings. The Beaneaters packed bags for the first of their two month-long western trips with a clearer idea of what was working for them and what was not. Stahl, who was batting over .530, had been a revelation in right field. Hugh Duffy, hitting his usual .360, was as solid as ever in left. And Herman Long, Fred Tenney, Bobby Lowe, and Billy Hamilton were producing as well.

Fielding was a concern. Selee assumed Long would round into form, but even by the relaxed standards of the time, the sixteen errors he had committed in fewer than a hundred chances did not constitute a performance up to his usual abilities. Collins too had been shaky with the glove. The pitching fortunes obviously rose or fell with Nichols, whose most recent work provided reason to feel upbeat. The biggest concern may have been with the Boston faithful, whose expectations far exceeded the club's 5-7 record. In the *Boston Globe*, Murnane did his best to allay rumblings at the 3rd Base tavern and other gathering spots.

"Collins, Long and Lowe are the strongest combination in the league today," he wrote. "Duffy, Hamilton and Stahl. Where can you match this outfield? Nichols, Klobedanz and Sullivan are a trio that cannot be matched outside of the Cincinnati club. I cannot see where the Boston team is weak." Murnane projected—correctly, as it turned out—that the team would win three of every four games on the western swing and during the western teams' visits to Boston during June. That, he ventured, would put the Beaneaters "close to the front by the time they leave for New York July 1."[18]

This was bold talk, especially since Klobedanz chose that moment to stage a brief personal walkout over seventy-five dollars he said the club denied him as a salary supplement. Boston owner Arthur Soden noted that the pitcher—young, single, and loose with a dollar—had already received advances through June 20 (he did not add that he had charged his pitcher interest on those advances). "If we thought the player was in hard luck and needed money, why I should not hesitate a moment," Soden said. "But [the team treasurer] must have some stopping place when it comes to continually advancing money."[19] The walkout ended about the time Soden's version of it hit the streets. Returning to Fall River, Klobedanz had been confronted by Charles Marston, his former minor-league manager, acting as a surreptitious agent for Selee. With the advantage of a night to let Klobedanz cool off, Marston was able to persuade him to get back on the train and rejoin the team, pointing out that the pitcher's petulance was ruining his career.

Since he was not scheduled to pitch the opener in Cincinnati anyway, the whole episode amounted to nothing more than a public airing of dirty laundry.

The First Journey West

To minimize travel expenses, teams in those days booked their two trips to the other ends of the east-west circuit in single gulps. With six cities to visit, excursions lasted as long as a month. The first of those, which took the eastern clubs west, began after the games on May 8 and did not conclude until the end of the month. For the Orioles, the trip was even longer because they traveled to Brooklyn and Philadelphia before heading west. At Brooklyn's Eastern Park, the trip did not open with a decision; the clubs played to a 3–3 tie and the game was called after eleven innings before a crowd of 8,500, including Jim Corbett. (The boxer, who took in the entire series, presented a portrait of himself to John McGraw and Wilbert Robinson with instructions that it was to be on display at the Diamond Café.) The Orioles were fortunate to escape the first game with a tie. After loading the bases with none out, thanks in part to a Brooklyn error, Willie Keeler lifted an easy pop-up that Brooklyn second baseman Jim Canavan simply dropped. Although Keeler was declared out on the infield fly rule, the muff allowed Robinson to score.

Even at this early stage of the season, Orioles backers saw complaints concerning rowdy behavior during the first week in Baltimore as evidence of a league conspiracy to deny them the pennant. One rumor circulating in New York had it that the sale of liquor had been prohibited in the bleachers in an effort to curb rowdiness.[20] That was provably false; liquor had been freely available for sale during the April home stand and would continue to be when the team returned home in June.

On Tuesday, Bill Hoffer and Brooklyn starter Dan Daub matched one another through eight innings, the Bridegrooms taking a 1–0 lead into the ninth. But in the top of the final inning, Jack Doyle's one-man exhibition of Oriole baseball—a combination of wit, bat, and legs—produced the winning two runs. With Joe Kelley at first and threatening to try for second, Dirty Jack feinted stepping out of the box as if to call time but then did not do so. Instinctively, the distracted Daub stopped his delivery, thus committing a balk. With Kelley at second, Doyle looked to make his own way on base, letting himself get hit by a pitch. Hurst refused to give him the base. Again the ball came in, again Doyle leaned into it, and again Hurst refused to pass him to first. Forced to swing, Doyle lined a game-tying two-base hit. Jake Stenzel bunted him to third, bringing the Brooklyn infield in on the grass for a potential play at the plate. That play came when Heinie Reitz shot a one-hopper at first baseman Candy LaChance. The Orioles believed in forcing the other guy to make a good play, and that particularly held for Doyle, who broke with the crack of the bat. LaChance did make a good play, fielding the ball cleanly and throwing on target to cut down the runner. Even so, Doyle hooked safely around the tag with what would become the winning run.

Sidelined for two weeks after his opening day injury, John McGraw made his return on Wednesday, pinch hitting for Arlie Pond in the ninth inning of a loss. He did not play the following day in Philadelphia but still managed to get himself ejected. The proprieties of recordkeeping (and the nature of the vulgarities themselves) usually leave us little by which to judge why a player was removed, but that is not always true and it is not true in this case. The Phillies had a veteran outfielder, thirty-seven-year-old Sam Thompson, who was nearing the end of a career that had made him one of the game's stars. McGraw suggested to umpire Tom Lynch that since Thompson would have no need for his glasses, perhaps Mr. Lynch would like to borrow them.[21] It probably wasn't an original suggestion even then, but it was, as it is today, a sure way to get the boot.

At least McGraw didn't have to hang around to watch his teammates throw away their third game of the season. The fourth inning was the worst of it. Due in part to the rudimentary nature of gloves, in part to the equally rudimentary nature of fields, in part to the unpredictability of a well-used ball, and in part to differences in skills, teams averaged 336 errors per 132-game season (or just less than 3 errors per game). (In contrast, today's teams make about 100 errors in a 162-game season.) Even so, what happened to the champions was a shock. After an opening hit, Doyle fumbled a ground ball while trying for a play at second. Reitz came over, fielded the ball Doyle had dropped, and threw it wildly, allowing the runners to reach second and third. One run scored on a ground out; then with a runner at third, Reitz fielded a grounder and threw to Robinson, who dropped it, allowing the second run to score. A couple more hits and the Phillies had five runs.

The Orioles rebounded the next day in an equally wild 13–11 victory that took three full hours to complete and sparked more than a little internal dissension. The problems came to a head during Philadelphia's eighth-inning rally against Joe Corbett, with the Orioles leading 13–10. After a lead-off walk, Doyle and Jennings came to the mound to lobby for Corbett to be replaced. Considering the ten Philadelphia hits to that point, Joe plainly was not at his best. On the other hand, five errors by the Orioles had rendered most of the Phillies' runs unearned. Hands-off managers such as Ned Hanlon (and Selee) generally left on-field decisions to the team captain, and that was where Doyle and Jennings directed their appeal. But Robinson, the Baltimore captain, would have none of it, and in the face of what had the makings of an insurrection, he told Corbett to keep pitching.[22] That decision looked even more questionable when Philadelphia's Lave Cross doubled to drive home the eleventh run. But Corbett struck out two of the next three men and then coolly set down the side in order in the ninth to preserve the victory. Willie Keeler slapped out two more hits. Hitting streaks drew little attention at the time, and nobody paid particular attention to the fact that Willie had hit in every one of his team's games to date.

McGraw returned to the starting lineup when the Orioles opened in Washington on Monday, May 10. For the first time since the season opener, the club's regular lineup took the field as a unit. The Senators administered a 13–5 hammering in a game nonetheless made memorable by a pair of fielding moments. Keeler made a catch so remarkable that it sounds fictional. Only the vagaries of ballparks of that era and the fact that disparate witnesses agree on the details of what they saw make the story believable. Washington's home park, Boundary Field, featured a six-foot right-field fence topped with three strands of barbed wire that the owners had strung in order to discourage bleacherites from coming onto the field. In pursuit of a first inning fly ball off the bat of Al Selbach, Keeler raced toward the barrier, leaped, reached his bare hand through the barbed wire, and caught the ball. His sleeve snagged on the barbs, badly gashing his arm as he fell . . . but he held onto the ball and stayed in the game. Then in the sixth inning, Doyle, Jennings, and Reitz combined for a triple play.[23]

Equally memorable was a 6–3 Tuesday victory for Baltimore, a game that became a running battle between the Orioles and Hurst. The kicking began in the third inning when Hurst called a strike on Doyle with Kelley trying to take second base. Kelley was called out and ejected for protesting, and Doyle, who believed the pitch had been ball four, beefed loudly and profanely enough to join him. Boileryard Clarke accused Hurst of squeezing Corbett and giving the Senators all the best calls. Keeler also attacked Hurst after being called out at third.[24] The reality was that the Orioles had only themselves to blame. Doyle, Reitz, and Clarke all failed to cover base runners on steal attempts, a cardinal failure among the Orioles, and in all cases the runners were safe. The series wrap-up, a 5–4 decision for Pond, was utterly uneventful by Oriole standards.

From Washington the Orioles traveled to St. Louis for a three-game mismatch series with the tail-end Browns. Winners of only four of their first nineteen games, the Browns were owned by Chris Von der Ahe. In the 1880s, Von der Ahe, a German immigrant brewer, built a Browns franchise that dominated the American Association. But a decade later he lacked either the financial wherewithal or the baseball savvy to field more than a shell of a team. Like most teams that visited St. Louis, the Orioles rolled up runs, winning 11–7, 20–3, and 14–5 in front of audiences of a few thousand. Again, McGraw provided the memorable highlight, standing astride third base to block Lave Cross's circuit of the bases. During Saturday's middle game, the home patrons jeered and hissed Von der Ahe as the score mounted, driving him from his box under a hail of fruit. The field, which combined elements of a ballpark and an amusement park, contained a Shoot-the-Chutes ride beyond the right-field fence. Reitz punctuated the game-long insults by hitting a home run into the lake at the base of the ride.[25]

The Beaneaters' trip west began in rocky fashion. During the fourth inning of their first game against the Pittsburg Pirates, Collins, Hamilton, and Duffy all committed errors within a few moments, resulting in three unearned runs for the Pirates. Although Nichols pitched well, those three runs were enough to decide the 4–2 game. Lewis shut out the Pirates in front of 3,400 the following day, escaping from a bases-loaded jam created in the first inning by two disputed bases on balls. Notwithstanding his shutout work, Lewis still found enough fault with Lynch's calls to keep up a more or less running verbal battle. Klobedanz, back on the mound on Wednesday, stopped the Pirates 3–1 on just four hits. In Cleveland on Thursday, Nichols did almost as well, besting Cy Young in a 4–1 victory that lifted Boston to .500 (at 8-8) for the first time. Rain on Friday forced the teams into scheduling a Saturday doubleheader, which they split.

The Beaneaters left for Chicago in high spirits. From the bottom of the league standings, they had worked their way to sixth place at 9-9, and although they still trailed the first-place Orioles by six games, they were already ahead of both the Giants and the Spiders. In addition, the coming week held series with the Colts and the Browns, two of the circuit's three weakest teams, raising the prospect of gaining even more ground. They got some help in the first game on Monday when Colts second baseman Fred Pfeffer bobbled three routine infield plays, setting up Boston's fifth victory in seven games since leaving home. Pfeffer had been a key member of the great Chicago teams of the 1880s, but he was now thirty-seven, past his prime, and a subject of derision in Chicago. He was hissed after each of the errors, booed loudly when he took his next turn at bat, and benched after the game.[26] He would join the forty-five-year-old Cap Anson in retirement at season's end. To add further spice to the occasion, Duffy and Stahl both homered in the ninth inning. The clubs split the final two games, and then the Beaneaters made short work of the St. Louis Browns. After Boston battered ace Bill Hutchinson 11–4 in the first game, Nichols shut out the Browns on four hits for an 11–1 win in the second game. In the series finale, Klobedanz rode a fourteen-hit attack to another 11–4 win. The 5-1 week boosted the Beaneaters, now 14-10, into fourth place, four and one-half games behind Baltimore. "I doubt if any club ever gave a better account of themselves on a western trip," reported Murnane.[27]

The atmosphere of the Beaneaters' road games was relatively tranquil compared to what was happening elsewhere in the league. In Cincinnati, for example, Pirates outfielder Steve Brodie drew a twenty-five-dollar fine from umpire Sheridan for arguing.[28] Two weeks later Sheridan needed police protection to escape fan outrage in Louisville following the Phillies' 7–1 victory over the Colonels.[29] Lynch forfeited a game to the Giants early in May, when Washington deliberately stalled in the fourth inning of a rainy game that the Senators were already losing 9–0.[30]

A Beaning and a Spiking

Things were decidedly more raucous and dangerous for the Orioles in Louisville and Cincinnati, especially after a routine shutout performance by Jerry Nops in the opener that featured only standard beefs lodged against umpire McDermott. The carping stepped up in the middle game of the series with Louisville, this one a 14–11 victory marked by what the *Baltimore Sun* described as "the worst [umpiring] the Orioles have encountered this season."[31] Whatever role the umpiring played, eight errors (three of them by McGraw) leading to twenty-two unearned runs strongly suggested that McDermott wasn't either team's only problem. The Orioles faced an additional concern: in the second inning a Chick Fraser fastball struck Doyle just below the left temple. Initial reports suggested the injury was relatively minor: "a red spot, badly swollen, painful."[32] But by the next morning the players were telling a different story. "It is lucky he was not killed," reported the *Baltimore Sun*.[33] Doyle, his face badly swollen, blamed a chronic illness that had dulled his reflexes for his failure to get out of the way. The fact is that a player's being hit in the head and sidelined for days at a time was a natural consequence of the way the game was played in the 1890s. Doyle would not be the last Oriole to go down that way.

The Orioles moved without Doyle to Cincinnati, where they ran into two challenges: the Reds, who were close on their heels in second place, and umpire Sheridan. Even before the arrival of the most hated team in the league, it had already been a bad week for Sheridan, who had almost literally been run out of Louisville a week earlier over his handling of a game with the Phillies. Angry bleacherites had poured onto the field to chase him. From somewhere, baskets full of eggs appeared. At the suggestion of Colonels owner Henry Clay Pulliam, Sheridan sought shelter within the team offices until most of the crowd dispersed. Even then, it required a cordon of sixteen police officers to escort him to safety. Pulliam made it plain that his had been merely a humanitarian gesture. "We will not stand any more of Mr. Sheridan," he wired to Nick Young. "We are willing to lose all the games on their merits, but we do not want to stand with our mouths open and get robbed and say nothing about it."[34] A second wire to Young, this one from an anonymous Louisville fan, put the proposition in more concise terms: "If you do not take umpire Sheridan away from here, you will be held liable for his funeral expense."[35]

McGraw was the first to have a run-in with Sheridan in Cincinnati. On first base, after forcing Hoffer in the eighth inning of the opening game, he took off on Keeler's double down the line, easily reaching third. Not content with that, he then challenged left fielder Eddie

Burke to throw him out at home. It was Orioles daredevil ball, but Mc-Graw had little chance of making it. Burke already had the ball as McGraw hit third, and he threw him out comfortably. But the easy play didn't prevent the beef that McGraw kept up until Sheridan threw him out of the game. The tantrum was especially costly when his substitute, Joe Quinn, misplayed a relay throw that set up a six-run game-winning Reds rally.

Quinn at least had an excuse. Dusty Miller, the target of the relay throw, had screened Quinn while running between second and third, getting away with the interference, which Sheridan did not see.[36] Miller scored when Hoffer failed to back up the play, allowing the throw to reach the fence. Hughie Jennings joined McGraw and Hoffer in getting roasted by their teammates following the loss. After McGraw had been tossed, Hughie rolled a meek bounding ball to Charlie Irwin at third, fired the bat away in frustration, and commenced a perfunctory, sulking jog toward first base. Irwin's throw sailed wide of the base, but by the time Jennings reached cruising speed, Farmer Vaughn had speared the ball and recorded the put-out. It was not Baltimore's finest performance.

The Orioles were on Sheridan with unified intensity for several offenses, primarily for what they perceived to be his central role in a decisive three-run Cincinnati rally on Friday. Until the eighth inning, Pond was working on a neat five-hitter. With one out, Dusty Miller sent a ball down the left-field line that Sheridan called fair for a double. Robinson had already been stirred to a froth twice. The first time was when Sheridan denied him a home run on a ball that bounced over the fence in the corner. By ground rule, a ball that left play, even on a bounce, was a home run. But a policeman had batted this ball back into play, and Sheridan ruled it fair and stopped Robinson at second. Later, Robinson reached for a foul tip, only, he claimed, to be jostled by Sheridan, which prevented him from making the catch. Now, joined by McGraw and Kelley, he argued that Miller's ball was well foul. The next batter, Vaughn, hit one that Quinn, who was subbing for Reitz, snared behind second and threw to first. Sheridan called the runner safe, touching off more howls. Two hits and an error later, both runners were across and Cincinnati had the winning runs. The decision moved them within a game and a half of first place.[37]

After the game, Robinson accosted Ned Hanlon. "Do you propose to play here tomorrow with this umpiring?" he demanded. If so, he informed the manager, several of the Orioles were ready to walk out. Hanlon tried to cool the walkout talk, but Young got yet another telegram calling for Sheridan's removal. "It was the worst skinning I have had for a long time," Hanlon wrote.[38]

The Orioles' problems in Cincinnati were not confined to the umpiring. Midway through the middle game, Reds first baseman Vaughn rounded third, only to find himself caught in what hometown newspapers described as a McGraw "stranglehold." He escaped in time to score.[39] In the eighth inning, McGraw grounded weakly to Bid McPhee and—to Vaughn's mind—tried to spike Vaughn as the out was recorded at first. "You owe me an apology," Vaughn is said to have yelled at McGraw. "I don't owe you anything," the runner responded, turning for the bench. Vaughn then fired the ball squarely into McGraw's back, and McGraw shrugged the incident off as barely noticeable. Sheridan reacted to the incident by ejecting McGraw.[40]

Whatever the validity of the spiking accusations, the Reds were serious about them and went out in search of retaliation in the third game of the series. They got it in a fashion that would have profound consequences for the entire pennant race. Midway through their 12–10 victory on Saturday, veteran infielder Biddy McPhee raced toward Robinson, who was holding the ball at home plate. McPhee went in with his spikes high, opening a gash in Wilbert's right thigh that coursed blood.[41] He had to be carried from the field, and he hobbled on crutches at the hotel that evening. Robinson told reporters that he did not believe the injury would prove to be serious, but Hanlon knew better.

Despite the fact that eight days and three cities remained on the road trip, he sent his catcher home to Baltimore on the evening train. The rest of the Orioles were equally glad to get out of Cincinnati. Between Sheridan and the hot-blooded Reds, and despite their still-shining 19-6 record, their lead had been shaved to one-half game.

National League Standings (Evening of May 22)

TEAM	WINS	LOSSES	PERCENTAGE	GAMES BEHIND
Baltimore	19	6	.760	—
Cincinnati	19	7	.731	½
Pittsburg	16	7	.696	2
Boston	14	10	.583	4½
Cleveland	13	11	.542	5½
Philadelphia	13	13	.520	6
Louisville	11	11	.500	6½
Brooklyn	10	14	.417	8½
New York	8	20	.286	12½
Chicago	8	16	.333	10½
Washington	6	16	.273	11½
St. Louis	5	20	.200	14

6. Streaks of June

Because schedules routinely called for teams to be away for as long as a month at a time, rabid fans looked to means other than the game itself to satisfy their rooting interests. As the Beaneaters prepared for their first long western foray in May of 1897, Lawrence McCarthy had an idea that he thought might please the masses and make him a little money.

McCarthy, who owned the Park Theater, decided to present "automatic baseball" on his stage. This type of entertainment, designed to allow fans to stay up to the minute on the events at distant parks, had surfaced in Baltimore, Philadelphia, and Cincinnati during the previous season. With the surge of interest in the pennant race, McCarthy sensed a market in Boston as well. In exchange for the ten-cent or twenty-five-cent admission price, patrons watched a board that reflected the movement of marionette ball players as relayed by wire. The May 10 debut, which coincided with the first game of the Beaneaters' western trip in Pittsburg, featured McCarthy's variations on the usual presentation. Instead of a display board, his stage featured a diamond with fences marking the limits of the field as a backdrop. The marionettes were replaced by automatons that were three-foot-tall replications of the players. Each took its proper position in the field, and each had a white bulb in its hand (to indicate a caught ball) and a red bulb at its feet (to denote an error). More bulbs were placed in

Fig. 13. Orioles first baseman Dirty Jack Doyle. His language, said the *Sporting News*, would embarrass "even hardened users of profanity." (National Baseball Hall of Fame Library, Cooperstown NY.)

front of the automatons to indicate ball movement, and four were suspended by wires to indicate ball movement in the air. If the player was retired, that was indicated by a flashing of the white light at the appropriate base. If he hit safely, a gong sounded once for a single, twice for a double, and three times for a triple. There was even an automaton for umpire Tom Lynch.[1]

The only automatons that had moving parts were the pitcher and the catcher, whose arms could be moved. As they entered the theater, fans were given scorecards with which they could record and track the action. The automatons representing the visiting Pittsburg players were distinguished by colored jackets.

As players batted, they were moved around the diamond as the action dictated. The first, Billy Hamilton, faced the automaton representing Pittsburg pitcher Frank Killen, whose white light went on. When Killen delivered the pitch, his light went out and the lights between the mound and home plate came on in succession, leading to the light in the glove of Pirate catcher Joe Sugden. Automaton Lynch called ball one.

"The spectators grew quite enthusiastic over the game," the *Boston Globe* reported the next day. "Once when Nichols sent three successive balls wide of the plate, a youngster in the gallery yelled, 'Git 'em over, Charlie; get 'em over.'"[2]

Theater re-creations were also a popular afternoon draw at the Music Hall down the street and at Ford's Theater in Baltimore. With teams in both cities now playing winning ball, but on the road from early May into June, the market was obvious, and the shows, which featured only the away games so as not to conflict with ticket sales, drew good crowds.

Arriving in Pittsburg, Ned Hanlon welcomed one catcher but bade farewell to another. Frank Bowerman, a twenty-eight-year-old who had had brief stints with the club in 1895 and 1896, reported to back up Boileryard Clarke while Wilbert Robinson recuperated from his leg injury. Back in Baltimore the wounded captain followed doctor's orders to stay at home and off his leg. He did, however, chat with neighbors and well-wishers, displaying what he characterized as his near-crip-pling injury. And having recovered his garrulous nature, Robinson re-sumed his criticism of Jack Sheridan's bias and incompetence as an um-pire. "It's a pity that President Young has not the interest of the game enough at heart to avoid placing a biased man in Cincinnati to um-pire games right along," he said. "He virtually robbed us of the first two after we had them won."[3]

As Bowerman arrived to take Robinson's place, Jack Doyle too de-parted. The rest in Cincinnati proved insufficient tonic for the bean-ing he had taken in Louisville, and the player and manager took advan-tage of a rainout to consult a Pittsburg specialist, who found a small fracture, continued swelling, and a lingering concussion. The physi-cian immediately ordered Doyle back to Baltimore.[4]

The Pirates Versus the Umpires

After the rain ended, the final week of the trip started well enough for the champions. They defeated Pittsburg 6–2, and this time it was the Pirates who complained about the umpiring. The key play came in the eighth inning of what at the time was a 1–1 pitcher's duel between Jerry Nops and Frank Killen, and again John McGraw was in the midst of it. With one out, McGraw had singled cleanly and then taken sec-ond when Hughie Jennings did the same. With Joe Kelley in the box, Sugden caught McGraw off guard. All the witnesses seemed to agree on McGraw's fate, including McGraw, who immediately unleashed a torrent of abuse toward Willie Keeler, the coach, for his inattentive-ness. Umpire Tim Hurst, however, allowed McGraw to remain at sec-ond, telling the Pirates that his vision had been screened and he did not see the tag. The call enraged Pirates fans and unnerved the team. Kelley walked, filling the bases; Jake Stenzel doubled, sending Mc-Graw and Jennings home; and before Killen recovered, the Orioles had scored five times.

The Orioles read the angry reports in the next day's Pittsburg news-papers without sympathy. When Ned Hanlon returned to the hotel after the disputed game, a telegram from Nick Young awaited him. Would Baltimore object if Sheridan were assigned to umpire in Cleveland, the Orioles' next stop? Most heartily, Hanlon replied. (Young assigned Hank O'Day to follow the Orioles to Cleveland.)[5]

The Pirates and Hurst crossed paths again the next day. In the third inning, he ruled Bill Hoffer safe on a pick-off play at first base, again to a profane chorus from the grandstand. The Orioles capitalized on that ruling for another four runs. Two innings later Hurst called Jesse Tannehill out, charging that he deliberately knocked Hoffer's throw to Tom O'Brien out of the first baseman's glove. At the end of the game, the bleacherites took out after Hurst, chasing him down the stairs to the clubhouse as he reportedly ran over a spectator in his haste to evade them. A barrage of punches and kicks followed, some of them by Hurst, until a hanger-on stepped in to help the umpire reach shelter. He waited in the clubhouse for ten more minutes until a sufficient force of police arrived to safely escort the beaten and bruised arbiter from the grounds.[6] Pirates backers openly predicted that Hurst would not have the nerve to umpire another game in Pittsburg that season—and they were right.

The two episodes touched off a week's worth of trouble between the Pirates and umpires. In New York, chaos erupted in the seventh inning after Sandy McDermott ruled the Giants' Ducky Holmes safe at second base. Pittsburg led the game 7–4, so it was a strange time for the Pirates to get swept away in a large-scale beef, but they did. Seven of the visitors' starting nine surrounded McDermott to argue the call, violating the league rule prohibiting players from leaving their positions in the field to argue. As the *New York World* described the scene, "Fists were shaken in the air while heavy oaths fell thick and fast. Now and then a hand reached out from the bunch of uniformed men and [McDermott] was shaken in the heat of fierce argument."[7]

McDermott raised his hand to silence the Pirates; the hand was pushed down. McDermott ejected Frank Killen, Dick Padden, and player-manager Patsy Donovan, but that did not quell the disruption.

While all this was going on, Giants fans in the stands poured down abuse on the Pirates, and matters threatened to devolve into what the *New York World* characterized as "a scene [that] recalled descriptions of Southwestern lynchings."[8] Finally, McDermott forfeited the game to New York. At this, fans poured onto the field spoiling for fisticuffs with the visiting Pirates. Recognizing the risks involved in pursuing the matter further, the Pittsburg players retreated to the visitors' locker room, where they took their aggressions out on the window panes. That in turn riled owner Andrew Freedman, who announced that he would deny Pittsburg the use of the dressing facilities during their next visit.

Three days later in Philadelphia the Pirates forfeited again, this time at umpire Jim McDonald's direction. The problems began during the fourth inning of a game in which the visitors trailed 4–0. McDonald ruled Sugden's drive over third base foul. The Pirates did not like the call, and their extended complaints led to the ejection of Donovan and fines for three players. When play finally resumed, the complaining still did not abate, and by then literal storm clouds had begun to gather. Assessing the entirety of the situation—the game was not official, the Pirates trailed, and he had heard enough—McDonald decided that the stalling was deliberate and dilatory, and he awarded the game to the Phillies. It remains the only time in major-league history that a team has forfeited two games within a week.[9]

The West's Final Battles

While the Pirates were battling the umpires, the Beaneaters won three of five on the final leg of their western trip to Louisville and Cincinnati, with one-run decisions in each city preventing a perfect week. They had only themselves to blame for the losses. In a 5–4 defeat in Louisville, Fred Klobedanz's one-out double offered a chance to tie the game in the ninth. But Billy Hamilton and Fred Tenney failed to drive him home. Then in the trip's final game in Cincinnati, Tenney's muff of a foul pop-up gave the Reds' Pop Schriver a second chance to hit with a runner at second. Schriver responded with a run-producing single that resulted in a 2–1 decision against Kid Nichols. Despite the losses, the team had concluded the trip with a 12-5 record that was a success by any standard. In addition, Boston could look ahead to playing virtually the entire month of June at home, with only a three-game trip to Brooklyn interrupting twenty-four dates at the South End Grounds. Among those twenty-four dates: Baltimore's first visit.

The Orioles arrived in Cleveland to take three more crippling hits, one of them in a most vulnerable spot, behind the plate. In the sixth inning of the first of the three games between the Orioles and the Spiders, Boileryard Clarke took a foul ball off the thumb of his bare hand, splitting it severely. Since the wound obviously would require weeks to heel, Hanlon had no choice but to send Clarke home and to entrust the catching duties to Bowerman, who had not even been with the club a week. At the same time, Stenzel came down with bronchitis and McGraw reported a sore arm.[10] With Doyle also out, a rainout of the middle game was an obvious blessing. For the Saturday wrapup game, Hanlon barely had enough hands to field a team. He sent pitcher Bill Hoffer to center field, Tom O'Brien to first, Joe Quinn to third, and Bowerman behind the plate. The four of them combined for eight hits and the Orioles won.

Baltimore crossed paths with Hurst again in Chicago, this time to Hoffer's chagrin. Rescued from center field by Stenzel's return, Hoffer presided over a 4–2 deficit as the game wound into the eighth inning. But relations between Hurst and the Orioles were sour almost all afternoon, starting in the first inning when, as far as the Orioles were concerned, Hurst overlooked Colts batter Bill Lange's blatant interference with Bowerman as Bill Everitt tried to steal second. In the third inning, Hurst again overlooked what the Orioles felt was Lange's clear interference as Bill Dahlen stole home. Moments later, with Lange now on first, Jimmy Ryan swung at and missed a low pitch that Bowerman trapped. As the catcher attempted to pick it up, Ryan reached out with his bat and knocked the ball several feet away. Lange took off for second. Hurst, who claimed not to have seen the interference, allowed the stolen base. In the sixth inning, he ejected Kelley for arguing.

By the eighth inning, Hoffer and most of the Orioles were operating on short fuses. Two hits and a double-play ball produced one run, and then George Decker sent a shot over Stenzel's head toward the crowd in center. Stenzel retrieved it and threw it in to Quinn, heading off Decker's attempt at a triple. When the runner tried to retreat to second, Quinn fired to Heinie Reitz, who tagged him for an apparent third out. Not so, Hurst said. He declared that the ball had reached the populace in center, making it dead and a triple under the ground rules. After more vitriol, Jennings was ejected. Now with a lineup that featured three pitchers—Joe Corbett at short and Arlie Pond in left—Hoffer turned the game into a farce. He lobbed the ball in, permitting six hits and five runs before Tim Donahue made the third out. The players left the field convinced that Hurst had joined the league-wide conspiracy to prevent their winning a fourth pennant.[11] However, they returned for Monday's concluding doubleheader of the road trip with enough presence of mind to win the first game 6–4. The deciding ninth-inning rally was pure Orioles. Jennings opened it by taking a fastball off his arm. He broke for second, and Kelley found the resulting gap for a hit-and-run single that sent the runner around to third. Stenzel drove Jennings in with the lead run and sent Kelley around to third with another hit. Then Reitz's fly to right drove the second run home. The second game ended in a 6–6 tie after nine innings so that both teams could catch their trains east.[12]

Abuse of Their Western Visitors

Although the Beaneaters still stood in fourth place, trailing the Orioles by five games, Tim Murnane gave voice to a growing level of confidence in Boston as the teams headed east. "I firmly believe the home team will pass all the teams higher up in the standing before long and be in a position to fight Baltimore for the lead when that team arrives here [June 24-26]," he wrote.[13] Others were picking up the same theme. "Keep your eye on those Beaneaters," suggested the *Chicago Tribune*.[14] The *Baltimore American*'s correspondent wrote that Hanlon had "changed his mind about the Boston team, and now believes they are the ones to be looked out for in the race."[15] Frank Selee agreed. "I have managed three champion teams," he said, "but the team I have this year is stronger than any [of them]."[16]

Murnane's only concern was for the wear and tear of the long trip. "Players are often known to play sleepy ball for a few days after returning home," he cautioned.[17] That concern failed to consider that the visiting St. Louis Browns—the first western club into town—faced the same trip east, and did so with far less talent. As it turned out, the Browns, not the Beaneaters, suffered from travel fatigue, surrendering fifty-one runs in three successive lashings.

The first of those games, a 25–5 rout, almost did not take place at all. The schedule called for a morning-afternoon doubleheader, but rain washed out the first game, and a liberal application of sawdust to the playing field rendered it barely usable for the afternoon game. Boston took full advantage, choosing to bat first and scoring in every inning except the ninth. Fred Tenney lobbed six hits to all parts of the park, Herman Long delivered three singles and two doubles, and Jimmy Collins hit safely four times. Jack Stivetts, making his return to competition, was the happy mound beneficiary.

The washed-out game was rescheduled as part of a morning-afternoon doubleheader the next day, a Tuesday, and this time Ted Lewis and Jim Sullivan picked up the easy victories. Long slapped out five more hits and Collins got four, one of which landed atop the right-field fence and then fell back inside the park, denying him a home run. The damage was minimal, with the home club scoring fourteen runs in the first game and twelve more in the second.

Cleveland followed St. Louis into town on Wednesday, and this time the tally was twenty-one runs, with Klobedanz enjoying an easy workout. In the first four games of the home stand, the Beaneaters had scored seventy-two times on seventy-eight hits, a yield of eighteen runs and nineteen hits per game on a .443 batting average. Other than Marty Bergen, whose hand injury had slowed his work at the bat as well, every Boston regular was batting above .300 for the season, and Hugh Duffy was pushing .400.

Selee had been trying for weeks to strike a deal that would unload Tommy Tucker, and he finally succeeded, selling him to the Senators for two thousand dollars. It was an emotional breakup; Tucker had been a Boston regular since 1890 and had been the star first baseman for all three pennant-winning teams. However, signing on with a ball club could never be confused with a marriage, and the thirty-three-year-old Tucker had already been supplanted by Tenney. At the same time, midseason personnel moves were rare, especially among the better teams. Other than the sale of Tucker, only the acquisition of reserve infielder Bob Allen (in July) and backup catcher Fred Lake (in September) would alter the cast Selee took to spring training in March. "Faithful at all times, Tucker took his medicine like a man," Tim Murnane reported.[18]

The prospect of a Kid Nichols–Cy Young match-up, combined with the Beaneaters' whirlwind offense, drew a crowd of close to eight thousand to the South End Grounds for the middle game of the series with Cleveland on Thursday. Notwithstanding the pounding they had been given the previous day, Patsy Tebeau's fiery Spiders presented an impressive attraction, featuring not only Young but also the outfield phenom, Louis Sockalexis, a full-blooded Penobscot from Maine. Fans and sportswriters had already begun referring to the club as the Indians. But whether Indians or Spiders, Tebeau's team took the field without its best offensive weapon. Outfielder Jesse Burkett, a .400 hitter during the previous two seasons, was at his off-season home in Worcester, after a beaning by Klobedanz the previous day. Without Burkett, any chance the Spiders might normally have had melted away before Nichols, although the final 6–1 score sounded modest compared to the barrages put forth previously. On Friday the Beaneaters, who were trying for their sixth straight win, led 2–1 in the third inning when rain and fog caused O'Day to call things off.

If not for Jimmy Collins, Boston's streak might have died the next afternoon against the Pirates. It was a physical game marked by flying hips and elbows delivered to base runners by larcenous infielders on both sides. With one runner retired in the second, Patsy Donovan tried to bunt for a base hit, only to see Collins race in and fire to Tenney. Seeing that he was going to be called out, Donovan grabbed at Tenney's wrist, causing him to drop the ball. A ruckus ensued when Lynch said he had seen no interference.[19] By then Boston already led 3–0 on Duffy's three-run first-inning homer. Klobedanz worked comfortably with a 5–3 lead going into the ninth inning. There might have been no need for heroics except that Long threw a one-out ground ball over Tenney's head. An out, two singles, and an intentional walk gave the Pirates a run and filled the bases for Harry Davis, a second-year player coming off a .239 rookie season. He cut at Klobedanz's first pitch and sent it toward the spot normally filled by the shortstop. When Long, who was leaning toward second, could not recover, Collins raced over, fielded the ball, and fired it to Bobby Lowe for the game-ending force out. "It was phenomenally quick ground-covering, and perhaps Collins is the only man playing ball who could have made the play," wrote Tim Murnane.[20]

Nichols took the mound on Monday, with his club eyeing second place. The star right-hander shut out Pittsburg 4–0. An eighth straight victory followed on Tuesday, this time 8–4, largely as a result of work by Collins. His over-the-shoulder catch of a foul down the left-field line caught fans' attention in the first inning. His leaping interception of a line drive turned into a double play in the second. And his snatch of a foul pop-up by Bones Ely, with two runners on base in the eighth, nearly took him over the low railing and into the stands. Each play drew louder and louder cheers. Collins added a run-producing double in the sixth and scored on Bergen's double as part of a three-run rally that proved decisive. The team that had started with six losses in its first seven games had only lost six more in the subsequent thirty-one. The Beaneaters had drawn within a game and a half of Baltimore in

the standings and were even with the champions in losses. "The Bostons are coming up so fast and at so steady a gait as to make them now
the champions' most formidable rivals for the pennant," observed
Sporting Life.[21]

Willie Hits, But Who Catches?

The Orioles came home with reason to be nervous. Despite their 11-5
record on the western swing, their leads of two and one-half games
over Cincinnati and three and one-half games over Boston looked in-
substantial. Doyle's return helped, but as the Beaneaters chewed up the
last-place Browns, Baltimore had to face the Reds, risking their grip
on the top rung in the standings. McGraw's sore arm would sideline
him for at least a week longer, and nobody knew when either Robinson
or Clarke would be able to return. The only good aspect of Robinson's
sidelining was that it gave him a chance to decorate the Diamond Café
with portraits of sports celebrities that he and McGraw had collected
on the western swing. It was an eclectic assemblage: bare-knuckled
boxers, including a life-sized portrait of John L. Sullivan and a portrait of Joe Corbett's brother Jim, and sketches of ballplayer after ballplayer. Dan Brouthers, the great former Oriole, was newly installed, as
were Ned Hanlon and his teammates on the famed Detroit teams of
the 1880s—Hardie Richardson, Deacon White, and Jack Rowe.[22] Robinson arranged for the current Orioles' team photo to get a prominent
display. He estimated that between the two of them, he and McGraw
had already collected five hundred images, creating a backdrop that
rivaled the one at McGreevy's 3rd Base tavern in Boston. Their am-
bitious goal was six times that many. The catcher's mood was upbeat
because he believed his workouts while the team was on the road had
gone well. Over dinner at the Diamond, Robinson assured Harry Von
der Horst that he'd be ready to play in a week.

 In fact, the Orioles' catching situation worsened almost by the game.
Bowerman and Quinn collided in pursuit of a foul ball during the Chicago wrap-up game, and both men showed the aftereffects. When they

detrained in Baltimore, Quinn's abdomen was black and blue and Bowerman's face was a reddened mess. He had been knocked cold for five minutes, leaving Hanlon at a loss as to who he might put behind the plate. Then, in the opener of the home stand, it happened again. As the Orioles rolled steadily to a 10–4 victory over the Reds, Cincinnati outfielder Dummy Hoy fouled a pitch straight back into Bowerman's mask. The ball broke one of the wires, driving it into the catcher's forehead, opening yet another spurting gash. Pond bandaged the wound well enough to get Bowerman back behind the plate.[23]

What Bowerman probably needed more than anything was a few days of rest, and the weather more or less provided it. The next day's game was halted by rain after four innings, a decided break for the Orioles, who trailed 6–0 at the time. Friday's scheduled series wrap-up lasted just three innings, but this time the rain victimized the home team, which led 6–3. For those three innings, the Orioles put on a superb exhibition of their version of baseball, mixing bunts, chops, and cuts in an array that proved maddening to the defense. You could think of it as "change of pace" hitting in the sense that it kept the pitcher and fielders off balance. Keeler opened the first inning with a base on balls, Jennings bunted and nearly beat it out, and then Kelley dropped down another bunt, this one for a hit. With the infield stepping in, Stenzel laced a drive through the hands of third baseman Charlie Irwin for a run-producing hit. With two runners still aboard, just one out, and the infield giving ground again, Doyle dropped another bunt, filling the bases. That brought up Reitz, who lined a single to center that sent Kelley and Stenzel home. Doyle scored on Quinn's force out, giving the Orioles four runs on just two hits that left the infield.

Last-place St. Louis followed the Reds into Baltimore, surprising a crowd of more than seven thousand by winning the Saturday opener 6–4. Despite the condition of the club and insistent reports of victory emanating out of Boston, those seven thousand fans treated the result almost as a delightful curiosity, applauding the work of former Oriole and previously winless pitcher Duke Esper in scattering fifteen Baltimore hits. It was an approach born either of the assuredness of winning three straight pennants or of a false cockiness, and it infected the entire city. "The Orioles can afford to lose a few games without danger," the next morning's *Baltimore Sun* rationalized.[24]

None of the defeats could be attributed to Keeler or Kelley, two of the few beacons of both health and performance. With fifty-seven hits in the first thirty-three games, Kelley was batting .445, a figure that didn't even lead his own outfield. Keeler had already topped seventy hits and ended the first week of June batting .446. More remarkably, but little noticed at the time, Keeler had not been held hitless in any of the Orioles' thirty-five games to date. He added another game to that stretch with a single in Nops's 4–2 victory on Monday. When more rain and a cold chill gripped the city on Tuesday, Von der Horst and Browns owner Von der Ahe agreed to cancel the game with the hope of a larger gate when the visitors returned in late August.

Cleveland was next, and the Spiders succumbed in all three games. To Orioles fans, the big news was the return of McGraw to his lead-off spot and third base position for the middle game. But again Keeler was the story, driving home all the runs in a 4–2 victory over Cy Young. The third game, a 5–4 victory for the Orioles, was settled with a typical Oriole two-run rally in the bottom of the ninth. Doyle started it with a Baltimore chop in front of the plate that he legged out for a single. Reitz followed with a hit of his own to left, bringing Bowerman to the plate for an obvious sacrifice. When Bowerman failed twice, Doyle lit out for third base and made it on a successful, if nervy, steal, scoring on Bowerman's base hit. With the game tied, Hanlon sent O'Brien up to pinch-hit for Nops, and he repeated Bowerman's performance, first failing to sacrifice and then finding a hole for a base hit. That filled the bases.

McGraw tried to work Cleveland pitcher George Cuppy for a game-deciding walk. He got the first three balls, but Cuppy refused to throw a fourth, so McGraw fouled off pitch after pitch. Finally he slapped one that shortstop Bobby Wallace fumbled, letting Reitz carry the winning run home. Afterward, an angry Cleveland manager Patsy Tebeau crossed paths with some well-liquored Orioles bleacherites, all to no good end. The fans verbally laid into the performance of rookie sensation Sockalexis, whom Tebeau urged to throw as many punches in retaliation as he chose. Only a police delegation could prevent a brawl.[25]

Louisville arrived in mid-June, and the Orioles made short work of the league's ninth-place team, winning the three games by scores of 15–6, 9–7, and 7–5. The big news was made off the field—specifically, above the left-field fence. Since April, Von der Horst had been concerned about the revenue lost to freeloaders sitting atop the roofs of houses, and he was galled by the fact that some of the building owners charged fees for access to the roofs, creating competition with his own bleachers. He had tried personal appeals, and he had gone to the city zoning office in search of toughened public safety enforcement. But none of that had curtailed the traffic. Now he unveiled his next solution—huge canvas tarpaulins that were unfurled across the top of the fence in an effort to screen the freeloaders' view of the field. Many of the fans did indeed climb down from the roofs, line up at the ticket windows, and pay their twenty-five-cent entrance fee. Not all did, however. At least one gentleman, presumably the home's occupant, went inside for a few moments and then emerged with a table, a soap box, and a chair, all of which he used to build himself a platform so that he could see over the screen.[26]

Robinson's appearance in uniform heartened the mood for the final game of the series with Louisville. Although he took the field only in a coaching capacity, the two thousand fans gave him a standing ovation. The captain assured his teammates that he'd be back in the lineup soon. Clarke, still incapacitated by the finger injury, was less enthusiastic. Of little use to the Orioles, he accepted an invitation to be a guest coach of the Princeton University baseball team. Hanlon initially vetoed the request, but he consented after Clarke assured him that he could practice as well in New Jersey as in Baltimore.

Jake Beckley Scores Too Quickly

The rain that lingered over the East Coast temporarily slowed Boston's rush to the top, washing out one game against Louisville and forcing a Friday doubleheader, which the home team swept. Cincinnati followed for games on Saturday, Monday, and Tuesday. With the hosts lagging two games behind Baltimore and the Reds trailing by three and one-half, the series amounted to an audition for the right to challenge the champions. The Reds were almost as hot as the Beaneaters, having won six of their last eight games on the road and having put together a ten-game winning streak of their own during the May visit by the eastern teams. Under the circumstances, the capacity crowd of eight thousand at the South End Grounds was no surprise.

What they saw was one part baseball and one part brawl, with the Reds falling behind quickly and then resorting to attacks on Hurst in an effort to make up ground. The Beaneaters retaliated, and in the home half of the fifth, Long drew a ten-dollar fine for arguing. "Mr. Hurst . . . had an off day, but as usual played no favorites," reported the *Boston Globe*.[27] The most energetic beef arose in the sixth inning, with the Reds facing a 3–0 deficit against Nichols. Tommy Corcoran led off with a single, and veteran first baseman Jake Beckley followed with a double, putting two runners in scoring position. One out later, rookie Claude Ritchey rolled a ground ball to Bobby Lowe. As he threw Ritchey out at first, Corcoran raced home with Beckley hot on his heels, having shortcut third base by a distance observers estimated at twenty-five feet.

It was the kind of larceny that teams often got away with, but Tim Hurst was having none of it. Although his back had been turned in order to make the call at first, he immediately signaled Beckley out for missing third. Both benches emptied on the signal, the Reds protesting that Beckley had actually retreated to third after Hurst's call without being retired—and thus should be safe. Boston, of course, contended that Beckley was out when he left the baseline. As was always the case with the magnificently self-assured Hurst, his original call

stood, and he told off Beckley and team manager Buck Ewing for trying to make him look like a chump.

"As I saw him coming, I said to myself, 'I've got you this trip,'" Hurst
said after the game.[28]

Boston won 5–1, took Monday's second game 5–3 behind Klobedanz,
and then rolled up ten runs on a wet field on Tuesday to make it easy
for Ted Lewis. The weather, which occasioned a twenty-two-minute
delay in the start of the game, probably held down attendance, which
was estimated at 2,600.

Cap Anson's aging Colts came to town just 17-26 and ranked eleventh in the standings. They then absorbed 14–3 and 19–7 beatings at
the hands of the Beaneaters, before falling in the final game by a more
respectable score of 7–3. Ten thousand fans overflowed the seating on
Saturday for the second game of the series, the latecomers taking up
spots against the center-field fence. They witnessed Boston players
doing things that were reminiscent of the Orioles. The second batter, Tenney, stepped in front of a pitch and allowed himself to be hit.
Caught off first, he ran out of the baseline to avoid being tagged by
Anson, got back safely, and was not declared out by Lynch. After Long
walked, Duffy stepped in front of Colts catcher Tim Donahue as he
tried to pick off Tenney, forcing the catcher to throw wildly. In short
order, both Tenney and Long scored. Then in the second inning, Tenney blocked Donahue as Hamilton tried to steal second, again with no
interference call forthcoming from Lynch. Later in the inning, Duffy
doubled and then grabbed second baseman Jim Connor, preventing
a play on Stivetts's attempt to score. Remarked the *Chicago Tribune*,
"Lynch's errors were almost as numerous as the Colts'."[29]

The final victory, obtained by Nichols, buoyed the Bostonians' record
on the home stand to a perfect 16-0. It had been a productive stand in
more ways than simply the victories. Top to bottom, the lineup was hitting. Duffy still led at .393, Long was up to .375, and with the exception
of Marty Bergen, all the other regulars were hitting between .310 and
.340. The pitching, while not overpowering, was more than sufficient.

After losing four of his first five starts, Nichols stood 10-5. Klobedanz, although giving up five runs per game, was 12-2, and Lewis was 7-2. At the gate, club owners enjoyed success as well, with the team averaging four thousand fans per game and netting thousands of dollars from every series. Visitors went home defeated but enriched. Published reports indicated that the Colonels cleared $1,200 for their doubleheader, and Anson's Colts netted as much as $5,000.[30]

Forty-four and Seventeen

Pittsburg wrapped up its eastern swing with three games against the Orioles, the home team winning the first two games handily. Keeler got one hit in the first game, a 10–8 decision for Nops, and three in the second game, an 11–9 victory in which Corbett benefited from the sixteen-hit support of his teammates. It was the forty-fourth consecutive game since the season's start in Keeler had hit safely. On the following day, June 19, Killen finally halted that streak, keeping Keeler hitless in four at bats during a 7–1 Pirates victory. The achievement drew only passing mention in any of the contemporary accounts. In fact, however, it was the end of a streak that would endure as the longest on record until it was broken in 1941 by Joe DiMaggio. Keeler's is still the longest season-opening hitting streak in history. During the streak, Keeler batted .418 and didn't even lead the team. Pitcher Corbett had twenty-two hits in fifty at bats, a .440 average.

Anyway, many of the fans were more taken with Robinson, whose reputation as a catcher was being supplanted by his reputation as a showman. He and McGraw invited W. R. Wallace, one of the leading pool players on the East Coast, to the Diamond Café after the first Pittsburg game for an exhibition match against Robinson. The first player to fifty balls was to be the winner. There was one catch: Wallace had to play with one hand. That was all the edge Wilbert needed; he beat the champion 50–38. After that, Wallace demonstrated his talents in more conventional fashion, winning a one hundred–ball match against the Maryland state champion.[31]

Having finished 10-2 in their home stand against the west—albeit with three rainouts—the Orioles looked ahead to the toughest stretch on their schedule: three games at home against the Giants followed by three-game trips to Boston and New York. Since his team's edge over surging Boston was only a game and a half, Hanlon assumed Baltimore's season-long grip on first place would be at issue during that nine-game swing and was glad to see Robinson reporting back for active duty. But Wilbert's own assessment of his fitness proved premature, and the Orioles suffered for it. After Bowerman caught for the first game, a 6–2 loss in front of 6,700 fans, Robinson played in the game against Jouett Meekin and failed to hit in three attempts. Baltimore lost again, 6–5. The double defeat sent Boston, victorious in Brooklyn, into first place by six percentage points. The Orioles reclaimed the top spot a day later when they beat New York's Cy Seymour and Boston lost in Brooklyn. Robinson suffered through a one-for-four day, his right leg red, puffy, and swelling again.

A sixteen-game winning streak ought to cement team harmony, but that was not entirely the case for the Beaneaters. During the middle game of their series with Chicago, Bergen lapsed into one of his moods, angrily accusing teammates of talking behind his back on the bench. It was a fully imagined slight—certainly his teammates did not know what to make of it—but it was real enough to Bergen that he left Boston and returned to his rural Massachusetts home, convinced that the club was against him. With few other options, Selee put Charles Ganzel in as catcher the next day. Ganzel had nothing approaching Bergen's defensive skills, but he was more emotionally stable and he could hit. Bergen stayed away for the entire three-game road series against the Brooklyn Bridegrooms, although all was forgiven when he returned to the team for the start of the Orioles series.

Bergen's absence may have contributed to the end of Boston's winning streak. After beating the Bridegrooms 11–6 in the first game, the visitors played sloppily in a 7–4 defeat that would have been more one-sided if Boston hadn't scored twice in the ninth inning. Brooklyn runners took particular advantage of Ganzel's weak arm, stealing three bases in key situations. "The wind was a little too strong against the throwing to second to suit Ganzel," Murnane reported.[32] But Ganzel was hardly the only problem. Doc Yeager's error in right allowed one run to score, and his pair of base-running gaffes cost two for Boston. In addition, Boston took plenty of issue with McDonald's umpiring. The defeat, coupled with a Baltimore victory against New York, ended their one-day stay in first, but they recovered sufficiently to hammer the Bridegrooms 13–2 the next day and retake the league lead by six percentage points.

Recalling a pivotal 1889 series with New York that drew more than thirty thousand for the three games, Murnane forecast larger turnouts against the Orioles. Looking past the question of Bergen's stability, he saw in Boston a perfectly put-together club: "Catchers who have effectually stopped base-stealing; pitchers with confidence that they were to be well-supported; an infield . . . on the alert for different kinds of hitting; and an outfield covering an immense amount of ground."[33]

National League Standings (Evening of June 23)

TEAM	WINS	LOSSES	PERCENTAGE	GAMES BEHIND
Boston	35	13	.729	—
Baltimore	34	13	.723	½
Cincinnati	30	17	.638	4½
New York	27	18	.600	6½
Brooklyn	24	24	.500	11
Pittsburg	23	24	.489	11½
Cleveland	23	25	.479	12
Philadelphia	24	27	.471	12½
Washington	20	26	.435	14
Louisville	19	28	.404	15½
Chicago	18	31	.367	17½
St. Louis	10	41	.196	26½

7. Sunday Misdemeanors

Three things were important to Frank DeHaas Robison: the Cleveland streetcar lines he ran, the Cleveland Spiders baseball team he owned, and the money he made from each. In 1891, when Robison opened League Park at the corner of 66th and Lexington Avenue (the junction of his Payne and Superior streetcar lines), he created the perfect convergence. Now Spiders fans would not only pay him to get through the turnstiles, they would also pay him to get to the turnstiles.[1]

Sadly for Robison, Spiders fans seemed oddly apathetic to the opportunity. Attendance was disappointing. Robison responded by improving the club. Cy Young, destined to become the winningest pitcher in the game's history, took the mound every third or fourth day. Jesse Burkett won two batting titles, and in both 1895 and 1896 the Spiders played for what was then the game's premier prize, the Temple Cup. They won it in 1895.

Still, crowds in the hundreds or low thousands were common at League Park. Robison hit upon another solution: Sunday baseball. One of the problems many baseball teams faced in the 1890s was that their games were played when few could actually watch them. The fifty-hour work week kept men occupied at their jobs during most of the daylight hours from Monday through Saturday. And when the work week was finally shortened, factories still did not close until noon on Saturday.

Fig. 14. Boston's infield, considered by some the best of the nineteenth century; *clockwise from top*: Fred Tenney, Herman Long, Jimmy Collins, and Bobby Lowe. (McGreevey Collection, Boston Public Library, Print Department.)

Baseball owners tried to compensate by scheduling their games late in the afternoon, often at 3:00 or 4:00 p.m. They could do this because most games could be completed in one and one-half to two hours. Even so, for most Americans the only real opportunity to catch a full game was between noon on Saturday and sundown on Sunday.

But Sunday baseball was illegal in parts of the United States and frowned upon elsewhere. The National League did not sanction Sunday games until 1892, and then it gave teams the option of refusing to play Sunday road games if players felt that it would undermine their morals or if ownership felt it would undermine their standing with home fans.[2] The Beaneaters, for one, took precisely that position. Playing professional games on Sunday was illegal by Massachusetts state law, and even though the club was not bound to adhere to that rule in other states, it did so to affirm its reputation back home as a Sabbatarian team. In fact, Maryland, New York, Ohio, Pennsylvania, and the District of Columbia all prohibited Sunday ball, leaving only the Browns, Colonels, and Colts technically free to schedule Sunday games. Among eastern teams, the Dodgers, and Orioles, Senators agreed to take part in Sunday games on the road, but the Giants, Phillies, and Pirates joined Boston in disdaining all Sunday play.[3]

This inequity set up several schedule biases. One outgrowth was the scheduling of one-game Sunday series, which required clubs that were playing a series in a city where Sunday ball was barred to make an overnight dash to a city where Sunday ball was legal. After playing the Sunday game, the team would then dash back to the previous city in time for the first pitch on Monday afternoon.

Because Sunday games were naturally better draws than those played on weekdays, teams that were able to play Sunday ball were thought to have a financial edge over the others. Ordinarily, it would be easy to point to the standings to refute the notion that Sunday ball was a financial advantage; after all, the western Sunday-playing teams were rarely pennant contenders. But particularly with respect to Robison's Spiders, there was another problem. Although Ohio state law specifically prohibited Sunday baseball, by 1897 the law was blatantly ignored in Cincinnati, where the Reds scheduled and played several such games to large audiences without interference from local authorities.[4] The games were brilliant successes by any measure, especially financially. A game between the Orioles and the Reds on Sunday, July 19, 1896, drew a crowd of 24,900, setting a National League attendance record. If the Reds could play ball on Sunday, Robison felt his Spiders ought to be able to do so as well.

In fact, he had had the concern for years. Nearly a decade earlier Robison had pleaded with the Cleveland city council to add a provision to its ordinances to specifically allow Sunday baseball. He hoped to use that provision as leverage to get around the Ohio state law. He won the ordinance change but lost the battle when law enforcement officers, stirred to action by Protestant ministers, broke up a Sunday game and arrested several of the players.[5]

Robison's biggest stumbling block was simply that the political situation in Cleveland was not the same as it was in Cincinnati. Cleveland was both farther east and farther north, and Clevelanders clung to many of the historically puritan sentiments evident in and around New England. Such sentiments, if they ever had existed in Cincinnati, had been eradicated. The breathing manifestation of those Cleveland sentiments was the city's mayor, Robert McKisson, whose election platform included opposition to Sunday baseball.[6] McKisson's rejection of Robison's various pleas for leniency prompted the Spiders owner late in 1896 to issue an open threat. He would schedule Sunday ballgames at home in 1897, and if they were not played, he would consider relocating the team. "St. Louis . . . possesses the weakest team in the league," noted the *Sporting News*. "Cleveland is the poorest patronage of the League cities, but has one of the strongest teams to represent it. . . . The Cleveland team in St. Louis would be a gold mine to its owners."[7]

As it was, Robison already had a close relationship with the ownership of the St. Louis team—the city farthest west in the baseball landscape and also the one that was warmest to Sunday ball. The connection dated to the 1891 merger of the National League and the American Association, when Robison (representing the National League) and the Browns' Von der Ahe were closely involved in the merger negotiations. Within a couple of years the relationship became financial as well as familial. By 1899 Robison moved virtually all of the Spiders' best players to St. Louis, and in 1900 he surrendered the Cleveland franchise altogether.

Jack Powell, Designated Criminal

Robison's frustration with Cincinnati is really a backdrop to the events of 1897. The first Sunday game scheduled in Cleveland in defiance of the state law was to occur when the Senators visited on May 16. But the game was in trouble virtually from the moment it was scheduled, and not merely because of Robert McKisson's opposition. Presbyterian and Congregationalist ministers rallied opposition, and they got support from an unlikely ally, the city's saloonkeepers. Although ball playing was prohibited as a violation of the Sabbath, no similar ordinance affected taverns—presumably because it was politically unwise to advocate such a restriction. Bar owners plainly feared the competition posed by opening the baseball grounds. "Men and boys will . . . go to the games and spend the seventy-five cents they would otherwise leave with us," one tavern keeper told *Sporting Life*. "We will lose three-fourths of this patronage."[8]

Robison pressed ahead, advertising the game widely, and by the time the gates to the ballpark were closed (a half hour before the 3:00 p.m. start), at least ten thousand people were inside and several thousand more lingered on the streets. But although the fans expected to see baseball, Robison did not. He and McKisson had already agreed to let events unfold in what amounted to a test case of the state law. Play would begin and then it would be halted, a certain number of players would be arrested and booked, one would be selected for prosecution on a misdemeanor charge of violating the Sabbath, and the courts would rule.

The afternoon proceeded according to script. In exchange for each ticket presented by a fan, Robison issued a check good for a refund in the event that the game was not played. He and Spiders captain Patsy Tebeau also juggled the team's lineup, including starting rookie pitcher Jack Powell at first base. Powell was to be the test case. After a scoreless first inning, Robison and a captain of the Cleveland police jointly appeared on the field to announce that the game had been stopped. All nine starters for each team as well as umpire Tim Hurst were arrested and taken to the booking station. There they visited with the police officers, signed the booking sheets along with some autographs, and were released on one hundred dollars' bail posted by Robison.[9]

The reaction within the sporting press was swift and far more sympathetic to the Spiders than to law enforcement. Remarked Elmer Bates in *Sporting Life*, "About seventy-five games of ball were played in the city yesterday (Sunday), the police not interfering." Bates also lambasted the ministers who "pointed out the probability of riotous demonstrations . . . with vivid apprehensions of a battle between the police and the spectators when the first game should be interrupted." Instead, Bates noted, "16,000 or 18,000 orderly, well-behaved, decently attired people came out . . . and even when the game was stopped the monster crowd gave no vehement demonstration of its displeasure and disapproval."[10]

Powell, the selected test case, was quickly tried and convicted of violating the Ohio statute. The quick verdict prompted Robison to cancel the next weekend's scheduled Sunday game with Baltimore and at the same time hire attorneys to pursue Powell's appeal. The basis of the appeal was straightforward: the provision in the state law violated Powell's rights by compelling him to observe a religious holiday. In less than two months, Walter Ong, judge of the Court of Common Pleas, upheld that argument, reversing Powell's conviction and throwing out the law. In order for baseball playing to be prohibited by law, Ong found, either it must be intrinsically immoral (a plainly unsupportable argument) or the Sunday prohibition must be religiously based. From there it was a simple determination that the ordinance's purpose was to unconstitutionally "compel the observance of that day as a day of religious worship."[11]

Robison had his victory and more. Although the state appealed, McKisson agreed not to interfere with the playing of future Sunday games until the Ohio Supreme Court ruled on Judge Ong's overturning of the original verdict. Partisans saw Ong's decision as a franchise saver. "The victory means that neither Detroit nor Buffalo will replace Cleveland in the big League in '98, but that the Indians will remain right here in the Forest City," remarked Bates. "Best of all, it means that 20,000 workingmen, heretofore deprived of an opportunity of seeing a National League game, can with perfect assurance of two hours of rare enjoyment go out to League Park on Sunday afternoon without fear of police interference in their effort to enjoy personal liberty."[12]

By year's end, the Ohio Supreme Court had overturned Ong's decision and upheld the state law, ending Robison's hopes for Sunday ball and initiating the events that would lead to the franchise's termination. In the interim, however, the Spiders did manage to get in four home Sunday games.

A Series to Light Up For

Powell's conviction was on appeal when the Orioles arrived in Boston for their Thursday-Friday-Saturday series. With first place at stake, more than forty-five thousand made their way to the South End Grounds to take in the three games. Back in Baltimore, hundreds more jammed the Ford Theater to watch the enactment of the games by marionettes.

Neither the Beaneaters nor the champs were at their physical best. For Boston, Chick Stahl had been sidelined since the Cincinnati series with what the newspapers generically described as "malaria," a catch-all term that often included syphilis and other problems considered unfit for public awareness.[13] Bobby Lowe too was out, having broken a finger during the Brooklyn series. Jack Stivetts and Doc Yeager took their places in right field and at second base, respectively. Ned Hanlon's catching situation looked increasingly serious. Boileryard Clarke could not even attempt to return for another week, and the doubts about Wilbert Robinson had been renewed by his weak showing against the Giants.

In the unlikely event that the home team required any additional motivation, a local cigar company supplied it, offering a box of cigars to each Boston player who hit safely in the opening game. With Kid Nichols facing Jerry Nops, the cigar company's tab didn't figure to be too high, but the company failed to count on the multitude of fans in attendance. With nearly twice as many ticket buyers for the Thursday game as there were grandstand seats, the excess crowd was penned behind ropes in the outfield, turning routine fly balls into easy hits. "As a baseball contest, the game was a pure farce," remarked the *Baltimore Sun*'s observer of a game played "in a space not much larger than a tennis court."[14]

The Beaneaters took better advantage of the tight dimensions, pounding out twenty hits for a 12–5 victory. Several of those Boston hits amounted to routine fly balls on a clear field, but the overflow crowd gave Willie Keeler, Jake Stenzel, and Joe Kelley no place to run under them. Although Boston papers made no mention of it, the *Sun*'s reporter thought Orioles outfielders had even more reason to beef. Keeler "was tripped and held by spectators in the ninth inning to prevent his reaching a fly that fell over the edge of the crowd," the *Sun* reported. As for Stenzel, "Whenever a Boston player's fly came near the crowd those in front would crowd up on it and let it fall in their midst (preventing) Stenzel from getting Duffy's fly in the first inning, and it cost a run."[15]

Hugh Duffy was certainly the biggest beneficiary. With five singles and a home run, he savored the prospect of six boxes of Perfectos. "Next to winning a ballgame, the thing that pleases me most is a quiet half hour with one of these cigars," Duffy told reporters afterward.[16] For Boston the only sour part of the game was the fractured finger that Marty Bergen sustained off a foul tip in the eighth inning.

With the wound in his leg fully reopened as a result of his premature return, Robinson sat down again before the second game for what would prove to be a long rest. Further misfortune struck when Willie Keeler was injured in the first inning. The Orioles had begun in textbook fashion, with John McGraw drawing a walk and Keeler bunting him to second base. But in his haste to reach first, Keeler tripped over the base and suffered a groin strain that would disable him for at least a week. One out and a walk to Kelley later, Stenzel drove the first run home. Jack Doyle followed with a ground double down the line, and the Orioles led 3–0. The lead lasted only as long as it took Boston to bat around in the bottom of the second; the Beaneaters scored five times thanks largely to Herman Long's two-out, bases-clearing double. The Orioles got one back in the third when Joe Kelley, who had forced Hughie Jennings, came around on Stenzel's double. Then in the fifth, Jennings, Kelley, Stenzel, and Doyle all hit safely, Heinie Reitz walked, and two outs later, McGraw offset Long's earlier bases-clearing double with one of his own. Now the Orioles led 9–5. It was 9–8 when the hometowners came up for their final shot at Bill Hoffer in the bottom of the ninth.

Hoffer had not been especially tough all afternoon, and by the ninth inning he was visibly tiring. Sensing his fatigue, the Boston fandom honed in with some of its choicest razzing, not all of it obscene. That expectant air was dampened, but only slightly, when the first two men went down.

With the game on his shoulders, Jimmy Collins found a hole on the right side for a single to get the tying run on base. Whether due to the fans, his own fatigue, or pure fate, Hoffer walked Charles Ganzel, putting the tying run in scoring position and the winning run on base. Frank Selee sent up Chick Stahl as a pinch hitter and Hoffer walked him as well. Now the place was roaring. Wrote Tim Murnane, "It was interesting to see McGraw, Kelley, Doyle and Jennings group around Hoffer as he was going to pieces. The ball was growing heavy and his eyes were fast losing their brilliant luster."[17]

Fred Tenney came next. The first pitch was a strike; so was the second. The third became a line drive on course for the gap in right, a solid hit that sent both Jimmy Collins and Charles Ganzel around with decisive runs. It touched off a scene portending of celebrations later in the year. The crowd burst onto the field and swept Tenney to its shoulders, carrying him to the grandstand to receive the public salute. So enthusiastic (if that is the proper word) was the reception that the hero emerged battered and bruised.[18] (He played poorly the fol-

lowing day and then sat out until the final game of the Brooklyn series on Wednesday.) The players finally were allowed to repair to the
clubhouse to dress, but the fans remained to cheer some more. They
would not leave until Tenney returned, this time in street dress, to receive a collection of change that had been taken up by the assemblage,
presumably in gratitude for the privilege of being able to pound him.
Boston, after opening the series with a half-game advantage, now led
by two and one-half games. Since the stumbling first week, the team
was winning at a staggering .833 pace, with thirty-five victories in forty-
two games. To make matters even better, Nichols was poised to come
back Saturday on a single day's rest. If ever a ball club looked invincible, it was Selee's.

A crowd of seventeen thousand—including Jim Corbett—strained
the confines of the Grounds to watch Nichols and Joe Corbett in that
Saturday wrap-up. The former champ came in search of takers for his
wager on his brother and the Orioles, and he found a hundred dollars'
worth of them.[19] Given the demand for tickets, Arthur Soden summarily raised the price on the quarter bleacher seats to a half dollar. That
left plenty of youngsters in mourning outside the park but otherwise
did nothing to stanch interest in the event. Despite the fact that he had
pitched just forty-eight hours earlier, Nichols was at his sharpest, limiting the Orioles to five hits. Corbett matched that performance, so as
the innings rolled on, the game assumed classic proportions, with neither team able to solve the opposing pitcher. Because of the series' importance, the league had assigned both Bob Emslie and Hank O'Day
as umpires. As the tension mounted, the clubs took turns playing each
of them in search of any call that might turn the outcome.

Murnane and others thought the visitors did a much better job
of lobbying. "Every Oriole was on his toes from first to last and nagging umpire Emslie at every turn," Murnane wrote. "The home team
played good ball, but was not on the lookout for its rights as the men
should have been. Because men are not batting is no reason they must
lay down and keep quiet."[20]

The Orioles threatened in the third when Reitz walked; then with two out, McGraw lined a single past Long, and the ball skipped past Duffy as well to put the runners at second and third. Nichols got Doyle on a foul pop-up. In the Baltimore eighth, Doyle drove a fly ball toward the bleachers in right, but Stivetts found room to get under it. Finally, with two out in the ninth, Stenzel took Nichols over the fence down the right-field line, and the ball bounced back onto the field but was declared a home run. Corbett was more than up to the task of holding that slim a lead, retiring Boston without incident in the bottom of the ninth. His brother, delighted to collect on his wagers, cut both Joe and Jake Stenzel in for a share of the winnings, purchasing a suit of clothes for each of them. As the Orioles climbed aboard their coach for the hotel, dozens of Boston youngsters gathered around. They weren't there to threaten the Orioles but to try to get close to the ex–boxing champ, who rode back with his brother and the team. His Orioles had lost two of the three games, but at least Harry Von der Horst had reason to smile. The estimated forty thousand people who paid to see the series returned about nine thousand dollars to the visitors as their share of the gate; the hosts' share was closer to fifteen thousand dollars.[21]

Rooters' Genesis

Following the prescribed Sunday holiday, Brooklyn made its first visit to Boston. Stivetts was the only plausible fill-in for Tenney at first base, so the weakened Stahl struggled out to right field, and the Bridegrooms agreed to Boston's request to use Ganzel as a "courtesy runner" for him. Since Ganzel was already subbing for Bergen and batting eighth, that raised the remote possibility of his being called upon to reach two different bases at the same time—a circumstance that would have been fascinating had it ever come about. It did not. What did come about was a 6–6 tie after eight innings, followed by two Brooklyn runs in the top of the ninth and three Boston runs in the bottom half, when Stivetts's easy fly for a routine third out was dropped. All three runs had reached base on walks to Ganzel, Billy Hamilton, and Herman

Long. It was the first of three one-run decisions in the series, with Boston claiming all three.

By the time of the Brooklyn series, the notion of an organized fan section had taken hold. Its size and composition was not yet recognized, nor is it known whether Tim Murnane authored the name or merely borrowed what he had heard from the fans themselves. However, his coverage of the Tuesday game includes this exhortation: "'Make 'em be good,' sang out a Royal Rooter as Collins went up to the cannon's mouth for business in the ninth."[22] Enthusiasm also gathered around the idea of the Beaneaters as a clean alternative to the widely despised Orioles. "Anything to beat Baltimore seems to be the sentiment and Boston appears to be the only club capable of the feat," reported the *Sporting News* after the series concluded.[23] But if the club now had the beginnings of an organized rooting section, it also had one less pitcher. During pregame warm-ups, Fred Klobedanz split a finger on his pitching hand and had to join Marty Bergen and Bobby Lowe on the sidelines.

As the race intensified, so did the cutthroat level of play. Between May 30 and June 4, eight players were ejected from league games, some for fighting, some for interference, and one (Louisville pitcher Bert Cunningham) for angrily throwing a ball out of the stadium. Even such ruffians as Cap Anson voiced concern. "In the old days, baseball was played with bat and ball," he told Chicago reporters. "Nowadays it is played chiefly with one's mouth. Disgraceful kicking, bad language and dirty ball playing generally would not have been tolerated ten years ago . . . the game is surely suffering in the public eye."[24] When he made the comment, Anson had three ejections ahead of him in 1897. Still, friends of a gentler game took their allies where they could find them. Henry Chadwick, the dean of baseball writers, wrote in his column in *Sporting Life* that the frequently profane practice of "kicking" had resulted in "a marked falling off in the attendance of ladies, when with anything like decent conduct thousands would be occupying the

grandstands." Added Chadwick, "The fact is reputable patrons have become disgusted with the scenes which have disgraced league grounds
at some of the cities—Boston and Brooklyn being excepted."[25]

The Pennant Race Hits Broadway

As the Beaneaters hosted Brooklyn, Baltimore moved on to New York,
where the Orioles were struck twice in one inning by crippling injuries.
McGraw opened the game by drawing a walk, but Doyle forced him
out at second. Jennings, the third hitter, was famous for being struck
by pitches. Like a lot of the Orioles, he saw it as just one more way to
get on base. He had in fact led the league in being hit during the previous three seasons and was hit fifty-one times in 1896 alone. He was
on pace to surpass that figure when Amos Rusie fired a fastball at his
head. The ball knocked Jennings out cold. Although neither he nor
the Orioles realized it immediately, he had suffered a concussion and
a skull fracture. Amazingly, after being down for several minutes, he
rose and insisted on staying in the game, trotting unsteadily to first and
eventually scoring one of three Baltimore runs in that inning. He took
the field for the bottom of the first, but when he lost track of a routine
ground ball, a doctor ordered him from the field. Keeler escorted him
away and put him to bed at the team's hotel, summoning more medical help.[26] By that time, Doyle was also out of the lineup, having been
hit in the eye by a bad hop that shot off the bat of New York lead-off
batter George VanHaltren. The loss of Jennings and Doyle left Hanlon to play the Giants with only McGraw, Kelley, Stenzel, and Reitz as
healthy regulars. Behind Rusie, New York won 4–2.

That evening the rumor mill wound into top speed regarding Jennings. Word circulated that he was near death, that he had been rendered delirious, that his career might be over. Those stories were not
entirely fictitious. He had in fact passed through periods of delirium
during the night, also reporting some paralysis in his arms and hands.
His speech was sometimes incoherent, his cognizance only occasional.
Nevertheless, Arlie Pond reported the next morning that he thought

Jennings would be able to play again within days or weeks, not months or years.

Doyle's doctor used leeches to reduce the swelling in the player's eye, but Doyle too was ruled out for the rest of the New York series. Boileryard Clarke, although he was not yet able to catch, volunteered to return to take over at first base. The battered Orioles lost again 8–2. They won the third game behind Corbett, despite again starting only four regulars and then losing one of them. Kelley, peeved at the work of umpire Jim McDonald on the bases, squawked and managed to get himself thrown out, leaving just McGraw, Stenzel, and Reitz available from Hanlon's regular team. With not enough position players to cover the spots on the field, Hanlon sent Bill Hoffer into the outfield to replace Kelley.

To fans not caught up in the pennant race, an eye-catching development in baseball occurred in Chicago on the final Tuesday of June, during a little-noticed match-up between the eleventh-place Colts and the tenth-place Colonels. Chicago opened with three runs in the first, scored five times more in the second, and chased Louisville pitcher Chick Fraser amid a seven-run burst in the third. That gave the home team a 15–1 lead. Jim Jones, a sandlotter who was making the only big-league appearance of his life, replaced Fraser, allowing another run in the fourth, three more in the fifth, one in the sixth, and two in the seventh. As the eighth inning began, the score stood at 22–7 in favor of the Colts. The Chicago hitters were just warming up. Cap Anson's team, which had chosen to bat first, added seven more runs in the eighth and another eight in the ninth, posting a final score of 36–7. In the more than 130-year history of the major leagues, no team has ever scored more runs in a single game. The Colts pounded out thirty-two hits, six of them by shortstop Barry McCormick and five by blessed pitcher Nixey Callahan. Due to nine Louisville errors, only nineteen of the Chicago runs were earned. Only.

The Beaneaters followed Baltimore into New York's Polo Grounds on July 1, where an audience of seven thousand gathered to watch

Amos Rusie and Kid Nichols. Repeating what was becoming a pleasant trend, Boston sealed the 5–4 victory in the game's final play. With runners at first and second, and amidst the din of the howling hostile gathering, Herman Long raced behind second base to snare George Davis's one-out grounder, beat Bill Joyce to second for the force, and threw out Davis at first. The play was vital because the runner at second, Mike Tiernan, cut third base and would have scored the tying run had both outs not been recorded.

Rain washed out the second game of the series, but Selee made news by signing backup catcher Fred Lake as a fill-in for Marty Bergen, who by this time had acquired a reputation for being physically fragile as well as emotionally unstable. Jack Stivetts outpitched Jouett Meekin for a 3–2 win in the final game, and as the team entrained for Philadelphia, Selee got some good medical news. Lowe and Bergen were both cleared to resume play, Tenney pronounced himself back at full strength following his post-victory pummeling by the home crowd a week earlier, and even Stahl gave signs of being ready to take over right field on a consistent basis. In Philly the team showed the same high level of ball, sweeping a July 5 doubleheader. Lowe's ninth-inning single drove home Duffy and Stahl for a 3–2 win in the morning game. Then, before nine thousand people at the afternoon game, Boston overcame a 5–3 Philadelphia lead in the final inning, scoring five times after two batters were out and just one was on base. The finish capped a remarkable string for the Beaneaters, who had won seven consecutive games, the first six by a single run and the seventh in a ninth-inning rally. It marked the team's ninth straight game decided either by one run or in the final inning (or both), and the Beaneaters' record in those games was 8-1.

Brawltimore

The next day's game was routine by comparison—a 6–2 victory in which even the Philadelphia partisans seemed to get behind the Boston visitors. Murnane reported that the exiting team was cheered in an implicit affirmation of the "anybody but Baltimore" theme.[27] For their part, the Orioles returned home for two quick games with the Senators before embarking on their second month-long road trip. They won both games, one of them a curiosity match in which Arlie Pond outlasted Washington's own pitching physician, Doc McJames.[28] Keeler returned for that game but was held hitless for only the second time all season. In the Friday second game, the crowd of 1,800 got a big surprise when Jennings appeared and announced his intention to play. His only offensive contribution amounted to getting hit by another pitch, but it came at a critical point. The Orioles trailed 4–1 entering the eighth, but then McGraw walked and Keeler delivered a hit-and-run single. When Jennings took a pitch in the ribs, the bases were filled with none out. A Washington error let both McGraw and Keeler score, and Jennings followed them home on Doyle's single to center, tying the game. With Kelley at third and Doyle at second, Frank Bowerman's base hit sent both of them across, establishing a 6–4 lead that Nops was able to maintain in the ninth.

But the western trip opened poorly in Cincinnati, where the Reds had beaten the Orioles three times in May. In 104-degree heat on July 4, they did it again, this time 5–4. The game was marked by six errors by the Orioles, two of them by Jennings. Cincinnati won again, 8–5, on July 5, thanks in good measure to three more errors by the Orioles, and they closed out the sweep with a 10–3 decision fueled by six more Baltimore errors. The Orioles had committed fifteen errors, and it was taking its toll on the always-volatile team chemistry. Doyle and McGraw—the latter already fuming because a Jake Beckley hip check had sent him flying during the game—snapped at Jennings and Reitz, and everybody snapped at the pitchers. Reported the *Baltimore Sun*, "The team is broken up by internal factional differences . . . carelessness and indifference . . . such as has never been shown before."[29]

Judging by the standings, something was wrong. Since concluding their home games with the visiting western teams with a 33-10 record and a one-game lead, the Orioles had won just five of fifteen times and had fallen into third place, six and one-half games behind the Beaneaters. Injuries to Jennings, Keeler, Clarke, Robinson, Doyle, and McGraw certainly had contributed. But with the exception of Robinson, all had been healthy in Cincinnati, where the team played some of its worst ball.

For their part, Beaneaters fans were encouraged, and not merely by the sweep of Philadelphia. Observed John Morrill in the *Boston Journal*, "It goes without saying that all of New England is baseball crazy."[30]

National League Standings (Evening of July 5)

TEAM	WINS	LOSSES	PERCENTAGE	GAMES BEHIND
Boston	44	14	.759	—
Cincinnati	37	18	.673	5½
Baltimore	38	19	.667	5½
New York	33	23	.589	10
Cleveland	31	28	.525	13½
Pittsburg	28	30	.483	16
Brooklyn	28	31	.476	16½
Philadelphia	29	33	.468	17
Louisville	24	33	.421	19½
Washington	23	35	.397	21
Chicago	24	37	.393	21½
St. Louis	11	49	.183	34

8. The Rise and Fall of Louis Sockalexis

The story of Louis Sockalexis is important in any discussion of 1897 for reasons that go beyond its bearing on the season's pennant race. It illuminates many of the social and cultural characteristics of the society within which ball games were played.

So let us begin by considering the dimensions of the Sockalexis phenomenon: He could hit a baseball harder than almost any man alive. He was an Indian playing a white man's game. His presence in the major leagues fed still-fresh stereotypes regarding the strength of the "noble savage." His downfall validated the classic cautionary tale of all great stories, be they comedies or tragedies. In the case of Sockalexis, it turned out to be a tragedy.

Beyond the plain fact that it was occasioned by liquor, the specifics of that downfall remain muddied by mythology. For decades the version of the story proffered by manager Patsy Tebeau, advanced by Hughie Jennings, and repeated by H. G. Salsinger, the famed sports editor of the *Detroit News*, held currency. The virginal Indian had been introduced to the hard stuff by his teammates in celebration of an especially remarkable performance in Chicago in late June. As Tebeau, Jennings, and Salsinger told it, Sockalexis's unfamiliarity with the power of bourbon made him a susceptible target, and soon thereafter it rendered him worthless.[1]

Fig. 15. When this formal portrait was taken in 1900, Louis Sockalexis was a twenty-eight-year-old baseball has-been. For three months of the 1897 season, he was the talk of all of baseball. (National Baseball Hall of Fame Library, Cooperstown NY.)

The story is almost certainly false. The reality (also proffered by Salsinger and validated by researchers) is that Sockalexis was already what we would call a "problem drinker" when Tebeau signed him out of the University of Notre Dame. His phenomenal half season amounted to the inevitable playing out of time until booze caught up with his performance.

The cautionary tale works only to the extent that we recognize the potential that those around him saw in Sockalexis. To grasp that potential, we need to look back at his undergraduate days at Holy Cross College.

Louis Sockalexis was a member of the Maine-based Penobscot tribe, whose presence at any college was a rarity in those days. But at five feet eleven and 185 pounds, he had an athlete's build that, combined with his natural speed and power, caught the attention of the region's sports programs.

Early demonstrations of his ability included the 1894 game between the Holy Cross Crusaders and visiting Harvard University. Like many colleges then and for years afterward, Holy Cross played on what was literally a field, open around the outskirts. A ball struck well enough might eventually reach the campus tennis courts, although it would have had to carry about 450 feet to do so. A batter striking such a ball could run as far as his legs could carry him or until a speedy outfielder could retrieve the ball.

That is precisely what occurred. With Sockalexis in center, a Harvard batter struck a ball to the edge of the courts. Knowing he had little time to make a play, Sockalexis chased down the ball, turned, and flung it with all his might toward the plate. To the astonishment of those present, the ball alighted on the pitcher's mound, reducing a sure home run to a triple. Following the game, two Holy Cross professors measured the distance between the mound and the edge of the tennis courts at 138 yards—414 feet. Sockalexis's ability to run a hundred meters in ten seconds flat had already made him a recognizable figure on and around campus; with this throw, he was on his way to becoming a legend.[2]

The legend grew quickly. By the time of his major-league debut, the story circulated that he had homered off Amos Rusie both the first and second times he faced "the Hoosier Thunderbolt" in an exhibition game. (Since Rusie did not play at all in 1896 and sat out during 1897 spring training, the only way this actually could have happened was if a barnstorming team featuring Rusie faced Sockalexis's club. No record of such a game exists, and today that particular yarn is viewed as very likely false.)

Following the 1896 college season, Sockalexis transferred from Holy Cross to Notre Dame. Major-league scouts followed, all agreeing there was good reason to do so. "I have seen him play perhaps a dozen games," remarked John M. Ward, the well-known former player and future Hall of Famer. "I unhesitatingly pronounce him a wonder."[3]

Sockalexis initially resisted the professional inquiries. But an incident reported in a February edition of the *South Bend Journal* suggests why he might have become more amenable to offers. The article also puts in doubt the notion that the great rookie was still a newcomer to the bottle the following June. The *South Bend Journal* reported on the Indian's arrest during a night of carousing. As the newspapers told it, he and a friend had barged into a local brothel named Pop Corn Jennie's and proceeded to tear up the place. Jennie called her friends at the city police department, and the ballplayer and his friend were taken into custody and then quickly expelled from college.[4] Accounts vary as to whether this incident occurred just after Tebeau signed Sockalexis to a $1,500 contract or, as some tell it, Tebeau leveraged the incident to get him to sign. What is known is that Tebeau posted bail and Sockalexis reported immediately to spring training. He was twenty-five years old.

"I congratulate you on securing Sockalexis," Ward wired Tebeau.[5] Others, however, were less enthusiastic. Tom Delahanty, brother of the great Ed Delahanty and a major-league hanger-on, told a reporter that "the league has gone to hell now that they've let them damned foreigners in."[6] Stories circulated that Sockalexis's new teammate, Jesse Burkett—a two-time league batting champion—baited Sockalexis with slurs. Burkett was known league-wide as "The Crab" for his irascibility, and in the 1890s, respectable white men needed no motivation to cast epithets at those of other races. Burkett had personal motivation too; he could easily view Sockalexis as a threat to his fame. In an interview with New York sports writer Joe Vila, Sockalexis denied such reports. According to Vila, Sockalexis said, "That is all bosh, for the white players can't do enough for me, especially Burkett, who is said to be jealous because I lead him in batting."[7] Since Burkett had been an assistant coach at Holy Cross during Sockalexis's years there, they could have developed a friendship. Whether Sockalexis was telling the truth or keeping team problems in the clubhouse must be left for conjecture.

Yet others plainly loved him. News reports described the athlete in terms suggestive of a superman. "He is massive with gigantic bones and bulging muscles," wrote a reporter in *Sporting Life*.[8] John McGraw and Hughie Jennings took one look at him playing the outfield and pronounced him the finest athlete they had ever seen. "A grand ball-player," agreed Tim Murnane after Cleveland's first visit to Boston.[9] Tebeau later said that within weeks of the player's debut, management had torn up the $1,500 contract and raised him to $2,400.

On the field he was a one-man version of Buffalo Bill's Wild West Show, which had a concurrent nationwide tour that provided a framework for such comparisons. "All eyes are on the Indian in every game," wrote *Sporting Life*'s Cleveland correspondent.[10] Sockalexis drew fans in numbers rarely seen. Vila saw the easy bond that formed between the young star and kids. "If the small and big boys find pleasure to shout at me, I have no objections," Sockalexis told him.[11] Yet much of that shouting was not friendly, as he himself acknowledged. "No matter where we play, I go through the same ordeal, and at present I am so used to it that I forget to smile at my tormenters," he said.[12]

A Living Parody

Sockalexis was seen through the parodies of the age. At home and virtually everywhere on the road, he was met with war whoops, some of them meant to encourage, others derisive. During Cleveland's June visit to Baltimore, McGraw wore a headdress onto the field in an effort to mock, rattle, and intimidate him.[13] "Columns of silly poetry are written about him," *Sporting Life* noted. "Hideous looking cartoons adorn the sporting pages of nearly every paper."[14] He was called the same names that all the other players heard but was also called a savage. "In many cases these demonstrations border on extreme rudeness," commented one writer.[15]

His April 30 home debut against the St. Louis Browns featured a home run. The next day he produced four hits in five tries, one of them a bases-loaded triple. "The red man has played good, steady ball," *Sporting Life* observed in mid-May. "Of course Sockalexis has much to learn about the game as it is played in the big league, but he is not only an apt but a willing pupil."[16]

In those days, racial parody was a widely accepted practice. The sport's overwhelmingly white audiences saw no inherent problem in artifices such as exaggerated dialogue and description. And the more exaggerated and abundant the artifices, the better. In his report on Sockalexis's first performance in front of the Baltimore fans during the second week of June, *Sporting Life*'s Orioles correspondent, Albert Mott, commented on the feedback from the Union Park bleachers. "They are funny, that's all," Mott wrote. "When Soxie came up to bat, there were some 'wow, wow, wows' and 'look at the injun' but—by implication, nothing more serious."[17] Mott himself referred to the Indian commonly as Soxie or Sockdolager and reported that Sockalexis's own teammates called him "Powwow."[18]

In his account of Cleveland's first visit to Boston a week earlier, Tim Murnane seized every opportunity—and Sockalexis provided plenty of them—to try to be clever at the expense of the visitor's culture. He compared Sockalexis's fleetness of foot to "the visitations of lightning from cloud to cloud [which] aroused the bleachers to a scalp dance."[19] Sockalexis is described in his first at bat as carrying a "war club." One day later, Murnane mused that "an Indian's presence on the ball field harks one back to the stirring scenes when clubs were used for other purposes than base hits."[20]

In short order, Sockalexis's teammates received the same media treatment. The *Boston Globe*'s coverage of the Spiders' series makes reference to such visiting players as "Silver Moon" (Zeke) Wilson, "Man With Curves in His Face" (Cy) Young, "Squawbush" (Ed) McKean, "Man With Hole in His Bat" (Bobby) Wallace, and "Plentybats" (Patsy) Tebeau.[21]

Sockalexis's first appearance in New York in mid-June captured the attention of the sporting world. This time Rusie was present beyond any question. So were fans—so many that Giants management penned them behind a roped-off area in right field for the game. In Sockalexis's first at bat against Rusie, he drove the ball over Mike Tiernan's head and beyond the rope. Under the ground rules, such a hit was in play, but by the time Tiernan had located it, Sockalexis had raced around the bases—a home run off Rusie.[22] And this time there were plenty of witnesses.

That Sockalexis was a sort of baseball asteroid who rose to fame and with equal fanfare exploded in ruin is plainly borne out by his record. Virtually all of his production was prior to July 1. It was a substantial half season. He was batting near .370 for the first sixty games, having driven in nearly forty runs and averaging close to two hits per game. But after the first week in July, he played rarely, fitfully, and ineffectively.

The Sockalexis legend traces his downfall to his performance during a midseason game in Chicago. As the story goes, the Spiders trailed by three runs at the start of the ninth inning, and Sockalexis arrived at the plate with the bases full and two outs. He slugged a grand slam. In the bottom of the ninth, with two runners on base, he made a game-saving catch in the right-center-field gap. Enraptured, his teammates escorted him to a nearby saloon for a hearty celebration that, by all accounts, succeeded in thoroughly liquoring up the Cleveland star. If it wasn't his first taste of bourbon, it clearly was one of his deepest.

The prospect of Sockalexis celebrating in a Chicago bar is plausible. Indeed, in late July the *Sporting News* carried a report of his involvement in a bar fight that June weekend. But the story remains more legend than fact. The first problem is its timing. Cleveland played in Chicago on June 24-27, but at that point Sockalexis had a solid week of quality ball left in him. The second problem is that in none of those Chicago games is Sockalexis credited with a home run, much less a game-winning grand slam. In fact, the Spiders did not score four runs in the ninth inning in any of the games in the series with Chicago.[23]

Today nobody knows precisely why Sockalexis broke down over the July 4 holiday; we only know that he did. It almost certainly involved a drinking binge, which Tebeau responded to by placing guards at the door to Sockalexis's second-floor room. If the manager thought the guards would prevent his player from sneaking out for booze, he was mistaken. In fact, it only encouraged the player to leave via the window. In the process, Sockalexis either severely sprained or fractured his ankle. The press reports assert the latter, but press reports of the time often contained hyperbole, and Sockalexis was able to play on the ankle off and on during the next few weeks. Whatever the diagnosis, his limited appearances, one- or two-day tests of the ankle's condition, were discouraging. If one takes the accounts of his teammates as fact, the Indian's persistent habit of hobbling down to the corner bar may have been a factor in the slow pace of his recovery. "He would get up during the night and walk a block on his plaster foot to get a drink of whiskey," Tebeau lamented years later.[24]

Despite the infrequency of his post–July 4 appearances, Sockalexis remained a matinee idol—"Socks' mail . . . is flooded with Cupid missives from palpitating maidens who pine for a photo," the *Washington Post* reported in mid-July.[25] But his play no longer merited the attention. Against Boston he committed two errors that led to seven unearned runs in an 8–2 loss in July. During that series, insinuations of a drinking problem became public. Sports reporters of the era rarely tarnished fans' images of their heroes, so when the *Cleveland Plain Dealer* reported that "a turkish bath and a good rest might be an excellent remedy" for Sockalexis, it amounted to a tell-all.[26]

The Birth of Darkhue White

The deeply held racial and ethnic biases into which the Sockalexis story played were by no means limited to the reception accorded him alone. America was profoundly affected by racial animus in 1897. M. Witmark and Co., one of New York's most popular retailers of sheet music, made it a practice to advertise its bestselling "coon songs" because, as the store's advertisements in the *New York Clipper* explained, the style "seems to predominate this year."[27] Among them were such favorites of the day as "My Gal Is a High Born Lady," "All Coons Look Alike to Me," and "Honey Does Yer Love Yo Man." In Boston, prejudicial attitudes surfaced at the ballpark, where the enthusiasm for baseball crossed racial lines but did not lead to a broadened exchange of interests.

In June, Tim Murnane had introduced into his reports an observer whom the city came to know as Darkhue White. Although Murnane presented and treated White as a real person, it seems impossible today to consider that he was not either a caricature (possibly of an actual fan), a composite of a fan, or a Murnane creation. As the season wore on, White was given a stronger presence, which paralleled fans' increasing interest in the game. In that sense, if only in that sense, he can be perceived as an Everyman.

Readers were told virtually nothing about Darkhue White, aside from his interest in the Beaneaters, during the summer after he was introduced. He first surfaced as an anonymous "colored man" who was admiring, while attempting to avoid getting in the way of, Jimmy Collins's pursuit of a foul ball during Boston's third win against the Pirates on June 8:

"'Aftuh yo, suh,' said a colored man to the foul that Collins went for in the eighth, and when the dandy third baseman seesawed up from the benches with the ball, he added, 'W'at he keech fo' dem balls? Nuffin sah, nuffin. Seems t' me ah nevuh see such a man's dat Mahs Collins.'"[28]

He returned with the name Crowhue White almost a week later in the account of the Beaneaters' victory in the second game of the series against Buck Ewing's Cincinnati Reds, this time with a postgame assessment of the tenth straight victory:

"'Seems t' me dat Mahs Buck got 'er pow'ful kerwallerpin ter day,' said Crowhue White after the game. 'But dey mowt jes 'es well try ter push de fus' base froo a knothole es ter win from Mahs Duffy's men w'en dey play ball like day hey Tenney. He done gets de drap on ebberyt'ing dat wobbles ovuh his way.'"[29]

The written record demonstrates that Murnane was willing to offer up virtually any dialect he thought he could parody in the interest of entertainment. In a different article he described "an Italian on a gravel car" who urged Fred Klobedanz to "watcha da pitch, t'row-a a crook."[30] During one of the Orioles' visits to Boston, an Irish lad was said to have remarked, "I'd like ter empire d' game w'en d'em Baltimore mugs are playin'." Just how would he handle McGraw, Jennings, and Doyle? "Just grab up a bat an' tap any kickin' bloke dat trun lip at me on d' mut . . . dat's w'at dere lookin' fur, see?"[31] As the mood suited him, Murnane would also from time to time introduce proper English gentlemen or fair damsels.

But day in and day out, White was his favorite. By June 19, during Chicago's visit, Crowhue White had gained a permanent identity as Darkhue White. The *Boston Globe*'s account of Boston's fifteenth straight win included this observation attributed to White: "Ye' pow'ful nice man, Mahs' Anson, but duh's no use yo'r tryin' t' joggle Mah's Duffy's pickaninnies, kase y' cain't do it. Yo heah me, Mahs' Anson."[32]

Insouciant Summer

Playing their best ball of the season, the Beaneaters had no need to be troubled by racial, tribal, or other issues of team or civic harmony. All they had to do was continue to win. This they seemed capable of doing indefinitely. As they passed the July 4 checkpoint and moved into Chicago to open their second western trip, all of the numbers augured well. The Beaneaters had won twenty-eight of their last thirty games, falling only to Brooklyn (to break their seventeen-game streak) and a week later to Baltimore. They had opened up a five and one-half game advantage, the largest by any team all season, and they led the three-time defending champions by six and one-half games. Even better, through the first half of the season, they were scoring almost twice as many runs as their opponents. They carried a .763 winning percentage into that western trip. Not in a dozen seasons had any team finished with a comparable record.

All of this success makes what occurred on the western trip explicable only by the recognition that baseball was then, as it remains today, an unpredictable game. Clark Griffith, the troublemaking Colts ace whose abortive efforts to restir the pot of labor unrest enlivened the league atmosphere in April, outpitched Kid Nichols to earn a 2–1, ten-inning decision. It concluded on Griffith's high chopper over Nichols's head and into center field with a runner at second. The next day the Colts won a second straight one-run decision, this time 8–7, in a contest invigorated by a brawl at home plate that saw two future Hall of Famers thrown off the grounds.

The game was tied 6–6, but George Decker occupied third base for the home club, having gotten there by virtue of two singles—his own and another by pitcher Danny Friend. Friend broke for second, hoping to draw a throw and allow Decker to score. Fred Lake, catching for Boston, did throw to second, where Herman Long cut the ball off and tried to run down the now-retreating Friend. Seeing Friend, Decker made his dash toward home with the go-ahead run, beating Long's return throw and Lake's tag. So said umpire Tom Lynch, anyway.

The Beaneaters disagreed, and they let Lynch know it, pouring out of the dugout in a mass protest. That brought Colts player-manager Cap Anson to the plate to defend his club's stake in the issue. Whatever was said between Lake and Anson must be left to the imagination, but it was sufficient to cause Lake to take a swing at Anson, striking him in the chest. The forty-five-year-old near-legend retaliated by grabbing Lake and throwing him aside, prompting Lynch to intervene and order Anson away from the melee.

Now Anson took out after Lynch, shaking his fists in the umpire's face in what was described in the Boston papers as a "vicious tirade." Lynch retaliated, and then Anson shoved the umpire and drew back his fist. Before Cap could throw a punch, Lynch ejected and fined him.[33]

Having settled that interruption, the umpire returned to the main order of business, persuading the Beaneaters—and in particular captain Hugh Duffy—that Decker really had been safe. More epithets followed, this time from Duffy, and these too were accompanied by gestures forecasting fisticuffs. So Duffy too was ejected, the first Boston player to be removed from a game by an umpire all season. (The Beaneaters were the last of the twelve major-league teams that year to lose a player because of his behavior.) The defeat was the first for Ted Lewis since late May, ending a run of nine consecutive wins. When the series finale went to Chicago, it was the first time the Beaneaters had lost three straight games since the season's opening week.

Through the remaining two and one-half weeks of that western swing, the Bostons played an insouciant brand of ball, winning as often as not but looking little like potential champions. Cleveland was the first stop, and the visit began ominously. As Boston approached the park, their bus crossed paths with a funeral procession, an ill omen among the superstitious players. Their opponents, a team that was now informally referred to as the Indians, had gone cold, in part because the one actual Indian on the roster was hobbled. Even so, Boston lost two of the three games in the series. Sockalexis played to unsatisfactory result in the first game, his injury especially showing up in the field when he failed to reach an easy fourth-inning fly ball by Bobby Lowe. The ball's fall eventually amounted to four runs. Sockalexis played "like a cigar sign," wrote Murnane.[34] He sat out the remaining two games, but during the last one, Cleveland snapped Klobedanz's thirteen-game winning streak, handing him his first defeat since May.

In Pittsburg two days later, a rhubarb enveloped the game's final play, obscuring the outcome for more than five minutes. The Pirates, who had chosen to bat first, led 5–4 with one out in the bottom of the ninth when Lowe walked. The ballpark atmosphere was fetid with both Duffy's vituperative jockeying of pitcher Frank Killen and the crowd's response, squarely aimed at the Beaneaters.

The rancor only intensified when Marty Bergen fouled off several pitches and then slid a single into left field. Lake grounded into a force play, but Bergen managed to interfere with the return throw subtly enough that he was not called out for doing so. The inning remained alive with the tying run on third and Billy Hamilton at bat. The fleet lead-off man rolled a slow bounder to Pirate second baseman Dick Padden and raced toward first as Bobby Lowe sped for home and Bob Allen, the pinch runner for Fred Lake, barreled around the bases. Observers agreed that first baseman Denny Lyons caught the ball contemporaneously with Hamilton's arrival; in fact, the two players collided and sent each other sprawling. Prone, Lyons was in no position to make a throw to home to catch Allen, who scored from first without a play. But did the two runs count, or had Padden's throw beaten Hamilton to first, ending the game? In the confusion, umpire Bob Emslie initially did not make a clear decision, a delay that brought both teams onto the field to celebrate their victory. Finally, Emslie gave a clear sign; Hamilton had been retired at first, neither run counted, and the Pirates had in fact won the game 5–4. Duffy's efforts at protest were ignored.[35]

It was neither the only outburst that day nor the most turbulent. In Louisville, fans attending the first game of a doubleheader with the Giants witnessed a fistfight between New York's George Davis and the Colonels' Fred Clarke, both of whom were ejected by Lynch. Ill feelings between the clubs ran deep because owner Andrew Freedman had denied the Colonels the use of the Polo Grounds dressing facility the previous month, alleging they had broken out a window in anger following an earlier loss.[36] To make matters worse, Lynch refused to umpire the second game of the doubleheader, asserting that he had already earned his wages for the day. That left the volatile atmosphere in the hands of former Colonel Jimmy Wolf, who was essentially the home team's designated substitute official. With Wolf's awarding of a walk to Louisville catcher Bill Wilson, forcing across the tying run in the ninth inning, the scene descended into chaos. The Giants rushed the umpire in protest, and at least two of them—Bill Joyce and catcher Parke Wilson—took swings at Wolf. Wolf retaliated in kind. By now Colonels fans were rushing out of the bleachers and onto the field to defend both their ballpark and their umpire. Backup Louisville third baseman Irv Hach tried to protect Wolf, whereupon Wilson turned his pugilistic attentions to Hach. The Louisville player swung his bat wildly at Wilson's head, but Colonels manager Clarke managed to divert the potentially lethal blow, in the process taking the whack himself on the shoulder. Recognizing that in the confusion no one had bothered to call a time-out, Ollie Pickering, the Louisville player who had advanced from second to third on the walk, broke for home. A policeman racing on to the field to help break up the fight accidentally sent Pickering flying, but none of the Giants even noticed. Pickering picked himself up and scored because Wilson—the man with the ball and thus the only one who could have made a play on him—was at that moment being physically restrained by the police.[37]

The matter did not cool even after the teams had left the field. The next morning Fred Clarke went to the Galt House, where the Giants were staying, and was confronted by George Davis. As the argument renewed, witnesses said they saw Clarke pull out a revolver and threaten to shoot Davis on the spot. Encouraged by Joyce, Davis sensibly retreated to the secure confines of his room and let Clarke go his way.[38]

The Beaneaters did win the third game in Pittsburg and moved from there to Cincinnati, where they took three of four against the second-place Reds in an atmosphere redolent with suspicion, rumors, and accusations. One rumor held that Reds manager Buck Ewing had dug out commonly used portions of the batter's box and filled them with sand, thus diminishing the footing for hitters. Then there was the matter of the poison. According to that rumor, Ewing had taken to "doping" the visitors' water keg with an unknown and presumably incapacitating substance. Joyce, whose Giants had preceded Boston into town by a week, fed the latter charges by very publicly carrying his own outsized demijohn of water onto the field.[39] This may have been out of fear, or it may have been one more manifestation of a running feud between the Reds and the Giants.

For the same series, Ewing had barred the New York players from either dressing at or practicing on the grounds, which was an apparent act of retaliation for Freedman's refusal to let the Reds do the same during their June visit to New York. "Of course the Reds will expect to be mistreated and misused when they again visit New York," concluded Cincinnati reporter F. E. Goodwin.[40]

Two more Boston wins in three tries followed in Louisville and again in St. Louis. The series in St. Louis was umpired by Horace McFarland, who was hastily recruited after Sandy McDermott disappeared. The recruitment of McFarland did not sit at all well with the Beaneaters, accustomed as they were to being overseen by veterans of the stripe of Tom Lynch, Tim Hurst, or Bob Emslie. McFarland ejected Bergen for arguing, prompting Tim Murnane to characterize his fill-in work as "absolutely wretched" while lamenting that "Nick Young should furnish good players with provocation to fight by appointing such tried and proven umpirical failures as McFarland to the staff."[41]

Fred Tenney might have had better reason than others to think ill of McFarland, but he was paying for his own sins. In the ninth inning of the final game of the series with St. Louis, Billy Hamilton reached first base and tried to add to his stolen base total. As Browns catcher Morgan Murphy prepared to throw, Tenney stepped in front of him, a commonly used interference technique that players usually got away with because the umpire was watching the play at second. As he threw, Murphy elbowed Tenney in the jaw, knocking him out. Play was halted for the several minutes it took to revive the batter.

Stalled by a Drunken Orgy

Baltimore took modest advantage of Boston's trials out west, winning ten of sixteen after leaving Cincinnati and picking up two games in the standings. After being six and one-half games behind Boston on the evening of July 5, they stood four and one-half out three weeks later. But Ned Hanlon's club had plenty of its own problems to work through, both physical and emotional.

Wilbert Robinson, of course, did not even make the trip, remaining in Baltimore to nurse his leg, operate the Diamond Café, and manage a team of practice players, known colloquially as the "Yanigans," through a series of exhibition matches.[42] Jake Stenzel was briefly left behind in Cincinnati to tend to his ailing wife. At first there was fear that her illness might be serious, but she recovered quickly and Jake was back with the team for its opener in Louisville.[43] Jerry Nops was less fortunate. Struck down by the 100-degree heat in Cincinnati, he labored through several sleepless nights and finally was ordered home to rest and recuperate.[44] Losing Nops, whose record was 12-4, was a serious blow to Hanlon's pitching plans, leaving only Joe Corbett, Bill Hoffer, and Arlie Pond as reliable starters. However, it probably extended the major-league career of George Blackburn, a midseason pick-up who had looked bad in his one start. Hanlon wanted to release Blackburn but decided against it when Nops took ill.

Most of the Orioles were as affected by the heat in Cincinnati as they were by the losses. In assessing the impact of those midsummer conditions, it is important to keep in mind that there was no air conditioning then. Players—and regular folks—relied on wet sheets hung to flap in the breeze and rudimentary fans to cool them through long, muggy nights. Although Louisville was as hot as Cincinnati, it still provided a bit of relief. The Galt House, where the players stayed, was larger, less susceptible to the outside temperatures, and situated on the Ohio River, which made it a bit more bearable.

Orioles fans who were following reports of the team's progress had good reason to wonder whether the heat problem was purely physical. As the team struggled, rumors of internal feuds resurfaced. The newspaper accounts of the Reds series had been full of instances of "selfish" individual play, a cardinal violation of the Orioles' scheme, and those reports only intensified when journeyman Louisville pitcher Bert Cunningham dispatched them 7-3 in the series opener. A second rumor—of debauchery—also circulated. No sooner had the Orioles left Cincinnati than the *Cincinnati Enquirer* published a disturbing note. It reported that four or five of the Orioles had engaged in a "drunken orgy" through the city's tavern and red light district following the third defeat.[45]

Hanlon, who believed in team play above all else, denied the most salacious of the rumors, but he was plainly disturbed by what he viewed as selfish individual play. He called an early morning practice on July 9, before the second game in Louisville, and read the team out.[46] Then the Orioles took the field and worked in spring training–like fashion on their classic retinue of bunting, hitting and running, slapping the ball, and working the count. The message appeared to get through. That afternoon they pounded Still Bill Hill for a dozen hits in a 9–4 victory. Stenzel showed renewed fire, sliding into Louisville's Charlie Dexter and slicing off part of his shoe. Rain washed out the Saturday series finale, but in St. Louis on Monday afternoon the Orioles gave an offensive exhibition that awakened memories of all of the legitimate aspects of their game that opponents had come to fear.

John McGraw opened the series by trying to bunt. He was thrown out. Willie Keeler followed with another bunt try, but he too was retired. The third batter, Hughie Jennings, also tried to bunt, but he fouled off the attempt and was retired.

Joe Kelley opened the second inning with the fourth straight bunt attempt, this time for a hit. Stenzel faked a fifth consecutive bunt and then hit away for a single, which allowed Kelley to reach third (although he never made it home). Joe Quinn tried to bunt in the third inning. Then, with one on and one retired in the fourth, Stenzel drew the Browns defense in with another feigned bunt attempt. Having caught them off guard, he drove a pitch to the wall and completed the circuit for a home run before the startled Browns outfield could retrieve the ball. After a single and an error, Boileryard Clarke laid down yet another bunt, this one thrown away by the rattled Browns infield for a run. Finally, with two on and two out, McGraw surprised everybody by bunting yet again, dropping it on the third base line and reaching first before a fielder could even touch the ball. By now thoroughly baffled, Browns pitcher Red Donahue let McGraw steal second and then served up a single to Keeler, a double to Jennings, a single to Kelley, and a triple to Stenzel. Having either faked a bunt or actually bunted nine times inside of four innings, the Orioles were well on their way to a 22–4 decision for Pond. The momentum from that win propelled Baltimore to victories in the final two games of the series. They headed for Chicago still in third place and three and one-half games out, but they looked more like three-time champions.

The momentum snagged when the Orioles ran into Griffith, the Colts ace. He beat them 5–3 in the opener of the four-game series, which included the playoff of a May tie between the teams, and then again 6–3 in the Sunday wrap-up. The whole series involved elements of low drama degenerating into farce and finally dirty play. The problems began even before the Orioles arrived, when Quinn's leg swelled badly on the train. He had injured it during a slide in St. Louis, and the doctors who looked at it found an infection, probably created by the black dye of his uniform seeping through the open wound.[47] With fever and inflammation, the diagnosis was obvious: blood poisoning. He was set down indefinitely. Then in the first game, Jennings's three errors let the three decisive runs score. He atoned for it the next day, running out a two-run home run in the top of the ninth to erase a 1–0 Colts lead and give Blackburn a 2–1 victory. A twenty-two-hit onslaught on Saturday made it easy for Corbett to record a 20–2 win in a game that almost literally became a circus. With the outcome long since settled, a Chicago partisan turned a horse loose on the field, presumably to provide amusement. It gamboled about amid shrieks of laughter from the twelve thousand in attendance at West Side Park, and the scene became even more anarchic when bleacherites took to throwing seat cushions at the players.[48]

While Saturday's game was a circus, Sunday's ended in rule bending. The Colts led 4–3 in the bottom of the seventh, when Bill Lange came to bat with one out and runners at first and third. It was a perfect spot for a double steal—a tactic the Orioles had practically invented—and Cap Anson put it on. But as Boileryard Clarke threw toward second, Lange jostled the catcher, whose throw wound up in short left field, allowing both base runners to score. Clarke hollered for interference, but umpire McDonald denied seeing the offense and let the runs stand.[49]

Trailing by three runs with only two innings to play, McGraw led off the eighth with one thing on his mind—reaching base. For this he had two favorite techniques—either taking a base on balls or allowing himself to be hit by a pitch. He took Griffith's first two pitches for balls, then eased his knee toward the strike zone for the third pitch, causing the ball to carom off of his leg. But McDonald denied him the base, judging he had put himself in the ball's path, and ruled that the pitch did not count. To a chorus of profane indignation—not only from McGraw but also from Jennings, Kelley, and Stenzel—but with the unanimous support of the 11,800 in attendance, McDonald held firm. Griffith threw a second time, and a second time McGraw leaned into the pitch and was hit. Again McDonald called it a "no pitch."[50] Now an incensed Griffith strode in, intent on spiking McGraw's plate-impinging foot. McGraw retaliated by taking his bat to Griffith's own feet. Divested of his best strategy, McGraw struck out on the next three pitches, and the Orioles surrendered.

Hanlon later talked about filing an official protest against McDonald's decision, pointing out that the pitches that struck McGraw had to be either balls, in which case his batter had drawn a walk, or strikes. But nothing came of his tempest, and the champions moved on to Cleveland, where they split two games with the Spiders and were rained out of the third. In the process, Hanlon lost Jennings again, this time when an errant throw tore a nail off his finger. The rainout eventually would loom as critical. Baltimore was scheduled to return to Cleveland for a single game on Sunday, but Tebeau saw no reason to play a doubleheader, and no rule in force at the time required him to do so. Once play shifted to the eastern cities, the distances made coming back for a single makeup game impossible. Canceled games were a relatively common practice at the time, but as the race wound to its final days, the inability to get this particular game in would play a large role in the Orioles' fate.

The opener of the Orioles' four-game series in Pittsburg—a series the teams split—was marred by a brawl that probably led to the resignation of Jack Sheridan from the umpiring staff. Two weeks earlier he had been subjected to an egg shower from the St. Louis patrons for calls the fans saw as favorable to the Brooklyn visitors. This time his awarding of first base on balls to an Oriole drew a sharp response from Pirates pitcher Emerson "Pink" Hawley. With a runner on first, the practice was for the umpire to move from behind home plate to behind the pitcher, and Sheridan's move put him in close physical proximity to the angry pitcher, who fired off more abuse. Sheridan replied with his fists, hitting Hawley in the face. Hawley retaliated with two blows of his own, knocking Sheridan out.[51] Hawley was ejected, but teammate Charlie Hastings got the substitute umpiring gig in place of the beaten Sheridan, calling the remainder of a 9–1 Orioles win. To his credit, Sheridan returned the next day, but the return was only temporary. His departure followed McDermott's resignation by only a few days.

One of the fill-in umpires, a man known only as McGinty, took charge of the July 24 game between the Spiders and the Phillies in Cleveland with incendiary results. McGinty was a loosely familiar figure in Cleveland, having filled in for three previous games around July 1, all of them Spiders victories. Phillies players believed McGinty favored the home team on ball and strike calls, and they had strenuously protested an early walk to Tebeau. So when McGinty waved Chief Zimmer to first base on balls in the ninth, the visiting players rushed him, suspecting a "fix."[52] Shortstop Sam Gillen took a swing at the fill-in ump, who responded by forfeiting the game to the Spiders. Phillies manager George Stallings filed a protest with the league office, but again nothing came of it.

McGinty's experience was even more harrowing than Hank O'Day's in Brooklyn, although that was because O'Day was unaware that he was being targeted. In the midst of a four-run, ninth-inning Giants rally that would lead to a 4–3 victory, an infuriated Brooklyn pitcher, Brickyard Kennedy, fired the ball at the umpire, whose back was turned. In addition to the obvious reasons why this was not a smart move, Kennedy forgot that the ball was in play. He missed O'Day, the ball sailed into the outfield, and George Davis easily scored the eventual winning run.[53]

Had Tim Hurst been umpiring instead of O'Day, the outcome might have been different. The next day in Cincinnati, a Sabbath gathering watched Hurst and Cincinnati catcher Heinie Peitz (not to be confused with Heinie Reitz, the Orioles second baseman) come to blows in the very first inning. No record exists of what triggered the episode, but Peitz apparently said something that caught Hurst's attention, for the umpire removed his mask and used it to belt Peitz in the chest. Peitz retaliated with a stiff right hand to Hurst's chin.[54] Then, just to show there were no hard feelings, they resumed play, with no fine assessed, no ejection, and no further incident.

That same Sunday in Louisville, the Colonels and St. Louis Browns played two of the several games in that city that were officiated by players. The Colonels named reserve outfielder Charlie Dexter, and the Browns selected ace pitcher Red Donahue, who was on his way to losing thirty-five games. Both teams were wretched, the Colonels sitting in ninth place and the Browns in twelfth. Following a relatively uneventful opener won by St. Louis, the Colonels led 5–1 entering the bottom of the ninth, when St. Louis right fielder Tuck Turner fouled off a pitch from Louisville's Bert Cunningham. Donahue, umpiring behind home plate, threw a new ball to Cunningham, who proceeded to roll it in the dirt, presumably to darken it and make it more difficult for the Browns hitters to see. Donahue objected to that practice and threw Cunningham a second ball. He soiled that one as well. A third and fourth ball entered and left play in the same fashion. When Cunningham dirtied a fifth ball, Donahue decided his honor as an arbiter had been soiled as well. He forfeited the game to his own team.[55] Colonels president Harry Pulliam protested the decision to the league office, which eventually ruled the game "no contest." Because neither team was ever in contention, there was no need to replay the game.

The Nation Takes Sides

With three games in Washington remaining on the club's longest trip of the season, Boston held first place by three and one-half games over the Orioles and Reds. The Orioles certainly had not been cowed into submission, concluding their own western swing with a 6–5 Sunday victory in Cleveland. However, there was little question about which team the country preferred. As the Orioles pulled out of Pittsburg, this editorial comment in that morning's *Pittsburg Dispatch* bade them farewell: "The most important point from a national standpoint is the superiority of the Bostons over the Baltimores as gentlemen. The latter have degenerated into a set of rowdies who resort to the smallest and dirtiest tricks ever seen on the ball field to win games. . . . How different it is with the Boston team."[56]

Orioles fans took great offense at what they viewed as signs of a league-wide bias against them. But beyond that, they were convinced that the Beaneaters lacked the backbone to stand up to their Orioles over the long haul. When the team returned to the east on July 28, sweeping a three-game series with the compliant Senators as Jennings returned to the lineup, they showed why their fans had such confidence. As was often the case when the Orioles looked good, their bunting and running games primed an offense that produced thirty-eight runs and forty-nine hits. As Albert Mott remarked in *Sporting Life*, "Yes, in the old antique base ball forms, Boston used to win, but the style of the game is modern. It don't go by main strength and awkwardness any more. It is brilliant base ball that has won the championship the last few years."[57]

Although Frank Selee tinkered only modestly with his basic roster, the flow of rumors and reports suggested that he was perpetually considering changes. One rumor making the rounds in Cincinnati during late July had the great Cy Young himself coming to Boston in exchange for a sum rumored to be between three thousand and ten thousand dollars. The names of Chick Fraser (in Louisville) and Pink Hawley (in Pittsburg) also surfaced. Ed Doheny, who had been lightly used by the Giants, was again rumored to be on his way to Boston, possibly in exchange for Charles Ganzel. In New York, any pitcher other than Amos Rusie and running mate Jouett Meekin (who between them pitched 71 of the team's 136 games) was deemed readily expendable. But neither Doheny nor fellow second-liner Dad Clarke intrigued Selee enough to force him to spend the time that it would have taken to negotiate a deal with Freedman. During the second western road trip, Selee used a day off to look at a Newcastle, Pennsylvania, pitcher named Charlie Hickman, eventually acquiring him, but to no great consequence.[58] Although Hickman enjoyed a ten-season journeyman's career that included eight different stops, he worked just two games for the Beaneaters that year—both of them in relief—encompassing thirty-eight batters, fifteen of whom reached base.

National League Standings (Evening of July 30)

TEAM	WINS	LOSSES	PERCENTAGE	GAMES BEHIND
Boston	55	24	.696	—
Baltimore	51	26	.662	3
Cincinnati	50	26	.658	3½
New York	46	31	.597	8
Cleveland	43	35	.551	11½
Philadelphia	40	43	.482	17
Pittsburg	37	42	.468	18
Chicago	36	47	.434	21
Louisville	35	47	.427	21½
Washington	29	49	.372	25½
St. Louis	20	47	.247	36

9. Day Jobs for Garroters

Given that the August 4 doubleheader between Cincinnati and Pittsburg featured two teams on the fringes of contention, there was little reason for fans outside the two cities to monitor the results. Indeed, the results were superficially uneventful, with Cincinnati winning the first game and the second halted in a 4–4 tie after six innings. However, in the tie game, the Cincinnati loyalists witnessed something unprecedented in 1890s baseball and unthinkable today.

The trouble flared after Pittsburg infielder Dick Padden blocked Reds base runner Bug Holliday as he attempted to take second base on his hit. Umpire Tim Hurst, a day removed from his fight with Reds catcher Heinie Peitz, not only refused to award Holliday second on interference but also ruled the runner had been tagged out retreating to first. Cincinnati partisans were among the league's rowdiest, and Hurst's call—which manager Buck Ewing immediately and vocally protested—set them off. Ewing had just turned his back on the umpire to return to the bench when a beer stein came flying from the stands in Hurst's direction. It was never determined who threw the stein, and the reports vary as to whether Hurst was actually hit in the leg, as he later testified, or the missile stopped several feet from him. What is undisputed is that Hurst, already enraged by the abuse he had taken from the fans over his call and now considering himself to be in physical danger, picked up the stein and fired it back. It landed amid a group of firefighters,

UMPIRE LYNCH
STRIKES DOYLE

Fig. 16. This woodcut depicts the fisticuffs between umpire Tom Lynch and Jack Doyle that marked Baltimore's second visit to Boston in August. Originally appeared in the *Boston Post*, August 6, 1897.

striking one later identified as John Cartuyvelle over the right eye. It knocked him out and opened a gash from which blood flowed freely. Six stitches would be needed to close the wound.[1]

Hurst's action proved to be as provocative as that of the original stein thrower, except that a lot more people were provoked. Enraged Reds fans, several of them the victim's firefighter cohorts, poured over the stands and onto the field to chase down the umpire. Police officers quickly moved in to shield Hurst from further assault. But it took five minutes to get the crowd off the field. The police actually allowed Hurst to complete that half inning before arresting him, hustling him into a patrol wagon, and taking him to the nearest police station. There he was jailed on a charge of assault and battery. It was only through the good graces of Ashley Lloyd, an officer with the Cincinnati front office, that Hurst walked out of the jail on bail that night.[2] Hurst later told the *Sporting News* that Cincinnati was "the worst city in the league for abusing umpires and visiting players," a place filled with the spirit of "win on the level if you can; if not, win anyway."[3]

THE POLICE ENFORCING UMPIRE
CARPENTER'S DECISIONS.

Fig. 17. Aided by three police officers, fill-in umpire Bob Carpenter enforces his ruling against a scowling Oriole during the final game of the series against Boston. Originally appeared in the *Boston Post*, August 8, 1897.

In Hurst's view, the beer stein attack was the culmination of a days-long attempt to "drive me away from the town." He had become a familiar face in Cincinnati, having worked seven of the team's previous nine home dates and twelve games in the previous two weeks. "I was daily threatened by cowardly spectators," he asserted. Hurst acknowledged that he had not handled the ongoing situation with studied detachment. "I sent back some equally hot compliments which didn't fail to hurt, I know," he said. More abuse followed. "These fellows . . . soon began calling me a crook, robber, thief, ex prize fighter, shortcard gambler, drunkard, murderer," explained Hurst. After the glass was thrown, he said, the crowd began to yell "kill the umpire," and he decided they meant it. He told the newspaper that others had told him the man he had struck was indeed the person who had thrown the stein.[4]

Less than a week later, Hurst appeared in court in Cincinnati, where he was found guilty and fined one hundred dollars. It speaks to the widely held view of umpiring as an impossible job that the league took no action against Hurst. In fact, he umpired a game in Cincinnati on the afternoon of his conviction. After all, the league presumably reasoned, he was already in town.

Meanwhile, commentators rushed to his defense. "Who blames Tim Hurst?" asked John E. Calvin, the Chicago-based correspondent for the *Sporting News*. "The conduct of the [Cincinnati] crowds toward an umpire when he gives a decision against the Reds is something awful."[5]

The arbiter's arrest necessitated the appointment of an emergency substitute. By custom that task fell to the home team's manager, and Ewing nominated Red Bittman, a one-time infielder who was in the stands. All proceeded reasonably smoothly until the seventh inning, when under gathering storm clouds the Pirates scored six times to break a 4–4 tie and take apparent command. Now a new din arose from the stands: calls rang through the park, with fans shouting that the threatening conditions made it too dark to play. Under the rules in force at the time, when a game was halted before the completion of an inning, the official score reverted to the score at the end of the previous inning. In effect, the Reds fans were screaming for Bittman to eliminate Pittsburg's six-run inning from the books—and quickly. Had Hurst still been on the scene, he would have ignored the howls of the assembly . . . but Bittman paid them full heed. After Dummy Hoy walked to open the bottom of the seventh and the first two pitches to Tommy Corcoran were declared balls, the substitute umpire raised his arms and declared that conditions were indeed too dark to continue play. Livid Pirates players poured invective down on Bittman. Making matters even more outrageous, within a few minutes of that call, the storm clouds broke and the sun returned, providing at least another half hour of playable daylight. By then, however, nobody was left on the scene to resume the game. "As deliberate a steal as has ever been made on the home grounds," the next morning's *Cincinnati Times-Star* characterized it.[6]

Team owners let the disgusting umpiring situation slide because they had larger problems to worry about. Due in part to the on-field atmosphere, in part to broader economic issues, and in part to the nature of a twelve-team league, financial problems were widespread. In Washington, attendance was off by one-third from the previous season. Under Von der Ahe, the St. Louis franchise was widely considered a wreck. Players complained of not receiving their full salaries, and again attendance was down. The Phillies were drawing 20 percent fewer fans to a facility that offered the league's lowest admission prices—twenty-five cents for all seats. That made it a concern for visiting teams too, because it reduced their share of the gate receipts. Attendance was also on the decline in Pittsburg and Cleveland.[7] Many attributed the falloff to the rowdy atmosphere at parks, but the aftermath of a nationwide mid-1890s economic decline might also have been a factor. The economic concerns may also have been overstated. In the summer of 1897, hordes of people were stampeding from all corners of the nation to the Klondike area of Alaska to seek their fortunes in newly discovered gold veins; it was decidedly a profit-conscious moment in history.

Whatever the reason for the decline in attendance, it occupied the league's attention. League president Nick Young went so far as to publicly raise the idea of contraction as a possible cure. "It would be cheaper to buy out some of the League clubs now struggling for existence," he suggested.[8] Under the agreement by which the American Association had merged with the National League after the 1891 season, a buyout could not take place for ten seasons without the unanimous agreement of the league's teams. But by 1897 that time frame was only a few years. (After the 1899 season, a buyout occurred, leading in turn to the elevation of the American League as a major-league competitor and to an even more bitter interleague war.)

Sparring of a Purely Verbal Nature

The fortunate teams did not need to concern themselves with such matters. For the Beaneaters and the Orioles, who were each enjoying banner seasons at the gate as well as on the field, any concerns were related entirely to the pennant race. Having put their two western trips behind them, both could look ahead to favorable August and September schedules. Baltimore still faced a demanding early August trip through Boston, Brooklyn, and Philadelphia. But beginning with the Bridegrooms' arrival at Union Park on August 16, Ned Hanlon's club would have the advantage of playing forty of its final forty-three games at home. Only a three-day September swing to New York would disturb the comfort of performing before the Baltimore audience.

Boston's advantage was not quite as concentrated, but it was sustained. Returning on August 5 from their thirty-game road trip, the Beaneaters could look forward to thirty-eight of their final forty-eight games at home, with only a four-game trip to New York, plus season-ending three-game visits to Baltimore and Brooklyn, requiring travel. Superficially, it seemed likely that the pennant would be won at home, and the only question was which home? Still, the matter of that final three-game series between the Beaneaters and the Orioles in Baltimore loomed. Never in the twenty-year history of the National League had possession of the championship come down to a last-week series between the contenders.

The teams' partisans sparred frequently concerning the Beaneaters' chances of ending the Orioles' three-year run. "Down deep in their hearts [Boston fans] know that Boston is the same old club and that Baltimore is the same old club," Albert Mott wrote, as the teams prepared for their third meeting in late July. "The temporary supremacy of Boston was due in great part to the temporary disability of Baltimore. When the natural conditions are restored then . . . Boston people should be glad that it is not worse than it is."[9]

Although he was more diplomatic about it, Ned Hanlon plainly agreed. In an obvious effort to stir feelings in advance of their third meeting, Tim Murnane presented Boston's Rooters this analysis of the rival skipper's comparison of the two teams:

> There's Jack Doyle, hasn't he a few acres the better of Tenney as a first baseman? Reitz is a standoff with Bobby Lowe. I will doff

my hat . . . to Herman Long, still on the whole as a fielder, base
runner and run getter I would pick Jennings if the pair were on
the market at an even price. McGraw's aggressiveness and inside
work . . . places him in front of Jimmy Collins. . . . Between two
valuable left fielders, Hugh Duffy and Joe Kelley, I would give Joe
the preference. Stenzel I should prefer to Billy Hamilton, though
I recognize that Billy is a great little man, and of course Billy Keeler is the daddy of Chick Stahl as a right fielder.[10]

Nor did Hanlon concede anything at the batteries. "Our catchers are
fully as good as the backstops of the Selee aggregation," he said, "and
we have more pitchers who can be depended upon than the beaneaters."[11] That, of course, presumed that Hanlon's catchers were healthy.
Wilbert Robinson still had not returned to play, although by the first
of August doctors allowed him to get into uniform. They forecast a
midmonth return, noting concern about the chance that the wounds
might reopen a second time if he came back too soon.

Frank Selee quickly put his disagreements on the record. "Tebeau
told me that Tenney is a much better all around man for first base than
Jack Doyle, so you see we don't all agree with Mr. Hanlon," he said. "I
wouldn't trade him man for man right through the list until I come to
Billy Keeler, who is certainly a wonderful player. As for McGraw being a better man on the inside than Jimmy Collins, I am not so sure
unless Hanlon means in the use of his tongue."[12]

The Orioles returned home on July 31 for the first time since early
July and greeted their favorite foe, the Phillies. Although Philadelphia
presented a respectable offense, featuring two-time batting champion
Ed Delahanty and rookie phenom Napoleon Lajoie, by the time the
clubs met at Union Park, the Orioles had beaten the Phillies nineteen
consecutive times in two seasons. Baltimore promptly made it twenty
and then twenty-one straight, with the latter win behind John Mc-
Graw (three hits), Hughie Jennings (two hits and a walk), and Jake
Stenzel (four stolen bases). Al Orth ended the streak on August 2 in
a 5–2 decision.

With the Washington series approaching, Selee turned his long interest in acquiring more pitching to Washington's principal starters, Doc McJames and Win Mercer. The Senators weren't much, standing solidly in eleventh place, and the transfer of either of those two would weaken them and bolster Boston precisely at the moment when the clubs were poised to meet five times in four days. McJames was a twenty-three-year-old right-hander in his second season, a veteran of thirty-three starts in 1896 and on his way to making forty more starts in 1897. The more highly regarded Mercer was also twenty-three but was in his fourth season. A workhorse even by 1890s standards, Mercer had won twenty-five of forty-five starts for the Senators in 1896 and would lead the league with forty-three starts in 1897. Ironically, both men would die young, McJames in an accident in 1901 and Mercer in a suicide in 1903.[13]

Selee offered the Senators seven thousand dollars for either pitcher, and he simultaneously sent feelers to Brooklyn about the availability of their ace, Brickyard Kennedy. However, none of these offers went anywhere. Having failed to obtain Mercer or McJames, Selee sent the Beaneaters out to beat them. Boston was a lame team, with Billy Hamilton slowed by a sprained ankle and Herman Long nursing a strained tendon in his knee. But the club was still good enough to beat McJames 7–6 on another ninth-inning rally, earning Kid Nichols his twentieth victory. With the score tied, McJames walked pinch hitter Hamilton, Fred Tenney bunted safely toward his predecessor Tommy Tucker at first, and Bob Allen sacrificed both runners along. Hugh Duffy rolled a grounder to Gene DeMontreville at shortstop, but despite the sore ankle, Hamilton's speed allowed him to beat the throw to home.

The clubs split doubleheaders on the next two days. The most notable aspect of the games was the league's decision to release Bob Emslie from his assignment to umpire both games of both doubleheaders. Instead, the task was given to a young Washington sports writer named John Heydler, who had umpired one previous Senators game and would work one more. Heydler, who a quarter-century later would follow

Lynch to the presidency of the National League, drew modest reviews. "Heydler had just five close decisions and all were given to the home team, helping it to victory," Murnane reported.[14]

The Beaneaters Call the Cops

On the eve of the season's third meeting between the Beaneaters and the Orioles, which took place in Boston, expectations ran high. A crowd of Rooters gathered at the 3rd Base saloon and walked to the train station, where they and assorted other fans constituted a healthy welcoming party. They especially saluted Long, who had played most of the season with a very sore fielding hand. Given the rudimentary nature of gloves, such injuries were common, and they generally damaged fielders' work both in the field and with the bat. That Long had persevered through it all, played almost every game, and was batting .320 made him very much a town hero. "Were the Boston club in the second division, Herman would be in the hospital, where he belongs," the *Boston Journal* remarked.[15]

Baltimore's victories over Philadelphia lifted the Orioles ahead of the Reds and into second place, so the three-game series pitted the two top-standing championship contenders against one another. Tom Lynch drew the umpiring assignment. Young decided the games were important enough to assign a second man to work the bases and appealed to Tom Connolly, a twenty-six-year-old New England Leaguer who had rejected a full-time position a few weeks before. Connolly initially accepted the assignment, which Young announced, but then turned it down, publicly citing his obligations to the New England League. The real reason, though, was that Connolly felt that the situation was poisonous, especially to a rookie. He had made up his mind to wait until 1898, when he assumed the league would accede to widespread calls to double the size of its umpiring staff.[16] And that is precisely what happened. Connolly was one of the call-ups and stayed long enough to officiate at 1,629 major-league games over a career that lasted into the

1930s. He worked eight World Series, including the 1903 inaugural series, and was inducted into the Hall of Fame in 1953.

As it turned out, Lynch could have used Hall of Fame–caliber help, for the series developed into combat and the combatants included Lynch himself. The mood was set even before play began, with the Baltimore partisans touting the superiority of their inside style of play and the Boston Rooters excoriating it.

"What manager Hanlon terms 'inside ball' . . . properly interpreted means turning tricks on both umpires and opponents," Murnane warned. "Vile language aimed at some sensitive player may disconcert him. Holding players, tripping and other dirty work is also called 'inside work.'"[17]

The Beaneaters, by contrast, would play clean, Murnane assured, "unless forced in self-defense." In that event, he said, "I am sure there will be hot times and play that will make Baltimore . . . cry for quarter."[18]

The Thursday game, pitting Joe Corbett against Nichols, was contested from the opening pitch. More or less continuously through the first three innings, Beaneaters accused Corbett of cheating forward off the pitching rubber, an allegation that finally drew a warning from Lynch. That brought McGraw, Jennings, and Doyle in for an extended debate with Lynch over whether Corbett had done anything wrong. If the idea was to rattle Corbett, it failed, for he gave up only two runs the rest of the way. The game was Baltimore's essentially from the start. McGraw opened with one of his customary bases on balls, and when Hamilton misplayed Willie Keeler's base hit, the Orioles had the dangerous top of their order at second and third. Jennings's clean hit drove them both home. He advanced on a passed ball and then scored on a Kelley single, and Kelley in turn scored on Doyle's hit. Boston touched Corbett for plenty of hits but never a timely one that might have enabled the home team to threaten the four-run hole that had already been dug. The afternoon was not all to the good for the Orioles, though. In the seventh, Jennings strained a groin muscle when Nichols took him out trying to turn a double play. He had to be helped off the field, but he returned the next day.

"Fo-teen men lef' on de wads, mm-mm," Murnane's Darkhue White muttered.[19]

The situation exploded on Friday when Baltimore built a fast 5–0 lead and then squandered it in a mass of fists and language, eventually losing 6–5. The Orioles "showed their true colors," said a disgusted Murnane. As long as they led, he taunted, they "acted like ball players." But as the lead evaporated, "they went into the air like a lot of frightened colts, and used abusive language to the Boston players, to umpire Lynch and to each other."[20]

For most of the game, the only ones doing the abusing were the nine thousand Boston patrons. They hooted as Chick Stahl lost a fly ball in the sun and hollered when Long dropped a grounder, the result being three unearned runs. Keeler's single, followed by a Kelley home run, yielded the final two runs off Fred Klobedanz, who trailed 5–3 entering the eighth inning. Duffy unsettled things with a one-out single; then after Stahl was retired, Jimmy Collins also singled, allowing Duffy to score. Now the nine thousand fans had something to root about, and root they did. From their positions in the field, Doyle and McGraw let fly at Lowe, the next hitter, hoping to throw him off his game. It didn't work. Instead Lowe smashed the ball over Stenzel's head toward the flagpole in deep center field. Collins scored easily, Lowe eased into third, and the game was tied. "Such cheering and coaching by the bleachers has not been heard at South End Grounds for many a year," Murnane remarked. The crowd, long since standing, raised its voices louder yet as Marty Bergen rifled a single to Keeler in right and gave Boston its first lead.

The Beaneaters had elected to bat first, meaning that Baltimore still had two more shots at Klobedanz. Doyle led off the bottom of the eighth inning, fouling easily to Bergen and then turning on Lynch. Whatever Dirty Jack called the umpire is not recorded for posterity, although the *Baltimore Sun*'s correspondent wryly described it as "mild for Doyle."[21] At any rate, when the Orioles took the field for the ninth inning, Doyle repeated his epithets and Lynch ejected him. More language followed, some from Doyle and some from teammates who had gathered to pursue the aspersions against Lynch's character. According to accounts from Boston sources, Doyle repeated the dirty words three times more. It is not clear who tossed the first blow, but Doyle punched and butted Lynch in the eye, blackening it, and Lynch decked Doyle with a full left to his neck. Kelley and Corbett raced to separate the combatants, and their involvement brought the Boston fans onto the field. "The cry was to mob the Baltimore players, and it doubtless would have been done," the *Baltimore Sun* reported, had not Boston players and police calmed the fans.[22] It took ten minutes, but the field was finally cleared for play to resume.

Compared with the eighth inning, the ninth was uneventful; all it featured was some bottles thrown Kelley's way, blatant interference, and a disputed game-saving play. McGraw had reached second on Long's one-out error, slightly wrenching his knee when he bowled over Tenney, who was blocking his path around first base. Tenney took off after McGraw but was held back by Lowe. McGraw left in favor of the slower Joe Quinn, a change that proved vital. Keeler fouled out to Long behind third, but Jennings stroked a clean single to Duffy in left. The Boston captain raced in for the ball and came up throwing. Lynch, probably in no mood to favor the Orioles with any close calls, declared Quinn out at home. "That Quinn was clearly safe was frankly admitted by some of the Boston writers," the *Baltimore Sun* told its readers.[23]

As far as Boston fans were concerned, the call and the outcome both stood as vindication. Arthur Soden announced that he would have extra police on hand the following day and that they would be ordered "to arrest any ball player using profane language."[24] Murnane all but called for Doyle's banishment. "If such men . . . are allowed to utter foul language with impunity and to apply obscene epithets to those doing their best to decide plays . . . the time will soon come when no person above the grade of garroter can be secured to umpire."[25]

Although he later rescinded the assertion, in the heat of postgame passion Hanlon virtually accused Lynch of throwing the game to the

Beaneaters. Alluding to his allegations of umpire crookedness during the July western swing, he said, "I know pretty well when a man makes an honest mistake, and I believe this was another case like that of Sheridan in Cincinnati."[26]

Lynch did not take the field for the Saturday finale because he was nursing his shiner in his hotel room. In his place the league assigned Bill Carpenter, one of the replacements for the recently resigned Jack Sheridan and Sandy McDermott. That the league should put its rawest rookie alone behind the plate for the decisive game of a series involving its two leading teams says everything about the state of umpiring at the time. No one professed to be more concerned than the league president.

"I don't know where to get acceptable men to umpire if this thing continues," Nick Young told *Sporting Life*. "Here is Connolly . . . said to be one of the best men in the business politely declining. . . . Sheridan came back from the west a few days ago and . . . vowed he could not stand the personal abuse heaped upon him."[27] Young revealed that he had asked Dan Campbell, a minor-league veteran, to join the staff. But, said Young, "he begs to be excused until the business gets semi-respectable."[28]

Under the circumstances, the best things Carpenter had going for him, other than his nerve, were the two policemen Soden positioned near the Boston bench. Following the previous day's brawl, Boston club ownership had appealed to the city for official support. It came not just in the form of the two uniformed officers stationed on the field but also in forty additional officers assigned to the larger grounds. Soden met with Carpenter in the Boston president's office on the morning of the game to urge him to use the police to maintain order.[29]

The Orioles, who were accustomed to dealing roughly with umpiring recruits, refused to be intimidated by the officers. In the first inning, Keeler was picked off at first, prompting the expected vehement protest. Carpenter called for the cops, and Keeler retreated quietly. Kelley tried to take up the debate, but Carpenter forcefully motioned him back to his bench, and after a few muscle twitches by the uniformed cadre, that's where Kelley went. McGraw, nursing a minor injury, threatened Carpenter from the bench on and off throughout the game, at the same time also managing to avoid arrest. But the sixteen thousand Boston Rooters who filled the stands and overflowed behind ropes on the field drowned out the Orioles' taunts with volley after volley of cheers, horns, and cowbells. "For once," said a pleased Murnane, "the Baltimore men were forced to play baseball with their hands and feet, cutting out cheap and abusive talk."[30]

Not that the back-and-forth all went Boston's way. Toward the end of the game, when Duffy raced in from left field to protest one of Carpenter's calls, the Baltimore bench chided the umpire with mock calls of "Police, police!"[31] But for the most part, the Beaneaters had the upper hand in the repartee, perhaps because they also had the upper hand on the scoreboard. Ted Lewis worked through all the distractions, limiting the Orioles to five hits, one of them a home run by Jennings. But the Orioles got only one more run for the entire game. Meanwhile, Boston touched Jerry Nops for three runs in the fifth inning.

After the game, a defiant Hanlon made no apologies for his team's treatment of the umpires. "Is it any wonder after the deal Lynch gave the Baltimores Friday that some of the players should have resented it?" he asked. "As a matter of fact," he asserted, "the Baltimore team for the past two or three years has been getting the hot end of the umpiring all over the country." Hanlon said Lynch was "at heart a Boston man, and I know it."[32] In *Sporting Life*, a more circumspect Albert Mott also blamed Lynch. "It is difficult to repress nature when being abused by players, but it is absolutely necessary that this should be done," he said.[33] And in the *Sporting News*, Jacques Eustace blamed the umpires for encouraging problems by their leniency. "Suppose that the umpire should put one or two of the best men of one team out of the game . . . the other team would have a decided advantage," he wrote. "The offending members would soon be given to understand that they shall thereafter do nothing that will debar them from continuing in the game.

There would be less kicking, better playing and the game would soon be on the level where a man is not afraid to take his best girl lest there be a pugilistic encounter in lieu of a decent contest."[34]

That was certainly not the view in Boston or much of the rest of the baseball world. "The champions got sore and began to express themselves in first class billingsgate," reported the *Boston Journal*'s J. C. Morse. He saw the Lynch attack on Doyle as regrettably necessary. "The provocation was as great as it could possibly be," he said, "and numbers will be found who will excuse anybody for acting as Lynch did under . . . such provocation."[35] The *Sporting News* applauded Soden's approach, saying, "The real solution . . . was that given in Boston on Saturday when two policemen were placed in front of the grandstand and summoned by the umpire every time he had any difficulty in enforcing his decisions." But long term, the *Sporting News* concluded, "are not two umpires better than one umpire and two coppers?"[36]

Another Corbett Picks a Fight

By this time, Doyle's problems plainly went beyond the umpires. *Sporting Life* reported that the player's own teammates had grown tired of his churlishness. "'Tis said that Scrappy Jack Doyle has but one friend on the Baltimore team, and that is himself," the newspaper reported. "What with Joe Kelley's badgering Hoffer and Doyle nagging Corbett, it would appear that the Baltimore fielders are not in accord with the Oriole pitchers."[37]

Having come into Boston trailing by three games in the standings, the Orioles left down by four games. At least the immediate schedule favored them; their next eleven games were against Brooklyn and Philadelphia, whose records were under .500. The Beaneaters, by contrast, faced a seven-game home-and-home series against the fourth-place Giants. The Orioles would use that schedule advantage to erase all but one game of Boston's lead.

But the favorable Orioles schedule could hardly have started less auspiciously. In Brooklyn, Corbett breezed to a 6–0 lead but then literally threw the ball away and stormed off the field in the third inning when his defense collapsed around him. If a pitcher ever had a reason to abandon his team in mid-inning, the Orioles afforded it to Corbett with their chaotic baseball burlesque. The episode began with a simple base hit. The next batter bounced back to Corbett, but Joe Quinn dropped Corbett's throw at second, allowing both runners to be safe. Fielder Jones also hit back to Corbett, but he could not make a play on what was scored as an infield single that loaded the bases. John Anderson sent a pop fly behind third, but it fell just out of McGraw's reach, and the first run scored. The next batter, Billy Shindle, laid down a bunt; McGraw fell trying to field it, and a second run scored. With the bases still full and nobody yet retired, Doyle let Candy LaChance's bounder get through him, allowing two more runs to score.

Doyle unwisely chose that moment to call time and walk to the mound in an effort to calm Corbett down. In one respect, he was an obvious candidate to talk to the pitcher because he and Corbett were best friends and roommates on the road. But even Doyle's "calming" actions could be inflammatory. In any event, the visit from the acid-tongued Doyle, who had just committed a critical error, did not have any calming effect. A walk and a single produced the game-tying runs; then Bridegrooms pitcher Jack Dunn bunted to Doyle, who threw home for a force out, only to watch Boileryard Clarke drop the ball. Now Brooklyn led 7–6.

Clarke's fumble, the fourth scored error of the inning, was the last straw. Corbett retrieved the ball, which was still in play, and threw it into the grandstands. Then he stormed off the field, oblivious to the fact that his rash behavior had allowed an eighth runner to come home. Clarke went into the stands and wrestled the ball away from a patron, throwing it to the plate, where several teammates had assembled. But they all got in each other's way and nobody caught the throw. The fumble allowed a ninth run home. It was 10–6 before Nops, the only relief pitcher in uniform that day, finally retired the side.[38]

Although Hanlon might have been expected to suspend Corbett for his damaging tantrum, the manager let his sixteen-game winner off with a conciliatory postgame upbraiding. "It was a foolish act, and I cannot account for it," he said.[39] Perhaps, he allowed, Doyle's intercession was to blame, but Corbett should have been used to that. "My players have been criticizing one another all year in this manner," he said.[40]

In fact, Hanlon sent Corbett back to the mound the following day for the second portion of a doubleheader, the makeup of an early May tie game that Corbett had also pitched. After the Orioles easily won the opener behind Arlie Pond, the teams tied again in the second game. They tried for a third time to settle the tie the next day, and Baltimore won after claiming the scheduled contest as well.

The Giants Are Laid Out

While the Orioles played in Brooklyn, Boston faced the first three games of an unusual week-long home-and-home series against Andrew Freedman's Giants. Under Freedman's management, the Giants were generally viewed in the first order of league miscreants, behind only the Orioles and the Spiders. Yet arriving in Boston on the heels of the Orioles, their public reception verged on acclaim. "These New Yorkers were able to put up the finest kind of game without resorting to . . . 'inside ball,'" Murnane asserted.[41] Home fans even applauded the umpires—Lynch and Carpenter—in a tribute that was far less about them than it was about Doyle. As Murnane recalled it, Lynch returned the favor, responding to his introductory cheers with his own backhanded slap at the defending champions. "Ladies and gentlemen, let us forget the trouble on the field here for the last few days and start all over again," he announced to the fans. "Bravo, Mr. Lynch," the crowd replied.[42]

The Beaneaters won two of the three games played in Boston, riding Klobedanz's 1–0 two-hit shutout in the middle game and then staging one of their late rallies in the finale. More impressive than the rally itself was the fact that it came against Amos Rusie, who had entered the game with a 17-7 record. The famed pitcher was making his first appearance in Boston in two years, and the fans gave him a lengthy ovation. But as the game wore on and their team fell behind, they were in a less sanguine mood. Some actually left—a rarity at the South End Grounds—as the eighth inning commenced. Those who did got a scolding from Murnane. "It doesn't pay to leave too soon" when watching the Bostons, he cautioned them the next morning.[43]

The good fortune started with first baseman Bill Clark's simple muff of Long's easy pop, which allowed the shortstop to reach first. The error also invigorated the Rooters, who were further engaged when Hugh Duffy rode a base hit out to center and Chick Stahl worked the Giant ace for a walk to load the bases.

From Nuf Ced McGreevy, John F. Fitzgerald, and every throat in the grandstand echoed the cheer, "Hit 'er up again, Boston!" Jimmy Collins took the cue, sending a rocket of a line drive over second baseman Bill Gleason's head and into right. Mike Tiernan cut it off quickly to hold the runners to a single base. Lowe was next. He drove the ball down the first base line, but Boileryard Clarke cut it off and forced Duffy at home. The Rooters, empowered by the cannonading but aware that only one run had crossed the plate, cheered on Marty Bergen. To their dismay, he drove a crisp one-hopper to George Davis, one of the game's surest hands, at short. But what looked like an inning-ending double play instead became two runs when the ball ricocheted wildly over Davis's head and into left field. Stahl and Collins both scored, enjoying a celebratory pummeling from their teammates as they crossed home with the tying runs. Now even the veteran Rusie began to feel the pressure, firing low and wide past catcher Parke Wilson. That wild pitch allowed Lowe to score the lead run. Bergen followed him a moment later on yet another bad-hop single, this one off Hamilton's bat, which vexed third baseman Jim Donnelley. For the Beaneaters, it amounted to an inning full of prismatic infield fortune—evasive hits past third and short, a mishandled pop at first, and a line drive out of the second baseman's reach.

With the club now four and one-half games in front, Murnane forecast even more intense interest in reports of the goings-on at the Polo

Grounds for Thursday's doubleheader and for the single games Friday and Saturday. That interest, he concluded, was likely to greatly profit the various real-time stage re-creations. "Without doubt, Music Hall will be packed to its immense capacity this afternoon by baseball rooters," he wrote.[44]

Those four games in New York presented Boston with a chance to deal the Giants' pennant hopes a near-fatal blow. Indeed, after Boston won both games of the Thursday doubleheader, by scores of 5–4 and 10–7, New York stood a distant fourth, ten games behind the leaders. But the Giants recovered to take the Friday and Saturday contests, handing the overall seven-game series to Boston by a thin 4–3 margin. Rusie, pitching on two days' rest, was heroic in the Saturday wrap-up, winning 6–4 in front of sixteen thousand spectators. Lame eighth-inning base running did in the league leaders, who saw Ted Lewis erased while trying for second and Lowe shot down while trying to score. It speaks to the drawing power of both Rusie and the visiting Beaneaters that the Polo Grounds attendance was about five hundred more than the combined total attendance at all of the five other league games that Saturday.

The Orioles Welcome Mr. Kelly

The split in New York gave Baltimore a chance to make up ground against their regular foils, the Phillies, in Philadelphia. They seized the chance and swept the series, drawing even with Boston in the loss column and moving within two games of them in the standings. The series marked Baltimore's introduction to the umpiring of Kick Kelly, the other replacement for the departed McDermott and Sheridan. The Orioles roughed him up in their standard fashion. The problems really began in the fifth inning, when a Philadelphia batter fouled a pitch into the press box seating area. Baltimore led 3–1 at the time. The common practice was to throw such a ball back into play, the umpire examining it and determining its fitness for further use under the lax standards in effect at the time. Kelly examined the foul ball and decided it was too damaged for use; he gave Corbett a new one. That angered Corbett and the Orioles, who did not like the idea of the Phillies getting to swing at a new baseball. Philadelphia went on to score two game-tying runs.

When the Orioles came to bat, a foul went into the seats—it happened to be off the bat of Boileryard Clarke—and was returned for Kelly's inspection. This time he decided it was suitable for play. Joe Kelley, acting as the team captain in Robinson's continued absence, argued the call and was ejected.[45] Clarke took up the cause and soon found himself alongside Kelley in the clubhouse. That forced Hanlon to put Frank Bowerman, who was nursing a fractured finger, in the game.

Things settled down, but only briefly. In the eighth inning, Tom O'Brien, who was Kelley's replacement, came up with Willie Keeler at third and Jennings at first. Umpire Kelly called O'Brien out on strikes, and the batter responded verbally, becoming Kelly's third ejection casualty of the afternoon. "The dictator of the diamond," the next morning's *Baltimore Sun* called Kelly.[46]

The three-game series with Brooklyn that initiated Baltimore's reassuring eight-team, month-long home stand was notable for three developments, the most vital being the Orioles' sweep of the series. Following up on the complaints against umpire Kelly, Nick Young paid another of his check-up visits to the first game, a 14–6 noncontroversial decision in favor of Baltimore. Young left, voicing great satisfaction with the way Kelly had handled matters. The second game of the series featured the even more reassuring presence of Wilbert Robinson behind the plate. With his May wounds finally healed, the catcher-captain delivered two hits and enjoyed the thoroughly delightful assignment of being the first to learn—from the press box situated directly behind him—that the Beaneaters had been beaten that afternoon. He shouted the news to the bench, and within seconds word was relayed through the grounds. The victory, which went to Corbett, moved Baltimore back to within a game of first place. The next day Bill Hoffer won his fourteenth decision to keep them there.

The League Suffers in Boston

The Beaneaters returned home for their longest stand of the season, a reassuring thirty-gamer that brought ten opponents to town—all of the teams except the Orioles. It looked like a good opportunity to expand their lead, and with fans in a pleasant mood, it looked like an even better time to make money. Toward the latter end, Soden authorized the sale of pictures of each of the players at the front gate, with the proceeds to supplement player salaries. The Beaneaters got a more immediate bonus when Arthur Dixwell, a local cigar merchant and one of the better-known members of the Royal Rooters, promised the players a box of cigars for each victory.[47]

Washington was the first to come to town, and the Beaneaters won two of three, falling 9–7 in the middle game when Senators pitcher Win Mercer's relief work, along with some infield shenanigans, quelled a late threat. After retiring Collins and Lowe to open the ninth, Mercer walked Bergen. Jack Stivetts, who had entered the game when Long was struck on the wrist by a pitch, dropped a floater close to the right-field line. But as Bergen rounded second, Senators second baseman John O'Brien sent the runner sprawling with a hip check, preventing him from taking third. "Emslie must have been in a trance," Murnane concluded.[48] The reality was that with the umpire focused on watching where Stivetts's hit landed, Bergen was fair game under the code of conduct for such situations. His safest course probably would have been to cut the base altogether. Hamilton followed with a hit, which filled the bases; then O'Brien retired Tenney to end the game.

The Pirates came to Boston for games on Thursday, Friday, and Saturday, and ran into an offense that went from very good to uncontainable. In the three games, the Beaneaters delighted their fans by crossing the plate forty-four times, winning 16–1, 15–2, and 13–12 in a wrap-up that may have exceeded any of their numerous previous comebacks for sheer implausibility. They trailed 12–7 with two out in the ninth and two runners on base. Hamilton stepped in against the backdrop of a crowd jostling for the exits. He sent a grounder to shortstop Bones

Ely, who misplayed it, allowing one run to score. Tenney followed with a smash clattering off the right-field boards, bringing two more runs home. The score now was 12–10, but there were two out and the tying run was merely at the plate. Worse, the tying run was Bob Allen, the midseason acquisition who was only in the lineup because Herman Long was still troubled by the wrist injury he had aggravated earlier in the week in a game against Washington. Allen got a high fastball and sent it on a line for the center-field depths, about as far as it was possible to hit a ball inside the South End Grounds. Tenney scored easily and Allen wound up at second. Stahl came next, and the fans who had stayed in the ballpark cheered in anticipation. The left-handed hitter slapped one past third and down the left-field foul line for another double, tying the game.

To a chorus that now sounded almost hoarse, Hugh Duffy came up to bat. Jesse Tannehill's first pitch was high and tight. Duffy set himself for the second and sent it out to center field, where Steve Brodie had no play. Stahl easily scored the winning run. Being a veteran player, Duffy knew what to do in these circumstances: he touched first and then made a mad dash for the clubhouse. Allen, less attuned to the protocol for staying healthy in the midst of a pennant race, lingered to receive the adulation of the throng, which surrounded him and administered the physical beating that perhaps he should have expected.

To compound the visitors' miseries, Boston players mixed deception in with their dominance. During one of the games, Pirates skipper Patsy Donovan was on third base when Elmer Smith lifted a fly ball out to Duffy. Donovan started to sprint home and then broke into a trot when he saw Bergen's casual posture at the plate. It was a ruse and a successful one; the ball shot over Donovan's head and he suddenly found himself blocked off the plate. "I have seen this trick worked before, but never was the picture of carelessness and unconcern more faithfully produced," remarked Donovan.[49]

The arrival of Louisville, the second of the six western visitors, for back-to-back doubleheaders portended no particular problems. The

Colonels, cellar dwellers during the previous three seasons, were by their standards enjoying the lofty strata of a tie for eighth place. Gangly rookie Honus Wagner had even become a modest attraction. But the Beaneaters performed as they usually did against western clubs, sweeping through the first three games before facing an unknown rookie out of nearby Brockton. The kid, Billy Magee, had been used only sparingly, mostly because he wasn't any good, as his 2-7 record and 5.50 earned run average suggested. But on that day, in front of his neighbors, Magee shut out the Beaneaters, and the Colonels left town having delivered an embarrassing 17–0 comeuppance to Boston's pride. It was the twenty-third time Boston had faced a team from the western half of the league at South End Grounds and the first time they had been beaten.

Philadelphia Courts Ned

Cleveland opened the swing of the western teams into Baltimore, sending Cy Young out to face the champions. It had not been Young's finest season to that point; it had been all he could do to maintain a .500 record, and his earned run average was at a three-season high. Against the Orioles, though, he showed his old form, shutting them out 3–0. It was the team's first such skunking all season, but the second was not long in coming. In the second game, on Friday, Jack Powell duplicated Young's performance, winning 6–0. By now the state of Hughie Jennings's arm had become a chronic worry. "It does not look as if Jennings could play again this season," Albert Mott wrote in what turned out to be a misdiagnosis of the situation. "At least any other man with his trouble couldn't."[50]

As if the sudden lack of offense and Jennings's health weren't enough to worry Orioles fans, a disturbing rumor surfaced out of the strangest of places—Eureka Springs, Arkansas. The rumor had it that the Phillies either already had finalized or were about to finalize an agreement with Ned Hanlon to manage their club in 1898. The explanation was reportedly simple: a twenty-thousand-dollar salary.[51]

In Philadelphia and Baltimore both, officials scrambled to shoot down the rumor. Phillies co-owner John Rogers denied the truth of such a transaction, "unless (team co-owner Al) Reach executed a flank movement yesterday." Hanlon went even further, telling a reporter that the story was "entirely incorrect," that he knew nothing of such a prospect, and that he had had no conversation with Rogers.[52] Fans read into those statements just enough wiggle room to give the rumor a touch of veracity, so it lingered for three more days until Hanlon was forced into declaring unequivocally, "I have absolutely no proposition under consideration . . . my intentions are to remain in this city."[53] Perhaps for fun, he then tossed a small grenade in the direction of the perennially underachieving Phillies. After noting that he made it a habit to thoroughly study all of his competitors, he added, "I never make any public criticism of any team or players, so I will not speak of what might be done in Philadelphia." Then he did exactly what he had just said he would not do, saying, "I know of three changes in the Philadelphia team which, if I could make, that team would be up front fighting for the pennant."[54]

The Orioles salvaged the Saturday wrap-up game against Cleveland, falling behind 6–0 but then tying the game with a six-run fifth inning and ultimately winning 12–6.

When rain washed out the opener of Baltimore's scheduled series with Chicago, it backed the Orioles into a stretch of eight games in seven days against the Colts and the Reds. To make matters worse, Willie Keeler lost a fingernail, although he only allowed it to sideline him for one day. With Jennings also questionable due to flare-ups in his long-sore shoulder, it left Hanlon again briefly fielding a patchwork lineup. Doyle came to the rescue with some base-running heroics, daringly running from first to third on a simple ground ball to first baseman Cap Anson in the ninth inning of a 2–2 tie, then scoring the winning run when the astonished Anson threw the ball down the left-field line. Pond officiated over the 3–1 victory in the third game of the series.

Doyle was the hero again in Thursday's opener of a five-game series against the Reds that included make-up games from two June rainouts. Leading off the ninth inning of a 2–2 tie, he beat out a popped-up bunt that Cincinnati pitcher Frank Dwyer trapped. That was Hank O'Day's opinion, anyway; Dwyer and the Reds argued strenuously that he'd caught it just off the ground. Reitz followed the argument with a line drive down the right-field line that sent Dirty Jack to third. The next hitter was Joe Quinn, who was filling in for Jennings, and he tried to hit a game-winning chop off the dirt in front of the plate. Shortstop Tommy Corcoran, who had drawn in for a possible play at the plate, snared the ball and threw it home, seemingly in time to get Doyle for the inning's first out. But Doyle snaked his way around catcher Heinie Peitz's lunging tag with a game-ending hook slide. The Orioles won again on Friday, 7–2, a decisive result that did not prevent Reds manager Buck Ewing from renewing what was becoming a running beef with Orioles fans and the supposedly intimidated O'Day.

National League Standings (Evening of August 26)

TEAM	WINS	LOSSES	PERCENTAGE	GAMES BEHIND
Boston	72	33	.686	—
Baltimore	67	32	.677	2
Cincinnati	62	36	.633	6½
New York	62	37	.626	7
Cleveland	53	47	.530	16½
Chicago	49	56	.467	23
Philadelphia	47	59	.443	25½
Louisville	46	59	.438	26
Pittsburg	44	58	.431	26½
Brooklyn	44	59	.427	27
Washington	42	60	.412	28½
St. Louis	26	78	.250	45½

10. Don't They Keep Warm?

The 1897 pennant race is an intriguing event for many reasons: Freed-manism, fighting, the reemergence of Amos Rusie, the rise of Louis Sockalexis, umpires, and the more or less ongoing struggle to find a balance between winning and bludgeoning are among the obvious ones. Many of these factors affected play among the ten National League teams not directly involved in the pennant chase.

A few incidents simply involved slack effort. On August 26 in Chicago, Colts ace Clark Griffith took the mound against his will after a dispute with Cap Anson. Griffith allowed doubles to the first three batters he faced and then, according to one account of the game, "became sullen and began to toss the ball over the plate."[1] Twenty hits later, the Giants had a 19–6 victory. The following day, star Phillies rookie Napoleon Lajoie showed up drunk for the start of the game with Pittsburg. He committed an error leading to two Pirate runs in the first inning and was yanked from the game.[2] In the last week of August, Pittsburg club owner W. W. Kerr briefly suspended the team's two star pitchers, Pink Hawley and Frank Killen, on grounds of indifferent play. Among their offenses was the hammering they had taken a week before in Boston. They were reinstated a few days later.[3]

The umpire situation was only slightly more stable than it had been the previous month, when Jack Sheridan and Sandy McDermott had

Fig. 18. The baseball landscape of 1897: The Bostons stand poised to challenge the hated champion Orioles (background) across a field littered with the bodies of their mutually dispatched opponents. Originally appeared in the *Boston Globe*, September 20, 1897.

quit. On September 8 in Washington, one of their replacements, Bill Carpenter, declared that the Spiders' Ed McKean had deliberately tried to get hit with a pitched ball. Cleveland player-manager Patsy Tebeau refused to let the game continue until McKean was awarded first base, so after several minutes Carpenter declared a forfeit.[4] The next day in Pittsburg, the Pirates defeated New York, 5–4, in the first game of a doubleheader. Giants captain Bill Joyce dawdled too long between games to suit the tastes of a tired umpire Hank O'Day, so O'Day walked off the field and left the teams to their own devices. With New York's Walt Wilmot and Pittsburg's Jesse Tannehill as emergency umpiring replacements, the Giants won, 6–2, in a game that was stopped after six innings because of darkness.[5] A week later, again in Pittsburg, Hawley struck out the visitors' Monte Cross, who responded with some vulgarities. Hawley responded with a sock to Cross's jaw. Both men were ejected.[6]

As they awoke on August 26, the Beaneaters led the Orioles by three games. By the following evening, Ned Hanlon's Orioles had erased that margin and actually taken a four percentage point lead. Then, like twin comets streaking across the night sky, the bitter rivals spent the next month spectacularly distancing themselves from the terrestrial portion of the league. Yet they never lost touch with one another. Frank Selee's Beaneaters won seventeen of their next twenty-one decisions; Hanlon's Orioles won nineteen of twenty-three. Between August 27 and the final game of their series in Baltimore a month later, Boston led by a half game seven times, Baltimore led by the same margin five times, and they were tied seven times. On six mornings, the teams woke to find one of them ahead by percentage points but trailing in the "games behind" column. As the chase unfolded day by day, neither team managed to open up a lead greater than ten percentage points.

Friday, August 27

Everything might have been different if Selee's club had managed to handle the Spiders during their second visit to Boston's South End Grounds. This was a different Cleveland club from the one that was swept in June. By this time, Tebeau had given up on Sockalexis, whose sore ankle and deep thirst had become chronic concerns. But Selee had his own problems in that regard: Herman Long remained sidelined with his sore wrist, and Bobby Lowe was also out. Kid Nichols took the mound to face George Cuppy. A slow-working slowball pitcher, Cuppy succeeded by getting on the nerves of opponents, and he left Boston's hitters frazzled in a 7–1 victory. Lowe returned the next day but dropped a throw in the first inning that set up the Spiders for five runs. From there Cleveland breezed along, with Jack Powell defeating Ted Lewis 10–4. At Union Park, Reds manager Buck Ewing beefed his way through a doubleheader loss to the Orioles that effectively buried his team's pennant hopes. Ewing's principal complaint was about umpire O'Day's perceived favoritism of the home team. Given that Bill Hoffer pitched a 5–0, three-hit shutout, Ewing had no argument in the first game. The second game was a tighter one, with pitchers Doc Amole and Ted Breitenstein tied 3–3 until Heinie Reitz's two-out single got Joe Kelley home and then Joe Quinn doubled Reitz across. That left the Orioles, although technically a half game behind Boston, actually four percentage points in front and moved the sports writers at the *Baltimore Sun* to imitative verse:

> *Oh, say can you see through the York road's thick dust,*
> *What so proudly we've hailed three years in rotation.*
> *Whose bright red, white and blue made the patriot bust*
> *With joy that once more we had licked all creation.*
> *The bleachers' wild shout*
> *Keeler lining them out,*
> *And Jack Doyle sliding in to old Anse's consternation.*
> *That championship pennant, oh long may it wave,*
> *O'er Buck Ewing's lost hopes, and the Beaneaters' grave."*[7]

Baltimore	69-32	.683	½
Boston	72-34	.679	—

Saturday, August 28

Boston beat Cy Young 11–5. Among the crowd of eight thousand was James B. Connolly, the Harvard dropout who a year earlier had won the first gold medal (in the triple jump) awarded at the rebirth of the Olympic Games in Athens. "James is indeed a loyal rooter," remarked Tim Murnane.[8] But to judge from the reporter's other observations, he was one of the few at that series; most, it seemed, had misplaced their enthusiasm when faced with their club's first fall from the top spot since late June. "The weak support in the way of applause given the home team . . . has caused the players much annoyance," he wrote.

Noting the partisanship of crowds in Baltimore and New York, he essentially accused Boston partisans of being too refined. "When [visiting players] find all hands and the cook out for the games, they find a much rougher road to travel."[9]

Spicier language made news in Baltimore, where Reds officials announced they were forwarding to league officials a transcript of John McGraw's verbal assault on Cincinnati pitcher Frank Dwyer in the first game of the series. "It was inside language by Hanlon's inside player," reported the *Boston Herald* with more than a touch of sarcasm, "and it should be enough to expel him from any first-class base ball organization."[10] The *Louisville Courier-Journal* added an editorial postscript with the comment, "Should Boston win the pennant this year it would be a big sendoff for clean baseball, and four-fifths of the baseball people are pulling hard for Boston on that account."[11] None of the uproar disturbed the Orioles, who beat Cincinnati for the fourth straight time, 7–2, behind Arlie Pond. Jake Stenzel's three hits included a double; Quinn, subbing for Hughie Jennings, also got three hits. The Orioles even provided fans with more spicy language. In retaliation for what he viewed as a dirty play by the Orioles, Reds pitcher Bill Dammann threw a ball close to Jack Doyle's head. Doyle walked toward the mound, swearing and gesturing toward Dammann. Joe Kelley joined him with more blue language.

Baltimore	69-32	.683	½
Boston	72-34	.679	—

Sunday, August 29

(No games)

Monday, August 30

The *Baltimore Sun* published the contents of telegrams sent by Ewing to the league office and to Boston manager Frank Selee after the

Reds' defeat on August 26. Ewing did not deny authorship of the telegrams; the one to Young invited him to "come over and see Hank O'Day steal the championship for Baltimore."[12] The telegram to Selee advised him, "With O'Day umpiring in Baltimore you haven't a ghost of a chance for the championship."[13] However, the umpire played little role in the Orioles' fifth consecutive victory over the Reds, this time by a 7–1 score. Joe Corbett did have a role, scattering seven hits. All fourteen of the Orioles' hits were singles, with Wilbert Robinson getting three of them.

The Beaneaters got even with Powell, winning 6–2.

Baltimore	71-32	.689	½
Boston	73-34	.683	—

Tuesday, August 31

The Orioles welcomed last-place St. Louis into town for four games that everyone assumed would be easy victories. The opener certainly was; Baltimore got seventeen hits behind Hoffer in a 12–5 decision. Observed the *Baltimore Sun*, "While there are some good ballplayers on the St. Louis team, taken as a whole it is entirely outclassed by the Baltimore club, which really ought not to lose more than one game in twenty to the Browns."[14]

Cap Anson's Colts arrived in Boston for the first of three games, but eleven innings of back-and-forth ball lent no clarity. Tom Lynch finally called it due to darkness, and the game ended in an 8–8 tie. The clubs agreed to replay the game on Friday. Hits by Chick Stahl, Hugh Duffy, and Bobby Lowe produced a tying run in the bottom of the ninth. Long tried out his injured wrist for seven innings and then gave up, pronouncing it still too sore.

Baltimore	71-32	.689	—
Boston	73-34	.679	—

Wednesday, September 1

By changing pitchers in the middle of an inning, Duffy stirred a tempest among Boston fans. The Beaneaters led 6–3 in the sixth inning when Ted Lewis lost his composure, walking two runners. In the seventh, Bill Lange singled; then Anson followed with one of his own. When Jimmy Ryan took two balls, Duffy called time, trotted in from left field, and motioned for Nichols, who had been warming up. Such a gesture, displaying a lack of faith in a pitcher, was rare in the 1890s; if a pitcher was to be taken out of a game, it almost always occurred between innings. Of Boston's 132 games that year, 115 were completed by the starter. Lewis's reaction to the move is not recorded, but some of the home fans rose to his defense, hissing the Boston captain. The *Boston Journal's* John Morrill ascribed mercenary motives to the hissers, suggesting that they had bet money against the home team. "If shoestring gamblers are to dictate the direction of a ballgame at the South End it is high time someone in authority should suppress those fellows," he asserted.[15] Whatever the fans' motives, Morrill's underlying assertion is unquestionably true: a betting proposition was easily found in the stands at South End, or most any other league park, in those days. But the boos of those fans must have been drowned out by cheers moments later, when Nichols retired the side at the cost of just one run, preserving an eventual 7–4 victory. "The ingredient Capt. Duffy has is 'sand,'" Tim Murnane argued, castigating critics of the decision to remove Lewis. "The time to change the pitcher is before the game is lost."[16]

Doyle and Quinn, both subbing for Jennings, each had three hits as the Orioles once again abused the Browns. This time the score was 11–5 behind Doc Amole, and the key was another seventeen-hit Oriole offense.

Baltimore	72-32	.692	—
Boston	74-34	.685	—

Thursday, September 2

Baltimore's string of seventeen-hit joyrides against the Browns ended abruptly, thanks to Willie Sudhoff. A rookie with only one major-league victory to his credit, Sudhoff allowed fifteen hits and put up with three errors behind him, yet still somehow managed to survive for a 4–3, ten-inning victory. The Orioles were all over him from start to finish; Willie Keeler had three hits, and Stenzel, Reitz, Quinn, and Robinson each had two. Yet none of the fifteen hits went for more than a single base. The only heartening news was Jennings's appearance as a pinch hitter in the final inning.

Rain washed out what was originally scheduled as the final game of Chicago's visit to Boston, forcing the teams into a Friday doubleheader. As a result, although the Orioles retained a one percentage point lead in the standings, they actually trailed the Beaneaters by a half game.

Baltimore	72-33	.686	½
Boston	74-34	.685	—

Friday, September 3

Boston pitchers Fred Klobedanz and Kid Nichols split the work as the Beaneaters swept their makeup doubleheader against Chicago by scores of 6–3 and 9–1. Again, the visitors accused Lynch of favoring Boston with his calls, this time in a dispute over a ball that struck home plate. Two Chicago runs had already scored and George Decker was at third base when catcher Malachi Kittridge bounded one off the plate. Marty Bergen grabbed the ball and tagged Kittridge, who had not run, claiming the ball was in foul territory. Lynch called him out. Then Bergen tagged a sliding Decker, prompting a double-edged Chicago beef when Lynch called Decker out as well. "The decision was so bad that the crowd hissed," the *Chicago Tribune*'s correspondent reported.[17]

In Baltimore the Orioles said farewell to the Browns with a twenty-five-hit explosion in a 22–1 victory for Corbett. The game concluded

a series in which the home team outscored the visitors 48–15 and out-
hit them 74–40, yet somehow failed to sweep. At least the 1,587 fans in
attendance had abundant reason to cheer; against call-up Percy Cole-
man, Doyle went six for six, Kelley had five hits, and Keeler had four.
Jennings was greeted with enthusiastic applause in his return to the
starting lineup, going four innings before retiring in favor of Quinn
with the game already out of hand.

Boston	76-34	.691	—
Baltimore	73-33	.689	1

Saturday, September 4

Bergen was the story for Boston, his play mirroring his unpredictable
temperament. He committed three passed balls but also threw out Cincinnati base runners. His two hits drove in four runs, and the Beaneaters defeated Cincinnati 7–6. With Long still out, pinch hitter Bob Allen had three hits and Jack Stivetts pitched just well enough.

Jerry Nops, finally recovered from an illness that had permitted
him to make one ineffective appearance in two months, returned with
a reassuring six-hit performance against the Pirates. Kelley came to
bat with two on base and got them home in unusual fashion—with a
home run into the bleachers.

Boston	77-34	.694	—
Baltimore	74-33	.692	1

Sunday, September 5

There were no games, which gave Hanlon time to wrestle with a big
schedule problem. He had wanted to use the coming Tuesday open
date to make up a previous rainout with Louisville, a game originally
scheduled to be played July 10 in Louisville. Travel demands eliminated any chance of both teams returning to Louisville to play the

game, meaning it would go unplayed unless the Colonels agreed to play it to Baltimore. Given the Orioles' circumstances, Hanlon could ill-afford to leave unclaimed any opportunity to pick on the eleventh-place Colonels. In one respect the calendar was a perfect fit; the Colonels had a doubleheader Monday in Washington, then a three-game series Wednesday through Friday in Baltimore. So adding the fourth game would be logistically simple . . . except for one problem. Louisville and Washington had played to a tie on Saturday, and that gave the Senators first claim on the Colonels' presence on Tuesday. Desirous of the gate, the Senators declared their intention to replay the game. That was all right with the Colonels, whose management much preferred to play the Senators than the tougher Orioles.

Monday, September 6

The season's only scheduled doubleheaders in both Boston and Baltimore were split-admission events. In Baltimore the Orioles took a 4–0 lead in the morning game, surrendered it during a six-run Pittsburg fourth in which they committed a series of fielding blunders, and then rallied to win 8–7. The afternoon game was a 7–2 decision behind Joe Corbett. John McGraw, Willie Keeler, Jack Doyle, Heinie Reitz, and Boileryard Clarke all came through with two hits. Save for the top of the fourth, the Orioles' brand of inside baseball dominated. They took the lead in the fifth inning of the morning game when Kelley opened by drawing a walk, Stenzel bunted for a hit, Doyle moved both runners along, and Reitz scored them with a double into the gap in right field. With the game tied, Robinson bunted Reitz to third and reached first safely himself, making Doc Amole's fly ball to Steve Brodie good for the lead run. The Orioles opened the afternoon game with a textbook illustration of their ability to get the most runs on the fewest hits. McGraw walked, Keeler singled, and Jennings sacrificed, and McGraw came home on Kelley's ground out. The fourth inning was classic Oriole ball in another way. McGraw opened with a bunt, took third on Keeler's hit-and-run single, and scored on Jennings's double. Again, Kelley produced a run—Keeler's—on a routine ground out.[18]

Pitching mismatches determined the outcome in Boston. Reds left-hander Ted Breitenstein, on his way to twenty-three victories, proved too much for Lewis in the 10:30 a.m. start. He defeated the Beaneaters 5–3 in a game marked by the home club's squabbles with Lynch. Watching their team trail throughout that morning game, Boston fans' hopes were raised when the scoreboard posted the Pirates' six-run fourth in Baltimore. Cries of "Hit 'er up again!" rose during an abortive seven-inning rally that began when Reds first baseman Jake Beckley bobbled Lewis's roller and Billy Hamilton beat out an infield chop. Fred Tenney sacrificed the runners into scoring position, setting up the tying runs for Bobby Lowe and Chick Stahl. But both men lifted easy infield pop-ups for the second and third outs. More heartbreak followed when the Orioles' 8–7 comeback victory over Pittsburg was posted. Baltimore was back in first place by percentage points. After the morning loss, Frank Selee demanded that Lynch not be assigned to future Boston games. Lynch, who was following his custom of refusing to work both games of doubleheaders, promptly complied, sitting out the afternoon contest. Reds manager Buck Ewing had no complaints. "If we had such a show in Baltimore from the umpire as we are getting in this city, we could have won games," he said.[19] In the afternoon, Nichols breezed to a 10–2 decision over Red Ehret.

Baltimore	76-33	.697	—
Boston	78-35	.690	—

Tuesday, September 7

No games were scheduled for either the Orioles or the Beaneaters. But they were busy in Baltimore.

Frustrated by his inability to get the Colonels into town a day early to make up the August rainout in Louisville, Hanlon lobbied manager Fred Clarke and owner Henry Pulliam to agree to a doubleheader during the visit that began on Wednesday. But Pulliam offered no reply to the Orioles manager's telegrams of inquiry. Orioles fans were left to contemplate the physical state of their team. Albert Mott boiled it down for them. "Jennings is still out of the game, and Nops is most dead. Robbie gives out, sometimes after a few innings . . . Willie Keeler is playing with one hand. Ned Hanlon has the croup. And Louisville's coming. The pennant's gone. The only thing now is an Oriole bunt for the Temple Cup."[20] An unusually downcast description of a first-place team about to open a series with a bottom-feeder.

Ever the fan, Mott found reason for gaiety in the play of his favorite Orioles. "The king of first base is Jack Doyle," he wrote in *Sporting Life*. "The intellectual inspiration that man has is remarkable. He will suddenly turn the complexion of a game in an instant by some act that must be an inspiration." Mott saw further intellectual breadth in McGraw. "Why that boy has done such hair-raising acts."[21]

Wednesday, September 8

In Baltimore, Nops reassured Orioles fans with his second strong performance since returning from illness. He allowed the Colonels just five hits—two of them by Honus Wagner—in a 5–1 victory. With McGraw sick, Keeler and Jennings took over at the top of the order, each collecting three hits. Their success was hardly a surprise given that Fred Clarke chose that day to test out a new signee on the mound, a peculiar twenty-year-old left-hander named George Waddell. He looked like a rube, so that's what everyone called him, Rube Waddell. Just up from the semipro circuits, but long on confidence, Waddell reportedly responded to Clarke's suggestion that he bail out the Colonels' frayed mound staff against the three-time champions by advising Clarke that all batters looked alike to him. He gave up eleven hits but showed moxie, striking out Stenzel at one key point and inducing Keeler to hit the ball after falling behind 3-0. Predicted the *Baltimore Sun*, "Waddell ought to become a star if his work yesterday was any criterion."[22]

Despite the victory, the day was far from perfect for Hanlon. He cornered the newly arrived Pulliam at the Grounds, only to be given a flat refusal of any interest by Louisville in rescheduling the August rainout as a doubleheader. Pulliam's perspective was simple to understand. Although in eleventh place, his team was a mere two games out of sixth in the tightly bunched second division. If he was under no requirement to make up the game, he wouldn't. "Harry wants to crawl up in the standing column and believes that this is not the proper place to crawl," explained the *Baltimore American*.[23]

Klobedanz startled the 2,200 Boston fans in attendance by allowing last-place St. Louis three runs in the first inning. Form held from that moment, though, and the Beaneaters won 17–5.

Baltimore	77-33	.700	—
Boston	79-35	.693	—

Thursday, September 9

What the Orioles had failed to do a week earlier—beat Willie Sudhoff—Boston managed to accomplish, albeit barely. Sudhoff and Jack Stivetts had fought to a 6–6 tie as they entered the bottom of the seventh. Consecutive singles by Hugh Duffy, Jimmy Collins, Bob Allen, and Marty Bergen sent one run across and filled the bases, prompting a chorus of "Win your own game, Jack" for Stivetts.[24] He complied with a line drive that split the left and center fielders for three bases. Having finally taken the lead, Selee took no chances, removing Stivetts in favor of Nichols, who shut out St. Louis in the final two innings of a 13–6 victory.

Keeler, Jennings, and sloppy Louisville fielding saved the Orioles. An error led to two runs in the first. Then with the score tied 2–2 and two out in the seventh, Keeler got his fourth hit of the game and Jennings followed with his second. Gambling with the lead run, Keeler raced around third in an attempt to break the tie and was rewarded when rookie second baseman Heinie Smith fired a hurried throw over the catcher's head.

Baltimore	78-33	.703	—
Boston	80-35	.696	—

Friday, September 10

The Browns jumped to an early 9–2 lead off of Ted Lewis. In no position to concede as much as a single game to the Orioles, and particularly one against the last-place team, captain Hugh Duffy pulled his starter after the first two runners reached base in the fourth. He called on Nichols for the second consecutive day; this time it was for a six-inning stretch. Nichols induced a Collins-to-Lowe-to-Tenney double play and then shut out St. Louis on three hits the rest of the way. Even that would not have helped except for Collins's stick work. His sixth-inning double drove home the first of four runs, his eighth-inning single set up another run, and his ninth-inning triple off the top of the right-field fence with two on base tied the game. A walk and an out later, Nichols rolled a grounder to Monte Cross, who threw home too late to get Collins's winning run. Cross was one of the Browns' few reliable fielders, and normally his throw would have retired the runner. But the previous day Cross had been badly spiked on the hand by Allen while trying to evade a tag; although bandaged, the bloody wound was still sore.

The Orioles led Louisville 6–5 when umpire Kick Kelly got fed up and called it a forfeit to Baltimore. By the second, Kelly had already heard plenty, ejecting Colonels catcher Charlie Dexter. As the innings rolled along, the Colonels' Fred Clarke, Bill Wilson, and Bill Magee all drew twenty-five-dollar fines, as did Joe Kelley. The final straw came under gathering darkness in the bottom of the seventh when Kelly called Keeler safe on a two-out, bags-loaded grounder that broke the 5–5 tie. The infuriated Colonels, believing the contest could not long continue anyway, surrounded Kelly and refused to resume play, so he ordered the game forfeited to the home team. It went into the books as a 9–0 decision. Doc Amole won, thanks in large measure to three Louisville errors that permitted five runs to score. Said the *Baltimore Sun*, "There was one redeeming feature about [the game]—it did not lack excitement."[25]

| Baltimore | 79-33 | .705 | — |
| Boston | 81-35 | .698 | — |

Saturday, September 11

A pregame shower held attendance down to four thousand in Boston, where Klobedanz scattered seven hits in a game in which the outcome was never in doubt. Boston scored three runs in the first inning and won 11–0.

In Baltimore rumors circulated that a five-hundred-dollar bounty had been offered by unnamed men to any Chicago pitcher who beat the Orioles in their three-game series.[26] The donor was understood to be somebody living in "the west"—meaning between Pittsburg and St. Louis—who wanted to see the "gentlemanly" Bostons defeat the "ruffianly" Orioles. Reporters traveling with the Chicago club supposedly confirmed the report, although those confirmations appeared only in the Baltimore newspapers, not in Chicago. Hanlon supposedly had lent his own confirmation, saying he had seen a written offer of a three-hundred-dollar payment from a man living in Louisville. Orioles fans took it as more evidence of the contempt the rest of the league held for their heroes. The *Baltimore Sun* sarcastically observed, "Perhaps other rich gentlemen . . . who are so intensely eager 'for the good of the game' may add other hundreds, and it may yet be worth a year's salary to a man to beat these horrible Baltimores only one game."[27]

If there was such a bonus, the first opportunity to claim it fell to Walter Thornton, who split time between the mound (sixteen games) and the outfield (fifty-nine games). He led 3–2 in the eighth when an error allowed Hughie Jennings to score the tying run. The Orioles might have won outright if John McGraw hadn't preceded Jennings's hit by getting called out trying to stretch his single into a double. McGraw's rage, which included roughly jostling umpire Jim McDonald, was described by onlookers as ranking with his most vitriolic of the season. McDonald, however, did not throw the third baseman off the premises. It was the season's third tie between the Colts and the Orioles, and the teams agreed to play it off as part of a doubleheader on Monday.

Albert Mott, meanwhile, reported a campaign among Orioles fans to purchase a new brick house for Hanlon. Mott may have gilded the story, saying the house would come "complete with a bay window and a ready-made family."[28] Nonetheless, by this time feelings for Hanlon plainly ran deep. "To get up and eat your breakfast, go out to a business lunch, go home to a family dinner, turn in at a proper hour . . . and feel assured that the result will be right . . . is a thing that only Baltimoreans can experience," Mott explained. "And who is responsible for all this? Ned Hanlon."[29]

| Baltimore | 79-33 | .705 | ½ |
| Boston | 82-35 | .701 | — |

Sunday, September 12

No games were scheduled, giving *Boston Journal* columnist John Morrill time to ramp up the Orioles-Beaneaters rivalry in anticipation of their upcoming series. Like Tim Murnane, Morrill was a former player (fifteen seasons in his case, including two as Murnane's teammate) who had turned to sports analysis. Morrill expressed amusement at unspecified complaints out of Baltimore regarding dirty play by the Colonels during their recent visit. "The Baltimoreans can see but one club in the field that has no faults," he wrote. "What they need down there is a few clubs to beat them at their own game." Of course, in Boston, beating the Orioles at their own game implied stooping to kick-'em-in-the-shins tactics. So be it, said Morrill. "The Bostons must make up their minds to play 'Baltimore' ball first, last and all the time," he wrote.[30]

Monday, September 13

In Boston, Royal Rooters Billy Rogers and George Appleton revealed plans for the big excursion to Baltimore the following week, promising a fare of twenty-five dollars per head if one hundred fans signed up.[31] "Nothing would encourage the players more than to have about 100 Boston friends present to see them tear up the earth with the champions," Murnane wrote. Fully aware of the atmosphere at Union Park, however, he advised that "if the rooters take the trip, they should carry fish horns and police rattles enough to partially offset the cannonading of that howling Baltimore mob."[32] Seeing a good promotion, several of the city's newspapers commissioned "official Royal Rooters badges" to be worn by their readers during the trip.

Murnane also found space to get in additional digs at the Baltimore atmosphere. He quoted Tim Hurst on supposed exchanges with Orioles players following defeats during the mid-August Cleveland series, which Hurst had worked. Murnane reported Hurst as revealing, "During one of the games, Joe Kelley passed me, saying, 'If I was Hanlon you never would umpire another game in Baltimore.'" Hurst was said to have replied, "What . . . not be allowed to umpire another game in this city for a lot of swell gentlemen like your crowd? Don't say that, old boy, you know all the umpires are stuck on umpiring for you people."[33]

Baltimore fans remained outraged over the reports that someone had offered a five-hundred-dollar bounty to any Chicago pitcher defeating the Orioles. Editors of the *Baltimore Sun* printed an anonymous letter, which they said represented the views of many in Baltimore. The letter described the offer as "the overthrow of baseball as a national game, and in fact as a game of any decency whatsoever."[34] The writer's point, which would redound during later betting scandals, was that if you could bribe a player to win, you could also bribe him to lose. In addition, an outside influence seeking to get players to defeat the Orioles might also try to get players to lose to the Beaneaters. "If the skill of a ballplayer is to depend upon the amount he is paid from the outside, the game will be looked upon as a scheme only to defraud the public," the writer argued.[35] The letter called for league president Nick Young to investigate the reports. But given Young's weak position and his unresponsiveness to other problems, including those involving player-umpire disputes, nobody held out much hope of such an inquiry actually being undertaken, and in fact it was not.

On the field the Orioles swept a doubleheader with the Colts. Bill Hoffer was his own best friend in the morning game, getting three of his team's eight hits, one of them a double. In the afternoon, McGraw doubled, singled, drove in three runs, and walked in an 11–4 victory that was called because of darkness after just five innings. The Beaneaters and Phillies were rained out, allowing Baltimore to resume first place by a half game and ten percentage points.

Baltimore	81-33	.711	—
Boston	82-35	.701	½

Tuesday, September 14

Long returned to the Boston lineup, and Nichols held the Phillies in check for a 6–4 victory. The victory, Boston's sixth straight, was also the first since September 6 in which the Beaneaters had scored fewer than ten runs. No big-league team has ever put together a longer stretch of double-digit offensive showings. The Orioles pounded Chicago's Thornton 15–8 beneath an eighteen-hit barrage. Kelley, Stenzel, and Reitz each had three hits; McGraw, Keeler, and Jennings each had two.

| Baltimore | 82-33 | .713 | — |
| Boston | 83-35 | .703 | ½ |

Wednesday, September 15

Boston breezed by Philadelphia, this time by a 9–1 score. It was the Beaneaters' tenth straight victory over the Phillies following two losses and a tie in the first three games they played in the season. With Long back at shortstop, the infield of Collins, Long, Lowe, and Tenney handled every chance flawlessly. Stivetts was not threatened, thanks in part to an offense that generated fourteen hits. Stahl laid out three of them; Tenney, Long, Lowe, and Bergen had two each.

Young and the Orioles separately moved to put the story of the rumored five-hundred-dollar bounty to rest. Young did so by issuing a statement dismissing concerns regarding the reports, although the statement tacitly acknowledged the existence of such an offer. "I have my doubts about the offer having been made seriously . . . and if it was I do not see how it could affect the honesty of baseball," he said. "Every Chicago pitcher who goes in against Baltimore will do his best to win—they all do. He can do no better than his best no matter how much he is offered."[36] The Orioles defused the issue in more concrete fashion, by concluding their sweep of Cap Anson's Colts 13–2. Fans took particular satisfaction in sweeping the long-time Chicago player-manager, who was playing his final circuit of the league, because he was seen as having taken sides in favor of the Beaneaters. Still, the 2,100 in attendance saluted his final at bat with a standing ovation. They applauded even more heartily for the sixteen-hit Orioles offense. Stenzel and Doyle got three hits each. McGraw, who had been hit on the elbow by a pitch on Tuesday, watched from the stands.

| Baltimore | 83-33 | .716 | — |
| Boston | 84-35 | .706 | ½ |

Thursday, September 16

The teams' twin September streaks had buried virtually every other league team. Only the Giants, eight and one-half games out of first, remained closer than seventeen games behind. Their slim playoff hopes rode on the outcomes of three games each with the Beaneaters and the Orioles during the week preceding their much-anticipated showdown. New York's team captain, Bill Joyce, had a particular problem. Because ace Amos Rusie had pitched in the previous day's game against Brooklyn—a Giants rout, as it turned out—he was unavailable for the entire Boston series. So Joyce would confront the Beaneaters with Jouett Meekin and two second-line hurlers. The first game, matching Klobedanz against Meekin, went to the desperate New Yorkers, 8–5, and left sour feelings all around. Murnane panned Klobedanz's work, finding that he not only pitched "weak ball, but was slower than an old horse cart covering ground."[37] Boston players tied into Lynch's work behind the plate, believing their man had been squeezed on balls and strikes.

The Orioles trailed 4–3 coming into the bottom of the ninth inning of the opener of their three-game series with the Phillies, and they promptly displayed both the best and worst of inside ball. McGraw led off, succeeding in working Philadelphia pitcher Jack Taylor for a base on balls. With Willie Keeler up, Baltimore ball presumed some sort of trick play would be next—and it was, with McGraw stealing second. Keeler failed in the first attempt to drive him home, lining out to center, but a wild pitch moved McGraw to third, and Jennings then smashed a two-base hit down the left-field line. That should have given either Kelley or Stenzel a chance to drive home the winning run. But Jennings let himself get caught off base while threatening a steal. With darkness at hand, the game was declared a 4–4 tie at the inning's end, and the teams agreed to replay it the next day.

Baltimore	83-33	.716	—
Boston	84-36	.600	1

Friday, September 17

With Nichols seeking his twenty-seventh victory against second-liner Mike Sullivan, it looked like New York's only chance was a rainout. The Giants almost got it when a storm soaked the grounds an hour before the scheduled first pitch. No such luck; the game began on time, and Boston scored six runs in the first inning on its way to a 17–0 runaway. Lowe, Long, Collins, Nichols, and Stahl each delivered multiple hits, which, along with a few walks, a couple of hit batters, and some poor fielding by the Giants, essentially rendered Nichols's shutout pitching a waste of effort. As if Sullivan hadn't had things tough enough, Andrew Freedman slapped him with a fifty-dollar fine following the game, citing indifferent performance.[38]

   With sixteen hits, Baltimore ran its winning streak to twelve games in the opener of a doubleheader against the Phillies. It was a typical Orioles attack: McGraw and Kelley each had two hits, Keeler and Doyle had three, Phillies ace Al Orth stopped nobody, and the outcome was effectively decided well before the 11–4 final score was posted. The decisive win makes the outcome of the afternoon game all the more difficult to explain. Facing an unheralded September call-up named Dave Dunkle, the Orioles succumbed 2–1 on just five hits. They took the loss out on umpire Bill Carpenter, blaming him for an inconsistent strike zone. But they knew they were as much to blame for failing to play their own style of ball. Trailing by one run in the seventh, Stenzel reached third on his single and another by Doyle, along with an error by Napoleon Lajoie. A squeeze—a standard Orioles ploy in that circumstance—would have gotten the tying run home. But Heinie Reitz swung away and popped harmlessly to Ed Delahanty in left. In the ninth, it was Jake Stenzel's turn to bunt for the tie; but he too was unsuccessful, and again the run did not score. This time Kelley was on third via a one-out triple. Stenzel popped up to second, leaving the winning streak riding on Jack Doyle's bat with two out. Doyle lifted a simple foul along third, and when Billy Nash caught it, the Orioles had lost for the first time since September 2. Dunkle became only the second pitcher all month to beat Baltimore, and there could be a good debate over which of the two—Dunkle or the Browns' Willie Sudhoff—would have been considered less likely to do so.

Baltimore	84-34	.712	—
Boston	85-36	.702	½

Saturday, September 18

Ten thousand fans enjoyed the weekend at South End Grounds, the crowd spilling out of the grandstand and forming three deep along the foul lines. Among them, of course, was Representative John F. Fitzgerald, joined for this day by state senator James Gallivan and alderman Charlie Bryant. Bill Joyce turned to rookie Cy Seymour, whose fifteen victories, 3.25 earned run average, and league-leading strikeout total all suggested he would be up to the task. He was not; the Boston rooters rattled him and the Beaneaters took an easy 9–3 decision. In the noisy first inning, Tenney lined a one-out single, Lowe drew a walk, Stahl singled, and Duffy and Collins both walked, forcing two runs home. Murnane described the noise from the Boston bench as "like the bing-bang of a tom-tom foundry, and the big crowd came in as the anvil chorus."[39] With two outs, Doc Yeager waited out another walk for a third run.

In Baltimore, fans took particular note of Joyce's decision not to use Amos Rusie against the Beaneaters but to instead save him for Baltimore. "What a glorious thing it will be," waxed Albert Mott, "to win the pennant while every club in the League, with the exception of Cleveland, has been specially conniving against it."[40] The Orioles dismissed Philadelphia 8–3 amid another fifteen-hit burst. The hits were easy to track; everybody, including pitcher Arlie Pond, got two, except

Jennings (one) and Robinson (a sacrifice and a walk). From Boston, Tim Murnane lobbed a grenade in the direction of the Baltimore players and rooters. "Next year," he wrote, "it is proposed to have the umpires in the Baltimore games located in a balloon above the grounds and announce decisions by means of a megaphone. For protection he may be given a few bombs to drop down to attract attention until he reaches the ground and gets away."[41]

Baltimore	85-34	.714	—
Boston	86-36	.705	½

Sunday, September 19

(No games)

Monday, September 20

Boston's game with Brooklyn was rained out and rescheduled as part of a Tuesday doubleheader. Frank Selee took the free afternoon to chat with reporters, speculating that he might use Nichols twice against the Orioles. The Orioles opened their final three-game road trip by scoring nine runs against Rusie at the Polo Grounds. Yet they still lost 10–9 in a game that featured thirty-seven hits. Joe Corbett twice surrendered leads, and Rusie himself drove in the winning run in the bottom half of the eighth inning with a two-out, two-strike single as darkness fell. The outcomes threw the race back into a virtual deadlock. The road trip meant that, back in Baltimore, operators at Ford's Theater opened their doors once again to a real-time marionette re-creation of the game. As usual, admission was ten cents, or twenty-five cents for preferred seating.

Meanwhile, team secretary Henry Borman announced that the sale of tickets for the Boston series would not begin until Thursday morning. The delay was an effort to minimize the prospect of the tickets falling into the hands of scalpers. Team officials mapped out what was described as "a plan of campaign" to distribute the tickets.[42] The campaign's points included the following:

1. A special detail of police was to be stationed at and around the team offices within the Baltimore American building at the corner of Baltimore and South Streets.

2. J. Albert Young, a team official, was assigned the duty of actually selling the tickets. Young was chosen because he was "one of the most skillful and rapid men in the country in this specialty."[43]

3. The line of purchasers was to form at the door to the newspaper office on South Street and extend down the street. Ticket buyers were to be admitted at the rate of four at a time. Officers were to be instructed to clear all others from the lobby.

4. Purchasers were to depart from the Baltimore Street entrance.

5. A total of 2,164 reserved seats were to be made available for sale; Young said it would take him just two hours to sell them.

Like a real-war battle plan, the plan of campaign would disintegrate once Thursday came.

Baltimore	85-35	.708	—
Boston	86-36	.705	—

Tuesday, September 21

What the Bridegrooms did to Kid Nichols before 8,560 in the first game had no precedent. Ominous portents arrived even in advance of the first pitch: Long reported with a sore hand, so Allen took his place. The first batter, center fielder Fielder Jones, walked after catcher Charles Ganzel twice dropped his foul pop-ups. A single, a fly ball, and another single over the drawn-in Allen's head—on what would have been the inning's third out, if Ganzel had made either of the foul catches—produced the first two runs. From there the Beaneaters uncharacteristically blew up. Lowe dropped a throw, Allen fumbled a bounder, and six more hits followed in quick succession, the sum of the damage being a full dozen Brooklyn runs before Nichols retired the side. The visitors added five more runs in the fourth, after which Selee finally decided that there was no point in further straining Nichols and brought in Charlie Hickman. "The worst exhibition of baseball ever seen on the grounds," remarked Murnane of the 22–5 outcome. He described Darkhue White as having fainted during the twelve-run first. When he was revived, Murnane reported, Darkhue asked, "Dat cake walk kem to a close?"[44]

During the 4:20 p.m. second game, the Beaneaters were everything they had not been a few hours earlier. Collins started a first-inning double play, and Ted Lewis held the visitors in check and hit safely twice himself during the 9–1 victory.

Before five thousand fans in New York, the Orioles pounded seventeen hits in support of Nops and climbed back into first, thanks to a 10–3 victory over Jouett Meekin. As was becoming almost customary, every Oriole shared in the offense, with Robinson and Nops delivering three hits each. In the first inning alone, hits by Jennings, Kelley, and Stenzel, a walk to Keeler, a throwing error, and a sacrifice fly produced three runs.

Baltimore	86-35	.711	—
Boston	87-37	.702	½

Wednesday, September 22

A strong, chilly wind dampened things for the Boston Rooters, but nothing could have chilled the day's news. A dozen hits permitted

Stivetts to breeze through a 12–0 victory that was called at the end of seven innings because of darkness. The scoreboard's posting of New York's 6–4 win over Baltimore was greeted with rounds of cheers. The teams now were in a virtual tie for the top spot as their decisive series approached. Willie Keeler had his worst day in weeks, getting only one hit in five trips. Organizers of the Royal Rooters' trip announced that seventy-five fans had already signed up and more seats were available. For Keeler, the poor bat work dropped his batting average below .430; even so, he led the league by about thirty points. Despite their second loss to the Giants, the Orioles continued to lead by one percentage point. But Boston led by a half game. At day's end, Selee thrilled Boston's Rooters even more, announcing that he had signed to manage the Beaneaters again in 1898.[45]

Baltimore	86-36	.705	½
Boston	88-37	.704	—

On that same afternoon the nation's chief executive paid his first visit to Boston since his election the previous November. President McKinley and his wife, along with Senator Henry Cabot Lodge, cabinet members, and state officials, arrived in North Adams to deliver an address. Such a figure should have been expected to draw a large crowd, and he did; an estimated forty thousand turned out to see the nation's leader. But it was a measure of the relative importance of the events that when the next morning's newspapers hit the streets, the president's visit shared top billing with the Beaneaters' victory over Brooklyn.

Albert Mott, for one, could have told the president's scheduler it was not a good time to visit Boston if the goal was to get headlines. Remarked Mott of the Orioles-Beaneaters contest, "Don't they keep warm? It is neck and neck. And won't that Boston series in Baltimore pull out some people?"[46]

National League Standings (Evening of September 23)

TEAM	WINS	LOSSES	PERCENTAGE	GAMES BACK
Baltimore	87	36	.707	½
Boston	89	37	.706	—
New York	79	45	.637	9
Cincinnati	70	54	.565	18
Cleveland	65	59	.524	23
Washington	57	67	.460	31
Brooklyn	57	69	.452	32
Pittsburg	56	69	.448	32½
Chicago	55	70	.440	33½
Philadelphia	54	72	.429	35
Louisville	51	73	.411	37
St. Louis	27	96	.220	60½

11. Fall in Baltimore

More than 125 of Boston's Royal Rooters were to detrain at Baltimore's Mt. Royal station on the morning of September 24 for the opening game of the most important series in the history of the National League. As he went to bed at the Eutaw House on September 23, Frank Selee knew he would be glad to see them. But the person he really wanted to see was Marty Bergen.

As night fell in Baltimore, the erratic Boston catcher's whereabouts was unknown to him or any other member of the team's party. Bergen had boarded the boat from Boston to New York after Wednesday's game, but he had disappeared in the big city that evening and had been neither seen nor heard from since.

Given Bergen's unstable personality, Selee fancied all manner of explanations for the player's disappearance. He could have gotten in a fight over some stranger's slight and been injured or thrown in jail. He could have taken offense at a comment that other players would have brushed off. If so, he might be back on his Massachusetts farm by now. It might not even have been a real slight; as the Boston players had already seen on several occasions, Bergen was capable of dreaming up a problem and then reacting to it. For the good of the team and the player, Selee put out a cover story: Marty was ailing, his arm was sore, and he needed a rest.

All Selee knew was that he didn't want to face Baltimore's lineup of devil-may-care base runners without his best arm behind the plate. It

Fig. 19. Outside the Eutaw House in Baltimore, the visiting Beaneaters, backed by more than 125 of their Rooters and a hired band (balcony), pose for a group picture on the morning of Saturday, September 25, 1897. The superstitious Billy Hamilton blamed this picture for Boston's loss that afternoon. (McGreevey Collection, Boston Public Library, Print Department.)

had not been that long since Doc Yeager had subbed for the injured Bergen during the club's season-opening series. The Orioles had run the bases at will and won all three games. Marty Bergen was one of the few catchers in the league—perhaps the only catcher—whose arm the Orioles base runners respected. Marty Bergen could control them . . . if Marty Bergen was here.

Selee didn't blame Bergen for his absence; he blamed himself. He suspected the problem was the exhibition game that the Bostons had scheduled for the previous afternoon in Orange, New Jersey. Sched-

Fig. 20. Flag and bean pot in hand, Louis Watson leads Boston's Rooters in cheers. (McGreevey Collection, Boston Public Library, Print Department.)

uling exhibitions on off days was a common practice for league teams and an easy way to pick up a few nickels. That's why Boston had agreed weeks earlier to play the game. But those few nickels were nothing compared to the stakes in this series—the pennant and the chance to end Baltimore's dynasty. Selee also wanted to prevent the Orioles from claiming the honor Baltimore had denied Selee three years earlier—a fourth consecutive league championship. With all that on the line, and given the reports of rain in New Jersey, he had done the logical thing, wiring his regrets and then proceeding directly from New York to Baltimore.[1] Hadn't anybody told Bergen? Was the team's defensive mainstay marooned in New Jersey?

Even the weather disturbed Selee's sleep. A heavy rain that hit the host city Wednesday evening continued into Thursday. The rain also made life miserable for the fans, who waited outside for tickets. To prevent speculators from taking advantage of the heavy demand, Orioles management had raised the price of reserved seat tickets to seventy-five cents and withheld their sale until the day before the game.[2] An additional rule was imposed: no more than two seats per customer, unless the customer was known to the Orioles management to have need of more. Against such preparations, scalpers resorted to their tried and true retinue of tricks. They enlisted boys to stand in line for them. They purchased tickets, changed clothes, and got in line again. This required more fortitude than the profession of scalper usually commanded, for it meant they would have to stand in line in the rain.

And it was a long line. When the seats finally went on sale, the cordon of rain-soaked fans stretched several blocks down Baltimore Street, from the baseball office to the corner of South and Baltimore.

That evening the Beaneaters did something that would have seemed incongruous most of the summer, given the contentious nature of the race. They socialized with the Orioles. Players from both sides were presented complementary tickets to the presentation of *A Man from Mexico* at Ford's Theater.[3] The theater management could not conceive of anything more rewarding in the way of publicity for its show.

As in Boston, all of Baltimore was abuzz with talk of the game. The *Baltimore American* expressed the myopia with which Baltimore alone viewed its heroes. "They have played the game in a way that has almost revolutionized it. . . . They have won the admiration of all who love good sport."[4] That was on the editorial page. The sports pages assumed a more openly defensive tone that was decidedly prone to suspecting a fix. "Umpires have been interviewed to the end that they wish the Bostons to win," the paper's sports page assured Baltimoreans. "Anything at all doubtful was always given against the Orioles. This was an unvarying rule. . . . To overcome it and win the flag would be a most remarkable achievement."[5]

Like most Orioles fans, the *Baltimore Sun* expected the home club to emerge with the victory. "If the champions will only play the kind of ball they are capable of, they are invincible," the newspaper told readers. At the same time it conceded that Boston played the steadier game. "It is doubtful, however, if the Bostons can stand the driving finish that the Orioles will give them—or ought to."[6]

Although Nick Young rarely assigned more than one umpire, he had from time to time assigned a second for an important series. This one certainly qualified. Hugh Duffy had argued often for expansion of that practice, saying, "The League can get twelve good umpires better than it can find six because the work will be lighter and the mental and physical strain much less."[7] The Boston captain was delighted to learn from personnel at the Eutaw House that both Tim Hurst and Bob Emslie had been seen in town.

The Rooters pulled in around noon from their all-night trip. Most of the chatter on the train had been about which team would win two of three, and the sentiment was by no means unanimous that it would be the Boston club. Not only were the Orioles three-time champions, they had also won five of the teams' first nine games, and they were at home. Most of the Rooters, however, expressed confidence in the Bostons.

Breakfast had been served promptly at 6:00 a.m., and the New York papers carried a fascinating rumor: Jack Doyle had been sold to Brooklyn.[8] This particular nugget turned out to be premature. Doyle, who had worn out his welcome in Baltimore, was to be sold, but only after the season was over—and to Washington, not Brooklyn.

At the Jersey City train station the Boston delegation had been met by a supplementary party that included Arthur Barrett, whose brother was a Massachusetts congressman, retired *Boston Herald* editor Jack Keeler, and humorist Augustus Howell. It is not known precisely how many people made the organized trip; contemporary accounts vary from about 125 to nearly 300.[9] The *Boston Globe*, which purported to have obtained a complete list, published 120 names but reported 125 in attendance.

But if the size of the traveling party is uncertain, this much is clear: it comprised a representative sample of the city's fan base. In the fashion of the age, the men, as well as the handful of women accompanying them, stepped off the train dressed more for an evening on the town than for a ballgame. They wore business suits, many with ties, and proper headgear. Congressman Fitzgerald was there, of course, as was Nuf Ced McGreevy, packing his ever-present megaphone. The front rank included Charlie Lavis, whose dignified appearance evaporated once he was in his grandstand seat. Equally recognizable was Louis Watson, who was thin and wore a handlebar mustache that drooped under the heat of the excitement. You could hear Watson's shrill voice from almost any part of the park, and you could spot him by the broomstick he carried to the games. Two items hung from the broomstick: an American flag and a bean pot. If one of the Orioles fans tried to keep Lou Watson from waving that broomstick to rally his team, there would be trouble.[10]

Friday, September 24

The Rooters arrived with three other signature items. The first was a medallion—or more precisely, medallions. The newspaper industry was highly competitive in Boston at the time, with nearly a dozen dailies. Several tried to outdo each other in promoting the Rooters' trip, to the extent of passing out commemorative medals for the fans to wear while in Baltimore. Each newspaper designed a slightly different medal that played on the Rooters' theme. The *Boston Globe*, for example, offered a brass bar with the inscription "Boston Rooters," which supported a red, white, and blue ribbon modeled after the American flag. From the flag hung an enameled medallion featuring Satan poised atop a beanpot.[11] The *Boston Herald*'s simpler medal featured a bar inscribed "1897 Boston Rooters," which also supported a flag-type ribbon from which hung a simpler brass beanpot.[12] Each newspaper tried to suggest to readers back home that their medal was far and away the most prized; the Rooters wore as many of the medals as they could lay their hands on.

The second type of signature item was noisemakers. Some could even be described as musical instruments. We know that at least one bass drum came down on the train from Boston, and the evidence suggests that trumpets, kazoos, and tubas also made the trip. But Rooters' instruments were more basic. Tin horns, cowbells, kitchen pans, and megaphones all were acceptable. When the spirit rose, the Rooters weren't above poetry either. One Rooter, Gil Burt, penned a parody of "Maryland, My Maryland" designed to bedevil Orioles fans as the Rooters marched en masse from the station to the Union Park. One of the defiant stanzas went as follows:

> *You've won the flag three times before,*
>   *Baltimore, my Baltimore.*
> *You'll have to fight to make it four,*
>   *Baltimore, My Baltimore.*
> *A club is after you it seems,*
> *From that far land of pork and beans,*
> *And of that pennant they have dreams,*
>   *Baltimore, My Baltimore.*[13]

The Rooters brought one final item to Baltimore with them: money. No record exists of precisely how much cash changed hands at and around the grounds. But given the confidence with which Orioles fans also approached the series, it seems safe to speculate that a visiting Boston loyalist seeking to put down a wager would have been able to locate a willing taker, either from Baltimore or from the frontiers of Orioles fandom. A large delegation from Bel Air, thirty miles to the north of the city, chartered a train of their own to get to the park and sat as a group behind home plate. Smaller groups came in from Frederick, Hagerstown, and Annapolis.[14]

Back in Boston, meanwhile, Rooters who had been unable to make the trip crowded into the Music Hall or other theaters, which set up competing simulations of the games. City newspapers estimated the turnout inside the Music Hall alone at four thousand, many arriving well before the scheduled 3:00 p.m. first pitch to ensure good seats. Along Newspaper Row, larger crowds gathered to watch the reports of events on scoreboards erected outside each of the newspaper offices. The dailies competed with one another to be the first to post telegraphed results. In Baltimore hundreds more lined up in three working lines outside the Orioles' ticket offices again on Friday morning to claim the remaining seats and any available standing room. By noon, after the ticket sellers had failed to dent the demand, they transferred operations up to the ballpark itself and continued to work. That filled Huntington Avenue with a volatile mixture of street cars, bicyclists, foot traffic, and people waiting in line. Two and one-half hours before the first pitch, one thousand fans already were in their seats, mostly filling the bleachers and overflowing onto the field. Some climbed the outfield fence, literally sitting or hanging on it if that provided their best view. Observers described every nearby roof as being filled. Considering the thirteen thousand estimated to be in attendance, the throng of freeloaders around the park, and the thousands more watching one re-creation or another, it seems plausible that more than twenty-five thousand fans in the two cities put themselves in position to view the game.

And that only included Boston and Baltimore. For one of the first times in the history of American sport, wire services set up entire communication networks so as to send developments nationwide more or less instantaneously. Perhaps only the Sullivan-Corbett and Corbett-Fitzsimmons heavyweight title fights had commanded such attention previously. Fifteen telegraph operators clicked off play-by-play to subscribing systems, either for use in remote re-creations or simply to keep groups huddled at thousands of bulletin boards and tickers in towns small and large apprised of what was happening. The game's outcome was the lead item on sports pages in cities as distant as Los

Angeles.[15] Most of the major newspapers in New York, Philadelphia, Chicago, Washington, and other cities sent or hired special correspondents, overflowing the Union Park "press box," which was really nothing more than a cordoned-off section of the grandstand. As a result, the dozen or so scribes who might normally attend a Boston-Baltimore game found themselves jousting and elbowing for space with dozens more. League president Nick Young had no such problems, enjoying the game with chief of umpires John B. Day from the private box of Orioles president Harry Von der Horst. Even better for Selee than all the Rooters in attendance was that Marty Bergen was in attendance too. He had indeed gone on to New Jersey for the canceled exhibition game, arriving on the overnight train. Had he not, the Beaneaters might have been questionable at three positions. Herman Long's arm was still sore, and Jimmy Collins took a bad-hop grounder in the eye during pregame warm-ups, which caused the eye to swell shut. Considering Collins's value to the team and the critical moment at hand, there was only one thing to do and Selee did it. He sent the team's batboy out to a nearby drugstore for leeches. By the first pitch, the leeches had done their duty for the Boston cause.[16]

As befitted the occasion, both managers sent their aces—Kid Nichols, 29-12, and Joe Corbett, 24-6—to pitch. From the first batters, the teams' competing identities asserted themselves. Billy Hamilton stepped in and took a ball, prompting Harry Rosenfield, the Rooters' designated cheerleader, to call for a chorus of "Hit 'er up again, BOSTON!" "An unearthly din," Orioles fans described it, and they would spend much of the afternoon trying to drown it out, with moderate success. After a strike, Corbett missed with another pitch. At least that's what Hurst said; John McGraw vehemently disagreed and let the umpire know it. Within a few seconds, Hamilton had struck out.

The Orioles found their step early. McGraw took a strike and four balls from Nichols, making his way to first amid the home crowd howl. When the reliable Willie Keeler failed to move him over, instead popping out, McGraw simply took off for second and stole it when Bergen's throw sailed high. Hughie Jennings got a fastball to his liking and slammed it past Long into left field, sending McGraw around with the game's first run. When Joe Kelley followed with a solid line drive over Hugh Duffy's head to deep left field, Jennings raced around and the Orioles led 2–0. With a potential third run in scoring position and just one out, Baltimore wasted a chance to deal further damage to Nichols. Jake Stenzel popped up and Jack Doyle went down swinging.

Through four innings, Corbett held Boston without a base runner, thanks in large measure—Boston fans insisted—to Hurst. They clamored when Chick Stahl opened the second by lining a pitch down the left-field line for an apparent double, only to see the plate umpire wave it foul. Of course, the hisses and jeers of "robber" were drowned out by cheers from the thousands of Baltimore partisans. They had brought their own bells and horns, and they were not shy about putting them to use in an effort to out-yell the Rooters. Stahl slapped the next pitch on a convenient hop to Jennings. In Baltimore's half of that same inning, Wilbert Robinson tried to bunt his way on base. Collins, who had built his reputation on throwing out the speediest Orioles at the top of the order, had no problem disposing of the portly catcher. McGraw led off the third with a line single, and the home crowd braced themselves in anticipation of what Keeler might make of that opportunity. Sure enough, he dropped a bunt down the third base line only to see Collins make the one-handed pickup and flash a throw across the diamond. Bob Emslie called him out amid only the mildest protest, and McGraw reached second as the play's consolation prize. He watched the rest of the inning from there, while Jennings rolled easily to Nichols and Long got in the way of Kelley's line drive.

In the fourth inning Fred Tenney finally gave the Rooters something to cheer about. It wasn't much—a walk—but when Bobby Lowe doubled past Stenzel into center field, it presented the visitors with their first scoring opportunity. Doyle helped them cash in on it, fumbling Stahl's line-hugging ground ball. With Lowe now representing the tying run at third, Duffy lunged at a Corbett off-speed pitch and popped it weakly behind the plate. Robinson put that away, and Doyle ended the inning with an easy play on Collins's roller to the bag.

The contest turned in the next two half innings. Stenzel opened the Baltimore half of the fourth with a soft line drive in front of Hamilton. The fastest player in the league first loped in on the ball, then decided he had a chance to make the catch and picked up his pace. It was too late; the ball hit in front of him and rolled through his legs. Stenzel reached third. Now Union Park vibrated with the sound of the home club's fans anticipating a two-run lead. But it was not to be. Doyle grounded directly at Collins, and Stenzel—caught too far off third base—was forced to try for home, where Collins's throw easily retired him. Then Bergen threw Doyle out as he attempted to steal second. With Collins's two plays on the Robinson and Keeler bunts and his throw to get Stenzel out, this was the fourth time in four innings that an Oriole had been retired on the bases.

Doyle's out also fueled the Rooters, whose cheers assaulted the home fans with nauseating repetition. Long stirred them further with a base hit to open the fifth. As Watson egged the delegation on with his bean pot, Bergen found a gap between Stenzel and Keeler, and the tying run scored. Satisfied with himself, Bergen pulled up at second, declining an opportunity to take third and forcing Nichols to try to bunt him there. The pitcher failed and fanned, as did Hamilton. Corbett elected to pitch around the left-handed Tenney, walking him and bringing Lowe to the plate. Again the grandstand and bleachers rocked with noise. Lowe's base hit gave Boston its first lead of the afternoon, 3–2.

Again and again, the Orioles tried their inside baseball, only to either botch it or see the visitors trump it. In the bottom of the fifth, McGraw tried to bunt his way on base but popped the ball easily to Nichols. Keeler opened the bottom of the sixth with a base hit, but Bergen cut him down trying to steal second to a chorus of Boston fish horns.

In the seventh, Corbett cracked under the accumulated pressure of the baiting visiting fans and the one-run deficit. Nichols opened with a base hit and Hamilton rolled an easy grounder out to him. But the pitcher threw hurriedly and wildly, retiring nobody and letting both runners take an extra base. When he followed that with a run-producing wild pitch, the score was 4–2. Tenney pushed a bunt toward Corbett, and it worked for a base hit and another run. The Beaneaters added a sixth run in the top of the eighth. Duffy walked against Arlie Pond, who came in to start the inning. Then he stole second on Robinson and scored when Long doubled into the populace behind the ropes in left.

Having constructed their lead on their offense and their arms, the Bostons set about to preserve it with simple glove work. In the bottom of the seventh, Tenney's one-handed stab of Long's wide throw brought the crowd to its feet. In the eighth, two walks and an infield hit filled the bases for Stenzel. The Orioles center fielder sent a vicious line drive toward left, only to see Long leap and snare the ball before it landed for two sure runs. "It was one of the greatest catches ever seen on a ball ground, and the Boston players had a laugh on the champions," Tim Murnane asserted. The Rooters had a particularly meaningful way of recognizing such plays, whether by the bat or the glove: they pelted their hero with silver coins on his return to the bench. Long enjoyed such a pelting as he trotted in from short at the end of the eighth.[17]

That may have been Long's richest moment of the afternoon, but it was not his finest. As 5:00 p.m. ticked away and darkness began to settle in, Doyle opened the bottom of the ninth with a line drive past Nichols into center field. Heinie Reitz followed with a bloop hit to right. With Boileryard Clarke on the coaching line stirring up the bleacherites (although they needed no stirring up), the atmosphere was so loud that telegraph operators could not hear the click of their keys. Most of the rattling was aimed at Nichols, who until that instant had not allowed more than one hit in an inning since the first.

Now the Orioles crowd joined in the strategy as well as the noise. In those days it was the custom for fans to politely return fouled balls onto the field of play so they could be used again. In fact, baseballs would be used until they were lost or so worn down that they were literally unplayable. Of course, a mushy ball was harder to hit; that was why home teams, given the option, frequently chose to bat first in that era. Now Robinson fouled a pitch back into the Baltimore loyalists, one of whom breached etiquette (but not strategy) by refusing to return the ball.[18] Under the circumstances, Hurst had no option but to throw a new white ball—one that would be easier to see and easier to hit—into play. Robinson raked the inviting target into left for a single that let Doyle prance home. Suddenly the tying run—in the person of pinch hitter Joe Quinn—was at the plate with none out. Nichols disposed of him, but McGraw scratched out a hit of his own to score Reitz.

With Keeler up next, the Boston margin reduced to 6–4, only one out, and Orioles at first and second, the park's seats were no longer in use. Not only did the fans strain the ropes separating them from the fielders in the outfield, but several of the more zealous Rooters escaped the bounds of the grandstand and slipped their way into foul territory by the Boston bench. The suspense was over almost before anyone realized it. Nichols sent a pitch low and away to Keeler, who punched it on a line past the pitcher. Acting on instinct, Robinson took three fatal steps toward third before realizing that Long would head off the ball. From there it was child's play for the Boston shortstop to step on second and complete a game-ending double play.

The posting of the final score touched off celebrations throughout New England, which then as now viewed any team representing Boston as representing itself as well. In Lowell and Salem, where re-creations of the contest were unavailable, crowds rushed to the carts that delivered the evening newspapers, claiming thousands of copies. Along Newspaper Row in Boston, the *Boston Globe* proudly related that "small boys yelled themselves hoarse" hawking the result to anxious fans.[19] In clubs, hotels, and homes around the town, celebrations echoed.

No place was hotter than the Eutaw House, where both the visiting players and the Rooters were headquartered. The fans tooted horns and cheered every step of the way from the ballpark to the hotel. When they got there, Frank Selee held an impromptu public interview, during which he essentially guaranteed victory in the pennant race. Congressman Fitzgerald decided that what the Rooters really needed was more noise, so he took up a collection to hire a band. That assemblage performed a concert for the visitors at the Eutaw House and then agreed to the important assignment of accompanying the Rooters to the grounds the next day.[20]

As the team came down for its postgame dinner, the Rooters, almost all of whom were hoarse by then, summoned up enough voice to stand in a long salute to each player. It was said that the building shook. Much of newspaper reporting, especially sports reporting, in the late nineteenth century has to be read with a wary eye toward rhetorical flourish. But given the Eutaw House's wood construction and the fact that it was already a half-century old, it is entirely plausible to take the assertion literally. The celebration continued long into the night, making the Eutaw House's bartenders possibly the only resident Baltimoreans who welcomed the visitors' win. The jubilation certainly meant a longer night for Selee and his players, who were trying to get some sleep upstairs. As he went to bed, Selee had a second problem: Collins. He had gone zero for four—although fielding five chances flawlessly—with that swollen eye, and in the relative calm and cool of the evening it had closed again. That meant that by morning, more leeches would make a banquet of the Boston third baseman's face.

Saturday, September 25

"There is no reason for despair," the next morning's *Baltimore Sun* advised the home team's fans. In a bow to the Boston Rooters, the *Sun* added a welcome and a caution. "They were hilarious at the result of the game, but it will be well for them to remember that 'he who laughs last laughs best.'"[21]

Before that day's game, the Rooters and the visiting players gathered on the hotel's front porch for a group photo. At least one player, Billy Hamilton, thought that was going too far. The center fielder, probably the most superstitious Beaneater, believed such a show of arrogance was sure to put a hoodoo on the club.[22]

Fans, meanwhile, pressed the search for tickets at the team office, and some of them resorted to subterfuges. A half-dozen fashionably dressed women presented themselves Saturday morning at the long line outside the downtown headquarters. In a display of gallantry, the waiting fans stepped aside to let the ladies move to the front. It turned out that scalpers had hired the women.[23]

Favored by the fact that it was Saturday, the crowd pressing in on Union Park was, if anything, larger and more rabid than the previous day's crowd. Von der Horst eventually put the paid attendance at about fourteen thousand, a club record. But as with Friday's game, thousands more watched for free, either from atop nearby houses and utility poles or by climbing the back fence. Among the paid crowd, an overflow again gathered in the recesses of left field. Two of the standees, unable to see the action through the throng in front of them, tried innovative measures. Each bought a beer keg, which they stood on until they were approached by two official-looking men who advised them that it was illegal under the city's laws to stand on a box or keg. The two dutifully stepped down, whereupon the official-looking men stepped up and watched the game from the kegs themselves.[24]

As it had done the previous day, the Baltimore police department sent fifty men to maintain order, again with indifferent success. Despite the fact that the Rooters occupied all of the space reserved for Boston fans, Congressman Fitzgerald somehow managed to secure room in foul territory for the band the visitors had hired. But although the park was full an hour before the scheduled 3:30 p.m. start, and although there was plenty of racket, the affair was carried off without any of the rancor that had marked much of the season. That may have been due in part to the fact that most of the Rooters had lost their voices. Harry Rosenfield, the chief cheerleader, surrendered his position to his designated aide, Dr. Isaac Louis, before Saturday's first pitch.[25] Back in Boston there was no rancor either—merely the cheers of thousands gathered at the Boston Music Hall. At the various offices on Newspaper Row that featured less elaborate but free play-by-play recountings, fans began claiming the best viewing spots by 8:00 a.m. for the 3:30 p.m. first pitch.

Fred Klobedanz took the mound against Bill Hoffer for the second game, to the strains of "There'll Be a Hot Time in the Old Town To-night," courtesy of the Rooters' band.[26] After just a handful of pitches, both teams had displayed their strengths. Hamilton led off with a smash past the pitcher's mound into center field. The second hitter, Fred Tenney, did the same, but Hughie Jennings was cheating toward second to guard against a stolen base and was able to flag it down for a force out. It was slick work, and even slicker was Jennings's handling of Bobby Lowe's one-hopper for an inning-ending double play.

Protests by Hugh Duffy and Fred Tenney, when Bob Emslie ruled that Willie Keeler had beaten out his one-out grounder to Long, set off cries of outrage in the Boston section of the grandstand. Klobe-danz threw Jennings out, but Kelley's base hit sent Keeler home from second with the game's first run. Orioles fans treated it as just another run; the Bostonians howled that they'd been robbed. But there was no robbery imputed in the Orioles' two second-inning runs, merely Collins's bad judgment compounded by bad execution.

After a single and a double, the Orioles had runners at second and third with two out and McGraw at bat. Given the game situation, Mc-Graw's .325 batting average, and Collins's reputation as a fielder, prob-ably the least likely strategy was a bunt. Yet that's what McGraw did. He pushed one a bit too hard toward the third base line. In the batter's haste to reach first, the bunt was imperfectly placed. Over the course of the season, McGraw had authored dozens of better bunt attempts; observers agreed this one was bound to roll foul. Collins raced in and tried to field the ball but instead kicked it into foul territory, letting Doyle at third and Hoffer at second both score. The Orioles led 3–0.

As a .300 hitter, Klobedanz could power his own offense as well as any pitcher. He lined a one-out single in the third and took second when Robinson let a pitch get past him. One out later, Tenney walked, filling the bases. Hoffer fanned a wild-swinging Lowe on three pitches. Then

Chick Stahl brought the crowd to its feet with a wallop down the right-field line, only to see it disappear at the last second into the crowd on the foul side of the pole. Hoffer got him on the next pitch.

In the fifth inning Klobedanz again rallied the spectators but not his teammates, sending a drive off the fence in center for a one-out double. Hamilton whiffed and Tenney lofted one that Stenzel ran under and caught.

Hoffer, who until that moment had essentially mastered all of the visitors' batters except for his counterpart, weakened in the seventh. Long started it with a double into the populace behind the ropes in left. Bergen drove Stenzel to the ropes again to run down his fly ball, and then Klobedanz got Boston's first run home with his third hit, a single. When Hoffer walked Hamilton and Tenney followed with a single, competing roars rose could be heard for blocks around. Lowe slapped a dangerous grounder to McGraw, whose throw to Jennings forced Tenney for the second out. Jennings's relay to Jack Doyle could have ended the threat, but Lowe won Emslie's call and Klobedanz scored to bring the Beaneaters within a run. Now it was the Orioles delegation taking out after Emslie, while the Bostonians defended him.

At that potentially decisive moment, Lowe tried to bring Baltimore's inside baseball to work against its creators, taking off for second as part of a double steal designed to get the tying run home. With two out, Robinson fired high toward second, but Hamilton failed to break on the throw, prompting Lowe to retreat to first. When Reitz threw to Doyle in an effort to get the fleeing Lowe, Hamilton finally did take off. Doyle turned the play to the plate with a hurried one-hop throw that sent Robinson sprawling after it. He, the ball, and Hamilton met in a heap a few inches in front of the plate. Although Hurst could have declared the runner safe due to Robinson's interference, he did not. Instead, Robinson gathered the ball and—still forming a human barricade between Hamilton and the plate—tagged him for the third out.[27]

Having survived that scare, the Orioles put the game out of reach in the bottom of the seventh. Keeler's single preceded one by Jennings that Hamilton bobbled, the scorer crediting Jennings with a double. Both runners scored on Kelley's single. The Orioles appeared poised for more when Stenzel followed with a double of his own. But Kelley played it safe, stopping at third. He was retired when Tenney took in Doyle's bunt attempt and fired to Bergen at the plate.

Boston's final threat produced a run in the eighth. But after three straight hits, Klobedanz finally failed, anxiously striking out with the tying runners on base and two out. "He could not have touched [the pitches] with a fishpole," Tim Murnane lamented.[28] Doubles by Robinson and Jennings produced a sixth and final Baltimore run in the eighth. With Lowe's game-ending ground out, the Orioles resumed the position atop the standings by the margin of one percentage point.[29]

Although conceding that the Orioles deserved to win, most of the Boston correspondents saw the outcome as a result of poor play by the visitors, especially Collins (for his lapse on McGraw's bunt) and Hamilton. The box score appeared to exonerate Hamilton; it showed two hits in three at bats, five put-outs, and no errors. But Murnane pointed to Jennings's ostensible single in the seventh that went for two bases and to the costly nap Hamilton had taken at third when Lowe broke on the potential double steal in the seventh. The *Boston Journal*'s Walter Barnes suggested that the outcome might have been influenced by Friday night's postgame shenanigans. "The Bostons lacked the dash which characterized their work of the day previous, and it is a question whether there was too much 'rooting' about the Eutaw House last night for the good of the players," he reported.[30]

At least nobody could find fault with the atmosphere within the park itself, a mood that after two games had strangely turned almost fraternal. Despite the season-long antipathies between supporters of the two teams, at game's end the Baltimore fans gathered in front of the Boston Rooters' seats. From the crowd, someone yelled, "Three cheers for the Boston team and Boston Rooters!"[31] That touched off a wave of cheers that washed back across the thousands on the field. "A marvelous change in attitude," remarked Barnes, who recalled instances where visiting fans were pelted with stones. "The good feeling has been so spontaneous that it does not seem possible that its sincerity is only a mask."[32] At the Eutaw House, Rooters seemed almost puzzled by their reception. "We expected to be obnoxious to the crowd here," one Rooter explained. Instead, the Rooters acknowledged being "agreeably surprised" when they were cheered for their sportsmanship following the Saturday Baltimore victory.[33] Suggested the *Baltimore Sun*, "Such an incident, so spontaneous and so hearty, ought to forever stamp the allegations of Baltimore partisans' unfairness as maliciously false and unjust."[34] While there was little chance of that occurring, the Rooters returned the salute with cheers of their own for their hosts.

Monday, September 27

While the Rooters spent Sunday in Washington (or took advantage of a railroad promotion to purchase one-dollar roundtrip tickets for Philadelphia), the Boston players enjoyed leisurely tours of the city's parks. Several, including Collins and Tenney, made the short walk that evening up Eutaw Street from the hotel to the Diamond Café at 519. N. Howard Street.[35] They were welcomed by Robinson and McGraw, the latter telling the Boston reporters, "Collins and Tenney are the greatest players that ever covered third and first base ... it's almost impossible to bunt on them."[36] For the first time since the series' opening pitch, Collins could see through his left eye unaided by leeches.

When Monday morning arrived, the train disgorged fifty more Rooters. Three and one-half hours before the first pitch, the box office was sold out of the day's reserved seats, and speculators commanded six to ten times the face value. Lines backed up two blocks. Even the trolley lines required ten minutes to make their way through the assemblage. By midday, railings around the ticket office had collapsed against the weight of those in line, and the fall of those railings in turn damaged the floor space, making even walking treacherous. Von der Horst himself took a turn in the ticket line.

Officials at the park extended the rope that held the overflow back; now it stretched across the entire expanse of the outfield and lapped over toward the infield foul ground. The police department added more officers to those already pulling extra duty. The *Baltimore Sun* compared excitement around town to that surrounding a presidential election, concluding, "This is the great day."[37]

The steps taken to manage the crowd proved inadequate to handle what would become both the largest paid audience and the largest overall crowd ever to see a baseball game. Excursion trains brought fans from Washington and Philadelphia as well as hundreds of smaller towns. By the time the teams came out for pregame practice, all the standing room and all the roped-off areas were full. Estimates at that early hour put twenty thousand people on the scene. Yet there was no letup. Fans piled against an outfield wagon gate, knocking it down. Officials estimated that seven hundred poured through before repairs could be made. One boy broke his arm in the crush and was hospitalized; a policeman sustained three fractured ribs.[38] Spectators climbed atop the fence from foul pole to foul pole. Some fans tore at the fence itself, removing slats for use as makeshift seats. The count went up to twenty-five thousand, then twenty-eight thousand, and finally thirty thousand. That did not count an estimated several thousand more who claimed rooftop perches or scaled poles for a view from outside. The *Baltimore Sun* reported additional crowds around its scoreboard outside the newspaper office. Commerce stopped.

Back in Boston, packs estimated at upwards of twenty thousand braved a raw afternoon to take up positions alongside the blackboard scoreboards erected on Newspaper Row. For the more fortunate, the Music Hall sold its capacity of seats for the day's re-creation well before noon.

The one group unruffled by the crowd was the Rooters, now numbering close to two hundred, who arrived with their own police escort. Crammed atop three thirty-foot-long horse-drawn barges, they formed a parade to the park in front of the coach carrying the visiting players. When they arrived, the players found the crowd, which had gathered as close as twenty feet from the field of play, denying them easy access to their own benches. Most simply plunked themselves down on the grass in foul territory.

Well before the game, the partisans renewed the mutual cheers with which Saturday's game had ended. The Boston Rooters' band struck up "Maryland, My Maryland," prompting a parkwide chorus. "Yankee Doodle" and then "Dixie" followed, the fans cheering as if they were one. Baltimore fans responded with cheers of their own. Their favorite: "Rah! Rah! Rah! Baltimore! We'll win the pennant three times more!"[39]

The clubs' managers chose their game starters, Joe Corbett and Kid Nichols, who pitched on just two days' rest. Selee could have turned to Ted Lewis, 20-11, who had rested since Tuesday and was the author of a shutout against the Orioles in the August series. "Just why Lewis is not tried is not clear," the *Baltimore Sun* remarked.[40] Or he could have used Jack Stivetts, 11-4, who also was rested and was coming off two starts in which he had allowed just one run. But Lewis was a rookie, Stivetts was a second-line figure, and neither had been tested under pressure like Nichols, already a thirty-game winner and widely considered the equal of any pitcher in the league. Hanlon's pick puzzled many Baltimore fans. Jerry Nops, 19-6 and undefeated since early August, had not pitched in nearly a week. And Arlie Pond, who seemed to have fallen out of Hanlon's favor despite an 18-8 record, had not started in nearly ten days. The *Sun* wrongly told readers it would be Nops. In the end, Hanlon granted Corbett his wish for a chance at revenge against the team that had beaten him in the first game.

That second-guessing gathered steam when Hamilton opened the game with a single that loosened the throats and lungs of the Rooters. Tenney walked, and Lowe delivered the expected sacrifice bunt, putting two runners in scoring position with one out for Chick Stahl. He drove a low liner back toward the mound that deflected off Corbett's fingers to Jennings. The shortstop threw Stahl out at first but could not prevent Hamilton from scoring. Worse, the ball badly jammed several of the fingers on Corbett's pitching hand, forcing him from the game. Hanlon motioned for Nops as a replacement. Tenney, in a daring example of Baltimore's own style of play, tried to steal home on a 1-2 pitch, but Robinson tagged him out, limiting the inning's damage to a single run.

It took the Orioles little time to rebound against Nichols. Keeler dropped a base hit over Lowe's head and reached second on a passed ball. Long, the fielding hero of Friday, kicked Jennings's grounder, allowing Keeler to score the tying run. Nichols, well off his game, followed a walk to Kelley by hitting Stenzel, filling the bases for Doyle. He sent what should have been an inning-ending double-play ball to Collins. But the Boston third baseman fumbled it and was fortunate to get a force at second as Jennings scored. Bergen's passed ball and Collins's muff, which was not scored as an error because he did record an out, set the tone for the tension-filled game, which would see the two best fielding teams in the league combine for eight actual errors. The lead change set a tone as well; it was the first of four in four innings.

Fans who favored Nops to start ahead of Corbett might have been reassured when he took the mound for the second inning with a lead. If so, their excitement was short-lived. A walk, an infield grounder, and Long's single plated the tying run; then Bergen backed Stenzel into the thunder of the pressing crowd for a fly ball that the center fielder dropped. It cost two bases in the short term and two runs when Nichols singled through second. The Beaneaters were back on top, now 4–2.

But they proved as incapable as the Orioles of playing through the cauldron of noise that the park had become. Providence favored the Orioles when Robinson opened the inning with a drive down the left-field line that Hurst ruled fair to the extended protests of the Beaneaters. Hanlon, who had not wanted to go to Nops to start the game, now let him go after a single inning of work in which he had allowed three runs, although just one was earned. He sent up Hoffer as a pinch hitter with instructions to take the mound as of the third inning. Given that Hoffer would be working on one day's rest, the move could only be viewed as a vote of no confidence in Nops. Hoffer singled deep enough that even the lumbering Robinson could score his team's third run.

With Hoffer running, McGraw sent what looked like an easy roller to Long. But the normally sure shortstop flung a wild throw into the crowd behind Tenney, permitting Hoffer to trot home with the tying run and letting McGraw advance all the way to third. After Keeler drew a walk, Nichols speared Kelley's grounder in time to retire McGraw at the plate, but Keeler reached third and then Kelley broke for second on a designed double steal. Lowe could have cut the ball off in front of the base and retired Keeler, but he let it go through and Kelley beat Bergen's attempt as Keeler scored the lead run. To the Orioles, Long's physical miscue and Lowe's mental one were gifts. But conceding that, the base running of McGraw, Keeler, and Kelley constituted the kind of freewheeling ball the Orioles had made their hallmark. Now they needed Hoffer to hold the lead.

He held it only briefly. With one out and Duffy and Collins on base, Hoffer fielded Long's bounder and threw the ball over Doyle's head. Duffy scored, tying the game 5–5, and Collins reached third. Bergen cracked a sharp line drive down the third base line. But McGraw reacted quickly, speared it, and threw to Doyle at first in time to double Long off the base.

Finally, in Baltimore's half of the third, somebody was retired without scoring. In the top of the fourth, the Orioles showed that they too could succumb to pressure. After Nichols was disposed of on strikes, Hamilton singled and stole second, colliding with Jennings as the shortstop tried to reach for Robinson's wide throw. Hoffer walked Tenney, Lowe lined a clean single to center, and Hamilton raced for home with the lead run. As he had done two days earlier, Robinson tried to block the plate, but Hamilton lowered his shoulder and leveled the catcher, scoring the tying run. Tenney scored his team's seventh run on Stahl's single. Lowe reached third on that play, and he too scored when Robinson misplayed Hoffer's first pitch to Long. Four innings were not yet in the books, and the Beaneaters had forced Hanlon to use three pitchers. They had scored eight times, but it was by no means certain that that would be enough.

From the bottom of the fourth through the sixth inning, the game proceeded in something resembling a normal pace and order. Collins lost an out in the fourth when the crowd prevented him from reaching what should have been an easy pop-up off of Keeler's bat—and Keeler followed with a single. But the home team did nothing with the opportunity. In any event, Collins made up for it in the seventh, climbing behind the ropes to outwrestle the fans for Robinson's foul. Hoffer, meanwhile, dispatched the Beaneaters on one hit over the next two innings. But he was tiring. That and the way the immense crowd impinged upon the playing area fueled a seventh-inning explosion.

Duffy opened the seventh with a sharp single. Collins got a fastball and rattled the crowd behind the ropes in right. With Beaneaters at second and third, Long drilled another fastball into the crowd in center, scoring both of them. Watching their pennant prospects recede into that outfield gathering, Orioles partisans snarled, complaining that on a normal field, Keeler and Stenzel would have run down both runners. And Boston wasn't through peppering the crowd. Bergen's base hit drove the inning's third run home; then Nichols too hit safely. When Hamilton followed with a sixth straight hit, Bergen scored to make it 11–5. By now Hoffer was plainly used up. Pitchers almost never asked out of a game. Certainly in the midst of an inning, such a gesture would have been regarded as a sign of surrender. Yet that's what Hoffer did, motioning to the Orioles bench in a plea for relief. He was in his fifth inning of work, two days after a nine-inning start, both times pitching against the league's toughest team, and he knew he was finished. Yet Hanlon ignored the gesture. First Robinson and then McGraw motioned to the pitcher to carry forward. Tenney broke the hit string with a sacrifice, but Lowe smashed the inning's seventh hit, scoring Nichols and Hamilton. The eighth hit, this one by Stahl, succeeded only in retiring Lowe, who had nothing to lose by trying to take third. But Duffy and Collins, both batting for the second time, drilled the inning's third and fourth doubles beyond the ropes. What a few minutes before had been an 8–5 contest suddenly was a 16–5 rout. When Long added his second double of the inning, a seventeenth run came around.

Perhaps as a mark of respect for their foes, or perhaps out of a desire to humiliate them, the Bostons refused to let up. Bergen reached first and Long third when McGraw bobbled the catcher's grounder; then Bergen ran for second on a double steal attempt. Jennings's return of Robinson's throw cut down Long as he tried to score the inning's tenth run, finally ending the side. The Beaneaters had sent thirteen men to the plate and delivered eleven base hits, five of them doubles. More remarkably, Hoffer failed to retire a single batter except Tenney, who sacrificed, although he was undermined in that effort by McGraw's boot. The other two outs came on Lowe's too-aggressive base running and Long's attempted steal of home.

The Orioles did not concede. Keeler opened the bottom of the seventh with a double, Jennings singled, and Kelley sent both across with a double over the crowd and off the center-field fence. Nichols never pitched a big game in better fortune than on this day, when he really had little speed, movement, or control of his pitches. When Doyle added a double of his own, Kelley scored, making the score 17–8. Under the circumstances, it was a noble, if futile, offensive gesture.

At the start of the eighth inning, Hanlon finally went to Doc Amole, who allowed single runs in that inning and the ninth. The Orioles scored twice more in their half of the eighth, thanks to Keeler's fourth hit of the day, a single that preceded doubles into the crowd by Jennings and Kelley. But those runs only made the final score a breathtaking 19–9. The three-time champions had not seen such an onslaught against them since early in the 1896 season, when the same Boston club had

scored twenty-one times. The numbers left plenty to digest: fifteen unearned runs, thirty-seven hits, and fifteen doubles (many of them into
the overflow crowd). Nichols had surrendered thirteen hits—four of
them to Keeler—and nine runs, yet he had pitched an easy complete
game victory. Despite all of the offense, the whole thing took less than
two and one-half hours to play.

Boston fans had come to the park with beans in their pockets; now
they hurled them into the air in celebration.[41] The two teams' fans
swarmed the field, many of them taking down portions of the wooden
barriers on their way. It would have been unfathomable before the series, but the bond forged by shared experience caused them to inter-
mingle without rancor; indeed, they did so with camaraderie. They
serenaded one another with favorite tunes: "Yankee Doodle," "Dixie,"
"There'll Be a Hot Time in the Old Town Tonight," and "Maryland, My
Maryland." The Rooters' band struck up a popular favorite of the day,
"The Blow That Nearly Killed Father."[42] So thick was the populace that,
viewed from the vacated seats, the once green field disappeared under
the human stampede. "Our sporting public treated the Boston nine
with the greatest consideration," the *Baltimore Sun* told its readers.[43]
The *Boston Globe* concluded, "Never was interest keener in America's
great national game than it is today."[44]

Murnane brought Darkhue White out of the mob to ridicule Hanlon's pitching staff. "Dah's a repo't heah to de effec' dat Mahs Corbett
an' Mahs Nops done tuck to de wudes, an' dat Mahs Hoffer an' Mahs
Amole . . . been driven ter'ble close to drink."[45] Selee and Nichols both
received dozens of congratulatory telegrams. From Boston, where he
had been called Monday morning, Congressman Fitzgerald wired Nichols to extend his "warmest congratulations." He advised the players
that Newspaper Row was "never so crowded and all Boston never so
pleased as she is tonight over your magnificent victory."[46]

The upbeat note on which the crucial series ended did not stay bitter
feelings against the Orioles in many quarters. The Louisville newspaper

called the outcome "a victory for clean, honest baseball. A throw-down to rowdyism."[47] Papers in New York and Washington also openly celebrated the outcome and took the Boston side in the final weekend.

The Clinching

When Orioles officials returned to the playing field the following morning, they looked upon a wreck of a park. "Not since the fire of 1894 has Union Park presented a more dilapidated appearance," the *Baltimore Sun* reported.[48] Spectators had virtually demolished the left-field fence, both by the weight of those sitting upon it and the slats taken down for makeshift seating. The ticket office flooring and railing were useless. Umbrellas, hats, canes, and other human residue transformed the field into a dump. Groundskeeper Morgan Murphy put the damage estimate at fifteen hundred dollars. He brought in eleven workers who filled four horse carts full of rubbish to be carried from the site. Carpenters were called in to temporarily repair the fences and gates.

For the Beaneaters there remained the formality of closing out the championship. The victories in Baltimore had left them one and one-half games ahead in the standings, although the two teams were even in losses, both with thirty-eight. Boston's advantage lay in the two early-season Orioles games that had not yet been made up—the May date in Cleveland and the July game in Louisville. Given that the Orioles had beaten the Spiders seven times in their eleven meetings and had won ten of eleven against the Colonels, victories in both games were likely. Those two wins would have narrowed the effective gap to a mere half game entering the final weekend. But in 1897 the exigencies of time and distance dictated that unplayed games be viewed as schedule quirks. The best the Orioles could do would be to finish with a .708 winning percentage. They would need to sweep a four-game series against the Senators to do that, and even if they did, Boston could still win by sweeping its three-game series in Brooklyn.

Because it was all they had, Orioles fans spent Tuesday and Wednesday morning clinging to the belief that the Beaneaters would lose at least once in Brooklyn. That belief, of course, ran counter to the long-held and still strong notion in Baltimore that the Orioles were the targets of a league-wide conspiracy, which at this point would ensure Boston victories. Whether they were right or wrong, the atmosphere in Brooklyn was openly friendly to the visitors, whose arrival was celebrated with banners and cheers. The warm reception could be attributed partly to the Rooters delegation that followed the team up from Baltimore, but there was no denying broader interest. The *Brooklyn Eagle* counted representatives from seventeen newspapers covering the season-ending games.[49] It was also true that the Bridegrooms players shed no tears at the prospect of losing such critical games to the Beaneaters.

In their wreck of a park, the Orioles fell on Doc McJames Wednesday for four quick runs on their way to the 6–3 victory over the Senators. McGraw's infield hit leading off the game set up the first of the four runs. Then with the bases full, two out, and a run already scored in the second, Jennings took a pitch in the head for a hard-earned run batted in, which made the score 3–0. A fourth run was scored in the third in classic Baltimore style. Stenzel led off with a walk, took third on Doyle's hit-and-run single, and scored on Reitz's roller. Nops pitched comfortably from there. But against the Bridegrooms, Lewis had an easy time keeping the Bostons on pace.

Hanlon sent Pond against the Senators on Friday in search of the next needed victory. But the doctor had no answer for a Washington offense that pummeled him for nine early runs. That news was posted in Brooklyn just as the Beaneaters finished their own 12–3 punishing of the Bridegrooms. Joined by former star player John M. Ward and Brooklyn captain Mike Griffin, Duffy, Stivetts, Klobedanz, and Long adjourned for a hotel near Washington Park where they could monitor the news out of Baltimore. The presence of the two non-Beaneaters was no accident. Ward, a respected attorney and player organizer, had been a vocal critic of Baltimore's inside style of play. Griffin's presence testified to the general sentiments of the league's players. Had the pennant been left to their vote, they would have over-whelmingly favored Boston.

The ticker reported no change through seven innings. "Hold on," Long said to would-be congratulators. "Those Orioles may pile up six or seven runs in the next two innings."[50]

There was no change in the eighth. Ward told fans the Beaneaters deserved to win because they played "not only the best ball but the cleanest." Griffin said a Boston victory would be an appropriate re-buke to "foul-mouthed ball players." Stivetts was first to pick up on the clicking of the wire for the ninth. "Nothing," he shouted, touching off one more celebration.[51] Telegrams of congratulation began to pour in: from team president Arthur Soden, from Albert Spalding, the grand old man of the National League, and from members of the Rooters as well. From Baltimore, Joe Kelley wired a congratulatory note: "You played great ball and deserve your victory," it said. Ned Hanlon wired congratulations "from the old champions to the new."[52]

Duffy simply looked forward to relaxing. "I have lost seven pounds in the last three weeks," he confessed.[53]

In Baltimore the Orioles lamented what might have been. Hanlon pointed to a lack of pitching, with Corbett, twice a loser to the Bea-neaters, a particular target. "How could we know that Corbett would not pitch in his usual form, and it was the one thing that defeated us," he told reporters.[54] If anybody deserved to be second-guessed in that game, however, it was Hanlon himself, who turned so quickly and for such a long time to Hoffer, who was on such short rest, even though he had fresh arms available. As much an idol as he was in Baltimore, Hanlon took some of that roasting on the city's streets and in the next day's papers. "It looked as if Nops were removed too early," remarked the *Baltimore Sun*'s correspondent, adding, "When the first symp-tom of flagging came Hoffer should have been replaced by Amole or Pond."[55]

The reality, which Hanlon perhaps could not bring himself to con-cede, was that his club had played superior ball only to be outdone by an even more superior team. History argues that the Orioles' final 90-40 record deserves to be appreciated at some length before it is consigned to the shelf on which runners-up gather dust. Since that 1897 season, there have been 313 divisional or league champions decided in the major leagues, and Baltimore's .692 percentage would have won all but fourteen of them.

But those who witnessed it also allocated some portion of the credit to Boston's rabid fan base. John Morrill cited the Rooters' presence in Baltimore. "The boys felt at home," he concluded.[56]

Afterword

One week after their climactic meeting, the champion Bostons and runner-up Orioles met again, this time for what was known as the Temple Cup. With only one major league in existence, there was no such thing as a World Series. But in 1894, to sate a perceived public desire for some type of concluding event, William Temple of Pittsburg donated a cup to be presented to the winner of a seven-game series between the league's first-place and second-place teams.

By the time the two teams took the field in Boston in early October, the future of Temple Cup play was already in trouble. One issue was a lingering dispute over the financial split. Temple had stipulated that two-thirds of the gate receipts should go to members of the winning team and just one-third to the losing players. But the league champions—in each of the three previous cases, the Orioles—had seen no reason why they should risk the lion's share of the pot against a runner-up. That led to the informal but recurring practice of "gentleman's agreements" for a fifty-fifty split. Inevitably, word got around that the teams would share the winnings regardless of who won, killing the perception that the series amounted to more than an exhibition.

Nor did it help the series' credibility that the regular-season champion usually performed without motivation in the postseason games. Only once in the four seasons of the series did the regular-season champions win the Temple Cup. Coming off their emotional to-the-wire

MARTIN BERGEN.
CATCHER OF THE BOSTON CLUB.

Fig. 21. Marty Bergen, moody catcher for the Boston Beaneaters, who in an apparent fit of insanity bludgeoned his wife and children and then slit his own throat in January of 1900. Originally appeared in the *Boston Globe*, September 23, 1897.

triumph in October of 1897, Boston won the first Temple Cup game and then lost the next four to the Orioles. William Temple withdrew the cup following the 1897 series.

By 1898 owners took two steps designed to reduce the amount of rowdiness in league games. They added a second umpire to work the bases at all games. During the turbulent 1897 season, forty-three different men, many of them active players, umpired at least one major-league game, and only five umpired more than eighty. In 1898 only twenty men officiated at major-league baseball games, and only five of those were not in the regular employment of the league. One of those five was Tim Hurst, who resigned his mask and indicator after 1897 to take over as manager of the St. Louis Browns. Twice during the season, manager Hurst was called on in emergencies to officiate at his own team's games. The league reverted to a single umpire for the first few years of the twentieth century, but by 1906 the idea of games umpired by a single arbiter was history.

In addition to improving the plight and status of umpires, owners agreed to refer allegations of the use of vulgar language to a board. As it turned out, the board considered no cases at all during 1898 and was disbanded after that season. In his 1960s history of the National League, Lee Allen quotes an anonymous writer as sarcastically concluding that during 1898 "not one reference was made to the maternal ancestry of any umpire; not once was any umpire or opposing player asked to accomplish the physically impossible."[1]

Under Frank Selee, Boston repeated its championship run in 1898, this time by six games over the Orioles. In Ohio the state supreme court upheld the validity of Cleveland's Sunday baseball prohibition, causing Frank Robison to shift home games to remote locales. After the 1898 season he purchased the St. Louis franchise from Chris Von der Ahe and moved his best players there. With attendance beginning to decline in victory-sated Baltimore, Hanlon did the same thing, obtaining simultaneous control of the Orioles and the Brooklyn franchise. After the 1899 season the Baltimore and Cleveland clubs, along with those in Louisville and Washington, were eliminated, and the National League took on the eight-team status that became familiar for decades afterward. One year later, Ban Johnson moved teams from his minor league into Cleveland, Washington, and Baltimore, put other franchises in Chicago and Boston, and declared war on the National League monopoly. Against Johnson's dynamism, Nick Young's inept and indecisive leadership ensured the outcome. Within two years, the National League recognized the American League as a legitimate major league.

Boston's Royal Rooters grew as an institution after 1897. When Jimmy Collins, Ted Lewis, and Chick Stahl moved to the city's American League club in 1901, the Rooters moved with them, cheering the club to pennants in 1902, 1903, and 1904. In 1903 Michael McGreevy, Louis Watson, and Charlie Lavis led a delegation of Royal Rooters to the first World Series in Pittsburg; they celebrated heartily when Boston won. One season later the Rooters paraded up Broadway for the concluding and climactic series between their first-place club and the runner-up New York Highlanders. Again Boston won, but this time there was no World Series because John McGraw's National League champion Giants refused to play.[2]

The Victims

Several of the Boston Beaneaters, so successful on the field in 1897, suffered off the field. For none was that more tragically true than Marty Bergen and his family. His inexplicable run-ins with teammates continued through the 1898 pennant-winning season. Responding to what he perceived to be threats on the bench, he told some teammates at the end of that season that he would "club them to death." His mental instability was exacerbated when his third son, Willie, died of diphtheria during the 1899 season. Distraught and also irrationally fearful for his own safety, Bergen left the team for periods of time, and the Beaneaters always welcomed him back. Although the concept of paranoid schizophrenia was not understood as a medical illness in those days, Bergen's actions seem consistent with that diagnosis. After the season, Bergen retreated to the solitude of his home, known as Snowball Farm, in Brookfield, Massachusetts.

A few weeks after the first of the year in 1900, Bergen's father Michael went to the farm to pay a visit. In the kitchen, he came upon the body of his granddaughter, Florence. The six-year-old had been bludgeoned with an axe. The horrified man staggered into the next room to be confronted with an even more grisly scene; the bloodied bodies of his daughter-in-law and grandson, Harriet and Joseph, also bludgeoned. Nearby was his son Marty's body. The tormented catcher had slit his own throat with a razor, nearly severing his head. He left neither note nor explanation. Selee attributed the murders and suicide to his catcher's ongoing hallucinations.[3]

Chick Stahl was among the several Boston and Baltimore players who gravitated toward team management following their playing careers. A star with the Beaneaters through 1900, he joined a legion of players who jumped to the new American League for the 1901 season, taking a starring role with Jimmy Collins's Boston Pilgrims. Stahl played with Boston on the 1903 and 1904 pennant-winning teams, which gave him four pennants in seven seasons.

But the Pilgrims—they were only then becoming known as the Red Sox—slid toward mediocrity after the 1904 season, and with the club mired in last place in 1906, management opted for a change. Although retained as a player, Jimmy Collins was relieved of his managerial responsibilities in midseason, and Stahl was given the job. At the conclusion of the previous season, the thirty-year-old had taken a bride. Visitors to their home reported that they were the picture of newlywed happiness, although rumors of infidelity would surface later.

Like other players' wives, the new Mrs. Stahl was unwelcome at the team's West Baden, Indiana, training camp. During the 1907 camp, teammates reported that their manager was unusually serious, withdrawn, and preoccupied with the lack of progress his team showed in workouts. To further complicate things, Stahl sustained a hobbling bruise on his foot, for which the physician prescribed daily treatments of a solution of carbolic acid.

On the morning of March 28, 1907, Stahl issued his usual workout instructions and sent his team ahead to the field. They assumed he would soon follow. Instead, he went into the bathroom, took the bottle of carbolic acid, and swallowed a large gulp. Infielder Bob Unglaub heard Stahl's death screams and reached the agonized player in time to hear him explain cryptically, "It drove me to it, Bob." He was dead before Unglaub could react, and no one has ever been able to determine precisely whether "it" was the team's play, his injury, marital problems, or a problem that nobody knew of.[4]

Consumption's Toll

In 1897 Herman Long had been the star shortstop of the championship team and the man who made the key play in the decisive first game of the critical series. To fans he seemed the model of an athlete.

But his skills deteriorated quickly after the glory of 1897, and he survived several of his final active seasons on reputation alone. Following his .322 average in 1897, he fell to .265 in 1898 and never hit even that high again thereafter. Possibly to alleviate the concerns that might come naturally to an aging star player, Long took to the bottle—hard. That of course exacerbated his decline. Released after a 1902 season in which he hit just .231, he signed on with the New York Americans for 1903 but moved quickly through Detroit and Philadelphia. It took the Phillies just one game in 1904 to recognize that Long was through.

He accepted an offer to play and manage at Toledo, but his managerial career was as checkered as the conclusion of his playing career. From Toledo he moved to Des Moines in 1905 and Omaha in 1906, each effort undermined by his increasing dependence on alcohol. To complicate the situation, he developed tuberculosis (then called consumption), the leading cause of death at that time. It was a disease to which chronic drinkers were especially prone. Made increasingly destitute by his own desultory habits, Long resigned the Omaha managerial position and traveled to Denver, hopeful that the altitude would provide some relief. Denver was a frequent destination for consumptives. But the move did not help Long, who died penniless in a fleabag hostel in December of 1909. He was just forty-three. When his death was reported, Henry Pulliam, who had risen to become league president, used it to advance the concept of a home for indigent ballplayers. But Pulliam killed himself just a few days later, apparently despondent over the cares of his office; and when he died, so did any momentum behind the creation of such a facility.[5]

Frank Selee had come to the job of major-league manager as a young, untested theoretician, and he rose to the pinnacle—five championships in eight seasons, three of them in succession. When the emergence of the American League sapped his club of much of its talent, he was re- leased and allowed to sign with the Chicago National League fran- chise. Selee immediately brought in a horde of youngsters, so many that the team acquired a new nickname in the newspapers—the Cubs. Frank Chance came from California, Joe Tinker from Kansas City, and Johnny Evers from upstate New York. That team finished below .500 in Selee's first season, 1902, but then improved by thirteen and one-half games. In 1904 the Cubs were nine games better yet.

But if his team was on the rise, Selee was not. At almost the same time that Long contracted tuberculosis, his former manager did as well. Selee tried to manage the Cubs from the bench in 1905 but gave up part way into the season and turned the job over to Chance. Then Selee made his own trip to Denver. It is not recorded whether he ever met up with his former shortstop there, but he lingered in the city for most of the next four years. He died on July 5, 1909, about six months before Long, having not yet reached his fiftieth birthday.[6]

Trials on the Periphery

An unusual number of the peripheral players during that 1897 season saw their fortunes fall precipitously as well, none more so than the promising Louis Sockalexis. Patsy Tebeau brought Sockalexis back for periods of both 1898 and 1899, but he never again showed even a glimpse of the talent that had so tantalized the fans. Released after just seven appearances in 1899, he returned to the Penobscot River area of Maine, where he could occasionally be seen paddling his canoe in search of clams. Having spent both his major-league earnings and his health, he took a logging job that paid twenty dollars a week, enough to live on in his meager style. On Christmas Eve in 1913, the other mem- bers of his logging team noticed that he had gone off into the woods alone. Following the trail, they found his lifeless body some distance away, the apparent victim of a heart attack. The story is told that as they loosened his garments, they discovered his clothes stuffed with old newspaper clippings that Sockalexis used to keep himself warm in the woods. The clippings supposedly were the stories of his glory days with the Spiders. Like much of the Sockalexis story, it is not possible today to say whether that particular aspect of his story belongs with the truth or the legend. He was forty-two.[7]

When contacted for his reaction, Tebeau lamented what might have been for Sockalexis. "Nobody ever heard of [Cy] Young or [Jesse] Burkett or the rest of us when the big Indian was around," he said.[8] The newspaper men had found Tebeau running a saloon in his old neighborhood in St. Louis. It was the place where Patsy was most comfortable, and he ran it for the remainder of his days. Those days concluded less than five years later. He had been in ill health and had recently returned from a trip to French Lick, Indiana, where there was a spa that was popular among those who sought healing treatments from sulfur-laced waters. Closing up a normal evening at the tavern, the fifty-three-year-old Tebeau locked the door from the inside, wrote a note to family and friends, and shot himself in the head. He was found dead the next morning.[9]

If there was a stranger on-field personality than Marty Bergen in 1897, it was the Giants' surly left-handed pitcher, Ed Doheny. Never comfortable around his teammates, he pitched sporadically until 1902, when he was picked up by the powerhouse team that Fred Clarke had constructed in Pittsburg. That team, which featured Clarke, Honus Wagner, and pitchers Jack Chesbro, Jess Tannehill, and Deacon Phillippe, won 103 games and finished first, ahead by 27½ games. Doheny contributed sixteen of those wins. He was still sharp in 1903, but his strange behavior worsened. He fought with teammates on the bench and away from the field, and he accused several of them of putting detectives on his trail. As with Bergen, the explanation was probably related to a psychiatric condition.

Despite the pennant race, Doheny left the team, but he returned and won four more games. Even so, and despite the fact that his Pirates were in a close pennant race with the Giants, Clarke judged Doheny such a distraction that he sent the pitcher home. He sat there and sulked as his teammates won the right to play in the first World Series. Convinced he was being unjustly deprived of both fame and income, the pitcher suffered a breakdown. A doctor and nurse were brought to his home; Doheny attacked both, striking the nurse with the leg of a cast iron stove. Police were called, and he held them at bay for an hour before being taken into custody. He was committed to the Danvers asylum in Massachusetts and remained there for the rest of his life, which ended in late December of 1916. He was only forty-three.[10]

The Forgottens

Jimmy Collins joined the first wave of jumpers to the new American League. Capitalizing on his fame, he accepted the position of player-manager of the Boston Pilgrims, burnishing his reputation by winning the 1902 and 1903 pennants and the first World Series. Removed in favor of Stahl during the dismal 1906 season, he continued as a full-time player through 1908 and then retired. At the time, and for years afterward, Collins was the standard by which other third basemen were judged.

Following his retirement, he took a position as president of the Buffalo municipal league. He had invested successfully in real estate and lived comfortably until the Depression wiped him out just as retirement neared. Instead of retiring, he took another job with the Buffalo parks department, living modestly if not as comfortably as he had anticipated.

Baseball opened its Hall of Fame in 1936, selecting five players for its initial class based on votes by two groups of authorities. The first was expert in pre-1900 baseball, the other in the post-1900 game. As with some other players whose careers straddled the turn of the century (notably Cy Young), Collins suffered by the division. Despite still being generally considered the best third baseman in the game's history, he finished only thirteenth among post-1900 greats and received a mere eight votes among the pre-1900 balloters. During the second election in 1937 (a unified vote), Collins moved up only to tenth over-all. He was still tenth in 1938 and twelfth in 1939. Plainly, memories of the now sixty-nine-year-old great were receding.

Worse, Collins suffered from medical problems that marked the beginning of the end. At age seventy, he and his friends launched an aggressive campaign for his election. Newspaper columnists tried to stir public sentiment; Collins and other former greats wrote letters of support. Their cause became a race against time when the Baseball Writers Association of America, which governed the election process, decided to hold votes only every three years. That meant no new class would be chosen until 1942. His health failing, Collins learned to his dismay that he had finished only fourteenth in the 1942 election. He succumbed to pneumonia following a two-week hospitalization in March of 1943.[11] His death reinvigorated discussion about his candidacy, but when the 1945 writers' vote was counted, he still stood just eighth, sixty-four votes short of the required number. A special Old-Timers Committee selected him that same year, also inducting teammate Hugh Duffy and Baltimore foes Wilbert Robinson and Hughie Jennings. Of the four, only Duffy was still around to enjoy the moment.

Duffy had jumped to Milwaukee's American League team when offered the chance to play and manage. But the club had little talent and did not draw well. In addition, Duffy was an easterner born and bred, and he had been a New Englander for all of his adult life. He retired for two years and accepted a player-manager position with the Phillies in 1904, but three years of indifferent play sent him home to Boston, where he became a coach at Harvard University and Boston College.

A beloved elder statesman in Boston, Duffy still found the lure of the big leagues occasionally irresistible. In 1910 he accepted the position of manager of the White Sox, staying for two nondescript seasons. When the Red Sox offered the local legend—then fifty-five—the chance to manage in 1921, he jumped again. Again he lasted just two ordinary seasons before returning to the college game with which he had become more comfortable.

In the mid-1930s, the seventy-year-old Duffy joined Collins in looking hopefully toward election to the Hall of Fame. After all, how could Hall voters overlook the credentials of a man whose .440 batting average in 1894 remained the highest ever recorded? How could they ignore his career .326 batting average or the key role he had played on five Boston pennant winners during the 1890s?

They could and they did. Duffy did not even surface on the list of vote leaders on the writers' ballot until 1945, when he picked up a token sixty-four votes in an election that required nearly three times that many for entry. As with Collins, the Old-Timers Committee moved to correct the obvious oversight. The result ratified Duffy's status as one of the game's elder statesmen, and as a Hall of Famer he continued to make public appearances for as long as his health permitted. Early in 1953 his heart finally began to fail, limiting his activities and initiating a slow decline that continued until his death in October of 1954, a month short of his ninetieth birthday.[12]

Kid Nichols, the third forgotten star, completed his third consecutive thirty-victory season—and the seventh of his nine-year career—in 1898. When he won his three hundredth game—all for the same team—in 1901, he became, and he remains, the youngest pitcher (thirty-two) ever to do so. What Nichols might have done had he continued to play must remain conjecture, because wear and tear forced his retirement in 1906. He left with 361 victories, a total exceeded at the time only by Cy Young. Today Kid Nichols is tied with Jim Galvin for sixth place on the all-time list, trailing only Cy Young, Walter Johnson, Grover Alexander, Christy Mathewson, and Warren Spahn.

Following retirement, Nichols moved back to Kansas City, where he joined Joe Tinker in running a business that distributed a new attraction—movies—to theaters around the Midwest. Using the proceeds of that business, he opened a bowling alley in Kansas City, which also did well. When he was not behind the counter of the bowling alley, Nichols was developing an exceptional amateur game. In 1935, at age sixty-four, he won Kansas City's city bowling championship.

Nichols had as much reason as any pre-1900 pitcher other than Cy Young to anticipate his election to the Hall of Fame. Yet in the 1936 election, he got a mere three votes. Like Collins, Nichols and his friends mobilized to try to sway the result. The Kid himself wrote letters to many writers who had never seen him play to advocate the merits of his candidacy. Year after year his effort proved futile. In 1949 the Old-Timers Committee finally selected the Kid in a class that included Three-Fingered Brown and Charley Gehringer. Nearing eighty and frail, Nichols made the trip to Cooperstown for the induction ceremony. But soon after, he was diagnosed with cancer of the neck. He fought the disease for a year before succumbing in April of 1953. Unlike his teammate Jimmy Collins, Kid Nichols had at least lived long enough to have a moment in the Cooperstown spotlight.[13]

The Slugger and the Parson

Bobby Lowe left Boston in 1902 to join his former manager, Frank Selee, in Chicago, where he played second base for two more years, eventually losing his job to Johnny Evers. Nearing forty, Lowe signed with the Detroit Tigers, enjoying one more flirtation with first place in 1907. But Lowe's days with that championship team were short; he retired seventeen games into the season. The Tigers eventually edged the Athletics by a game and a half for the pennant.

Lowe lived a comfortable, quiet life in retirement. He was hired by the city government in Detroit and worked there for thirty years until retiring in 1941. He lived ten more years in Detroit before he died in 1951 at age eighty-six. But for a slugger in New York, he might have been forgotten. In 1932 Lou Gehrig muscled up four home runs in Philadelphia, becoming only the third player ever to do that. When the Yanks next visited Detroit, one of the newspapers got the idea to introduce Gehrig to Lowe, who had been the first. So the one-time player, now a gracefully aging sixty-seven and as slight of build as ever, put on his best suit and went to Navin Field, where he dutifully had his picture taken and swapped stories with Gehrig. The photo was used nationally, as was Gehrig's introductory question to the frail gentleman: "Did you really hit four home runs in one game?"[14]

In many respects, Ted "Parson" Lewis enjoyed the most notable career of any of the old Beaneaters. He played through 1901, after jumping to the Pilgrims. But at heart he was too intellectual to view the game as a long-term arrangement. He earned a graduate divinity degree and accepted a position as an instructor at Columbia University, moving after a few years to Williams College. He ran as a Democrat for the House of Representatives in 1910 on a platform that included direct election of senators, states rights, support for a federal income tax, labor reform, and reduced tariffs. But Lewis was no politician; in heavily Republican Massachusetts, he lost that year and again in 1914.

With his education credentials, Lewis took a faculty position at the University of Massachusetts Agricultural College. He became head of the department of languages, was named dean in 1914, and served several terms as acting president. He was formally named to the position in 1926, but faculty political pressures were mounting, and Lewis resigned a year later to accept the same position at the University of New Hampshire.

In each of his administrative capacities, he was allowed to indulge his many and varied interests: language, baseball, and politics. He was known to play catch with poet Robert Frost on the campus grounds at New Hampshire, and he wrote voluminously until his death in 1936. "I thought there might be a feeling against me because I was college bred," Lewis once wrote of the reception he expected in the rough-and-tumble 1897 game. "I was wholly mistaken."[15]

Three Managers, Fifteen Pennants

Several of the old Orioles enjoyed notable managerial careers. John McGraw was first among them. An Oriole through 1899, McGraw began a thirty-three-season managerial career in 1899, leading a team depleted by syndicate baseball to a credible fourth place. He was still only twenty-six. Signed by the Giants in 1902, he quickly eased out of a player's role, retiring from that capacity altogether in 1906. As incendiary in the dugout as he had been on the field, McGraw browbeat the Giants to the 1904 and 1905 pennants and won the World Series in the latter season after refusing to play against Boston in 1904. More pennants came in 1911, 1912, and 1913, again in 1917, and then he won four straight between 1921 and 1924. McGraw thus accomplished something that his Orioles had denied Boston in 1894 and that Boston had in turn denied his Orioles in 1897. In 1932, when a health-impaired McGraw realized he was losing his competitive edge, he summarily announced his retirement in midseason. He returned to the field just once more, managing the National League team in the first All-Star Game in Chicago in 1933. His life had been all glory, but it had worn him out; he died in February 1934 at age sixty-one.[16]

Robinson, his partner at the Diamond Café, played under McGraw in Baltimore in 1899 and then went west with him to St. Louis in 1900. He returned to Baltimore to play with the new American League team in 1901 and 1902, but when that club was moved to New York, Robinson stayed behind, tending to the Diamond and playing occasionally for the city's entry in the Eastern League. In time, McGraw called and asked him to work with his pitchers in spring training. The job became a full-time coaching position that put Robinson in the center of New York's 1911-13 pennant races. But when the Giants lost the 1913 World Series to Philadelphia, McGraw blamed Robinson and fired him. Given the volatile nature of both men—especially McGraw—the firing blossomed into a full-blown feud, which lasted for sixteen years, until they reconciled in 1930.

It did not take the old catcher long to find work; he was named manager in Brooklyn and within three seasons had the Dodgers in the World Series for the first time. Brooklyn repeated in 1920 but then rarely challenged during the remaining twelve seasons of Robinson's supervision. When the 1931 season ended, he was sixty-eight, a winner of 1,399 games and a loser of 1,398. He probably planned to retire at season's end anyway, but that opportunity was preempted when the

Dodgers announced the appointment of Max Carey as manager for 1932. Robinson lived long enough to mourn the passing of McGraw in early 1934, but he suffered a stroke in August of the same year and died a few days later. With his 1945 election to the Hall of Fame, he joined McGraw, who had been chosen by a special Centennial Commission in 1937. Both men were recognized primarily for their managerial exploits; in McGraw's case, at least, that assessment gave short shrift to a noteworthy playing career highlighted by a career .466 on-base average that remains the third best of all time, behind only Ted Williams and Babe Ruth.[17]

Hughie Jennings followed McGraw and preceded Robinson into the managerial ranks, taking over in Detroit in 1907 and promptly steering that team to three consecutive pennants. His career winning percentage after only three seasons as a manager was a stunning .606. Although he managed thirteen more seasons, Jennings never again got a team closer than second place. But it did not diminish the quality of his life, and it certainly did not diminish the excitement in his life. Whatever he did, Hughie always seemed to be in the center of strange and harrowing events.

While studying law at Cornell University, Jennings decided one night to take a dip in the college's indoor pool. He raced there, stripped, and dove in headfirst, failing to notice that the pool had been drained. He suffered several fractures. In December of 1911 Jennings was at the wheel of an automobile that overturned on the bridge across the Lehigh River near Philadelphia. He sustained a fractured skull, a concussion, and a broken arm. Again there were concerns for his life. But when the 1912 season began, Jennings was on Detroit's sidelines.

Unlike other players of that era, Jennings did not need to manage, for he had completed his law degree and obtained a law license. He even practiced occasionally. Combined with his income from the Tigers, the income from his law practice left him comfortable, so when he stopped working in 1925 he was able to retire comfortably to the Poconos. Although calling it a fortune might be extravagant, the Jennings nest egg was variously estimated at between $87,000 and $150,000 by the dawn of 1928. But in late January of that year, the popular figure contracted meningitis, a fast-spreading, often fatal ailment. He was hospitalized, and the daily bulletins published in newspapers around the country contained no good news. He died one week after being stricken, on February 1, 1928. The reports of his death included a bedside admonition directed toward the game's leaders: "Keep it clean and honest," he told them.[18]

The Outfield

Joe Kelley was transferred to Brooklyn in the syndicate swap of 1899, remained there through 1901, and then jumped briefly to the Orioles in 1902. After a half season he jumped back, signing with the Reds as a player-manager. But Kelley lacked McGraw's managerial acumen, a particular problem since he was competing against McGraw for the pennant. He quit after four seasons, only one of them with the team averaging above .500, and played only sporadically thereafter, mostly in the minor leagues. Retiring to Baltimore, he lived comfortably, working various city and state jobs, drinking when he chose, and relaxing when he felt like it, which was most of the time. He died in 1943 at age seventy-one, and his accomplishments faded into the background noise until they were resurrected in the late 1960s by a renewal of interest in the game's early history. When that occurred, Joe Kelley's career .317 batting average and central role on three championship teams made people wonder how he had ever been left out of the Hall of Fame. He was quickly inducted in 1971 by a vote of the Veterans Committee.[19]

Alone among the Orioles greats, Willie Keeler never tried his hand at managing. Keeler stayed active in baseball for another decade, helping Brooklyn to the 1899 and 1900 pennants, and marking his fifteenth consecutive season above .300 with the New York American League team, which only began to be called the Yankees in 1906. But his retirement as a player paralleled the onset of a heart condition that seemed to run through the family. Increasingly, the lifetime bachelor found his movement restricted to the area around his Brooklyn home, then to the home itself. The decline was slow but inevitable. He died on New Year's Day in 1923, only fifty years old. Hall of Fame voters may have forgotten many of his contemporaries, but the writers did not forget Keeler's aphoristic batting philosophy, "Hit 'em where they ain't." He was elected in the fourth election in 1939, becoming the Hall's nineteenth member.[20]

Manager, Umpire, Scout

Of all the Orioles, the one perhaps least likely to be asked to run a team—and also least likely to live to a ripe, old age—was Dirty Jack Doyle, who was traded by Hanlon to Washington after the 1897 season. Yet in midseason of 1898, with his new team floundering in eleventh place, Doyle was asked to take over as manager. The experiment lasted seventeen games—the Nationals going 8-9—before Doyle was relieved of the managing responsibility and traded to the Giants. Mellowing hardly at all, he wore out his welcome at seven stops until 1905, when at age thirty-five he quit on opening day. Doyle drifted through a succession of baseball-related jobs, including—in the ultimate of ironies—a term as an umpire in the minor leagues. His greatest success came as a talent scout, especially for the Cubs, for whom he worked for more than thirty years. Among the finds credited to Doyle's diligence were almost every regular on the Cub teams that won four pennants between 1929 and 1938: Gabby Hartnett, Stan Hack, Billy Jurges, Billy Herman, Riggs Stephenson, Phil Cavaretta, Sheriff Blake, Charley Root, Bill Lee, Guy Bush, Augie Galan, and Pat Malone. Doyle had recommended and signed them all.

He never apologized for the acerbic style of his play, but he never discussed it in any great detail either. "It wasn't a matter of being rough or dirty," he said late in life. "I was a hard-nosed base-runner . . . [but] with the dead ball, games were won by very small margins."[21] In other words, the end justified the means. He continued scouting virtually until his death, which came on New Year's Eve of 1958. The man who had played the game so brutishly died peacefully at age eighty-nine, having outlived almost all of his contemporaries.

Serenity at Cebu

If Arlie Pond did not live as long as Doyle, he certainly lived more exotically. The pitcher who had come to Baltimore to study medicine, and who had agreed to pitch only as a sidelight, left the game early in 1898 when war broke out with Spain. Assuming his services would be needed in the war, he joined the medical corps and was sent to the Philippines, where he remained following the cessation of combat. There Dr. Pond set up clinics committed to fighting the typical jungle maladies: malaria, yellow fever, leprosy, and cholera. It was said that over the course of his life he inoculated one million Filipinos against smallpox.

Dr. Pond lived well on the island, operating from a Cebu plantation home that featured a thatched roof and woven palm leaf walls. He learned golf and became skilled enough at tennis to claim the national championship of the island.

In September of 1930 the physician, then fifty-seven, was struck by severe intestinal pain and taken to his own hospital. The diagnosis was obvious: appendicitis. But with no outside medical help able to reach that remote location, Pond simply suffered until the rupture developed into peritonitis and killed him.[22]

Final Glories

Following his retirement as a player in 1901, Bill Hoffer, who had absorbed that merciless beating in the decisive game of the 1897 season, worked on the train line from Cedar Rapids to Iowa City for twenty-seven years. He watched as his old teammates passed from the scene one by one, until only he, Boileryard Clarke, and Jack Doyle remained. By the time Doyle died, cancer had taken hold of Hoffer, who succumbed in July 1959 at age eighty-nine.[23] Clarke, a long-time coach at Princeton, survived him by one week, dying from complications of a hip fracture on July 29, 1959, at age ninety.[24]

Their manager, Ned Hanlon, had been gone since 1937. Lasting in Brooklyn until 1905, he led Cincinnati after Joe Kelley's dismissal, but he failed to get the Reds above sixth place and retired after the 1907 season. His teams had won 1,312 games, the most of any manager at the time.

Still popular in Baltimore, "Foxy Ned" caught on as a member of the city's park board, where over the course of more than two decades he advanced to the status of elder statesman. But as with Selee and many of the other stars of that era, his death extinguished the memory of his accomplishments, and when he was thought of at all, it was as the overseer of the least gentlemanly team ever to gain success on the field.

That did not change until the early 1990s, when Hanlon's teenage great-great-grandsons took up their ancestor's cause. As had Nichols's and Collins's friends in a previous age, they lobbied for Ned's election to the Hall of Fame. Confronted with the evidence—five pennants between 1894 and 1900, more wins than all but a handful of managers, and his revolutionary impact on the game—the Veterans Committee assented. In 1996 Ned Hanlon got his Cooperstown plaque. Frank Selee followed him three years later.[25]

Appendix

FINAL NATIONAL LEAGUE STANDINGS, 1897

TEAM	WINS	LOSSES	PERCENTAGE	GAMES BEHIND
Boston	93	39	.705	—
Baltimore	90	40	.692	2
New York	83	48	.634	9½
Cincinnati	76	56	.576	17
Cleveland	69	62	.527	23½
Washington	61	71	.462	32
Brooklyn	61	71	.462	32
Pittsburg	60	71	.458	32½
Chicago	59	73	.447	34
Philadelphia	55	77	.417	38
Louisville	52	78	.400	40
St. Louis	29	102	.221	63½

LEADING NATIONAL LEAGUE BATTING AVERAGES, 1897

1. Keeler, Baltimore	.424	6. Lajoie, Philadelphia	.361
2. Clarke, Louisville	.390	7. Jennings, Baltimore	.355
3. Burkett, Cleveland	.383	8. Stahl, Boston	.354
4. Delahanty, Philadelphia	.377	9. Doyle, Baltimore	.354
5. Kelley, Baltimore	.362	10. Davis, New York	.353

1897 STATISTICS: BALTIMORE ORIOLES (LEAGUE LEADERS IN BOLD)

Batting

PLAYER	GAMES	AT BATS	RUNS	HITS	DOUBLES	TRIPLES	HOME RUNS
Keeler	129	564	145	**239**	27	19	0
Stenzel	131	536	113	189	43	7	4
Kelley	131	505	113	183	31	9	5
Reitz	128	477	76	138	15	6	2
Doyle	114	460	91	163	29	4	2
Jennings	117	439	133	156	26	9	2
McGraw	106	391	90	127	15	3	0
Quinn	75	285	33	74	11	4	1
Clarke	64	241	32	65	7	1	1
Robinson	48	181	25	57	9	0	0
Corbett	42	150	27	37	6	1	0
O'Brien	50	147	25	37	6	0	0
Hoffer	42	139	20	33	8	1	1
Bowerman	38	130	16	41	5	0	1
Nops	30	92	7	18	2	2	0
Pond	33	90	16	22	3	0	0
Amole	11	28	1	3	0	0	0
Blackburn	5	13	1	1	0	0	0
Maul	2	3	0	1	0	0	0
Cogan	1	1	0	0	0	0	0
Total	1,297	4,872	964	1,584	243	66	19

Pitching

PLAYER	GAMES	GAMES STARTED	COMPLETE GAMES	SHUTOUTS	SAVES	INNINGS PITCHED	HITS	HOME RUNS
Corbett	37	37	34	1	0	313.0	330	2
Hoffer	38	33	29	1	0	303.1	350	5
Pond	32	28	23	0	0	248.0	267	4
Nops	30	25	23	1	0	220.2	235	5
Amole	11	7	6	0	0	70.0	67	0
Blackburn	5	4	3	0	0	33.0	34	2
Maul	2	2	0	0	0	7.2	9	0
Cogan	1	0	0	0	0	2.0	4	0
Total	156	136	118	3	0	1,197.2	1,296	18

RUNS BATTED IN	BASES ON BALLS	HIT BY PITCH	SACRIFICES	STOLEN BASES	AVERAGE	ON BASE PERCENTAGE	SLUGGING AVERAGE
74	35	7	12	65	.424	.464	.539
116	36	10	3	69	.353	.404	.481
118	70	7	9	44	.362	.447	.489
84	50	11	6	23	.289	.370	.358
87	29	1	2	62	.354	.394	.448
79	42	46	17	60	.355	.463	.469
48	88	9	8	44	.325	.471	.379
45	13	3	3	12	.260	.299	.337
38	9	9	0	5	.270	.320	.320
23	8	1	1	0	.315	.347	.365
22	4	1	1	4	.247	.271	.300
32	20	2	2	7	.252	.349	.293
16	6	2	2	2	.237	.279	.331
21	1	2	1	3	.315	.331	.377
7	3	1	2	0	.196	.229	.261
6	11	1	3	2	.244	.333	.278
5	1	2	0	0	.107	.194	.107
0	0	0	0	0	.077	.077	.077
0	0	0	0	0	.333	.333	.333
0	0	0	0	0	.000	.000	.000
821	437	115	72	401	.325	.394	.414

RUNS	EARNED RUNS	BASES ON BALLS	STRIKE OUTS	WILD PITCHES	HIT BY PITCH	BALKS	WINS	LOSSES	EARNED RUN AVERAGE
173	108	115	149	13	22	0	24	8	3.11
188	145	104	62	4	17	0	22	11	4.30
131	97	72	59	4	15	0	18	9	3.52
107	69	52	69	4	9	0	20	6	2.81
34	20	17	19	2	6	0	4	4	2.57
30	25	12	1	0	1	0	2	2	6.82
8	6	8	2	0	4	0	0	0	7.04
3	3	2	0	1	1	0	0	0	13.50
674	473	382	28	28	75	0	90	40	3.55

Fielding PLAYER	POSITION	GAMES	PUT-OUTS	ASSISTS	ERRORS	DOUBLE PLAYS
Amole	pitcher	11	2	19	3	0
Blackburn	pitcher	5	2	7	0	0
Cogan	pitcher	1	0	0	0	0
Corbett	pitcher	37	21	76	16	1
Hoffer	pitcher	38	22	64	4	4
Maul	pitcher	2	0	1	0	0
Nops	pitcher	30	10	38	4	0
Pond	pitcher	32	16	52	6	2
Bowerman	catcher	36	155	29	10	1
Clarke	catcher	59	191	38	15	2
Robinson	catcher	48	186	36	8	2
Clarke	first base	4	35	2	0	4
Doyle	first base	114	1,105	75	25	72
O'Brien	first base	25	205	9	7	7
Quinn	first base	2	14	1	1	2
Quinn	second base	11	24	36	4	3
Reitz	second base	128	282	449	29	62
Kelley	third base	2	0	1	0	0
McGraw	third base	105	112	182	38	16
Quinn	third base	37	41	81	7	6
Corbett	short stop	1	0	0	0	0
Jennings	short stop	116	335	425	55	54
Kelley	short stop	3	2	7	1	0
Quinn	short stop	21	56	57	3	10
Corbett	outfield	1	0	0	1	0
Hoffer	outfield	4	7	0	0	0
Keeler	outfield	129	217	12	7	2
Kelley	outfield	130	240	15	11	3
O'Brien	outfield	24	38	6	2	2
Pond	outfield	1	0	0	0	0
Quinn	outfield	6	7	1	0	0
Stenzel	outfield	131	264	12	20	2

PASSED BALLS	AVERAGE	LEFT	CENTER	RIGHT
	.873			
	1.000			
	.858			
	.956			
	1.000			
	.923			
	.919			
21	.948			
8	.939			
10	.965			
	1.000			
	.979			
	.968			
	.938			
	.938			
	.962			
	1.000			
	.886			
	.946			
	.933			
	.900			
	.974			
	.000	1	0	0
	1.000	2	1	1
	.970	0	0	129
	.959	**130**	0	0
	.957	13	1	10
		1	0	0
	1.000	1	5	0
	.932	0	131	0

1897 STATISTICS: BOSTON BEANEATERS (LEAGUE LEADERS IN BOLD)

Batting

PLAYER	GAMES	AT BATS	RUNS	HITS	DOUBLES	TRIPLES	HOME RUNS
Tenney	132	**566**	125	180	24	3	1
Duffy	134	550	130	187	25	10	11
Collins	134	529	103	183	28	13	6
Hamilton	127	507	**152**	174	17	5	3
Lowe	123	499	87	154	24	8	5
Stahl	114	469	112	166	30	13	4
Long	107	450	89	145	32	7	3
Bergen	87	327	47	81	11	3	2
Stivetts	61	199	41	73	9	9	2
Klobedanz	48	148	29	48	8	5	1
Nichols	46	147	20	39	5	0	3
Allen	34	119	33	38	5	0	1
Lewis	38	113	15	28	0	1	0
Ganzel	30	105	15	28	4	3	0
Yeager	30	95	20	23	2	3	2
Lake	19	62	2	15	4	0	0
Sullivan	13	33	3	6	0	0	0
Tucker	4	14	0	3	2	0	0
Hickman	2	3	1	2	0	0	1
Mahoney	2	2	1	1	0	0	0
Total	1,285	4,937	1,5,74	1,574	230	83	45

Pitching

PLAYER	GAMES	GAMES STARTED	COMPLETE GAMES	SHUTOUTS	SAVES	INNINGS PITCHED	HITS	HOME RUNS
Nichols	46	40	37	2	3	**368.0**	362	9
Klobedanz	38	37	30	2	0	309.1	344	13
Lewis	38	34	30	2	1	290.0	316	11
Stivetts	18	15	10	0	0	129.1	147	5
Sullivan	13	9	8	1	2	89.0	91	1
Hickman	2	0	0	0	1	7.2	10	0
Mahoney	1	0	0	0	0	1.0	3	0
Total	156	135	115	8	7	1,194.1	1,273	39

RUNS BATTED IN	BASES ON BALLS	HIT BY PITCH	SACRIFICES	STOLEN BASES	AVERAGE	ON BASE PERCENTAGE	SLUGGING AVERAGE
85	49	4	27	34	.318	.376	.376
129	52	6	13	41	.340	.403	.482
132	41	7	8	14	.346	.400	.482
61	105	6	4	66	.343	.461	.414
106	32	4	13	16	.309	.355	.419
97	38	3	5	18	.354	.406	.499
69	23	2	17	22	.322	.358	.444
45	18	4	2	5	.248	.295	.318
37	15	2	1	2	.367	.417	.533
20	5	4	3	1	.324	.363	.466
28	7	4	2	4	.265	.316	.361
24	18	0	3	1	.319	.409	.387
8	6	0	7	3	.248	.286	.265
14	4	1	3	2	.267	.300	.362
15	7	0	3	2	.242	.294	.389
5	1	0	2	2	.242	.254	.306
3	0	0	1	0	.182	.182	.182
4	2	0	0	0	.214	.313	.357
2	0	0	0	0	.667	.667	1.667
1	0	0	0	0	.500	.500	.500
885	423	47	114	233	.319	.378	.426

RUNS	EARNED RUNS	BASES ON BALLS	STRIKE OUTS	WILD PITCHES	HIT BY PITCH	BALLS	WINS	LOSSES	EARNED RUN AVERAGE
152	108	68	127	6	5	0	31	11	2.64
198	158	125	92	7	23	1	26	7	4.60
177	124	125	65	8	10	1	21	12	3.85
75	49	43	27	2	5	0	11	4	3.41
56	39	26	17	0	2	0	4	5	3.94
5	5	5	0	0	0	0	0	0	5.87
2	2	1	1	0	0	0	0	0	18.00
665	485	393	329	23	45	2	93	39	3.65

Fielding PLAYER	POSITION	GAMES	PUT-OUTS	ASSISTS	ERRORS	DOUBLE PLAYS
Hickman	pitcher	2	1	1	0	1
Klobedanz	pitcher	38	8	47	2	4
Lewis	pitcher	38	6	46	3	1
Mahoney	pitcher	1	0	1	0	0
Nichols	pitcher	46	29	62	3	1
Stivetts	pitcher	18	3	36	2	0
Sullivan	pitcher	13	4	16	2	1
Bergen	catcher	85	351	66	16	4
Ganzel	catcher	27	103	26	8	1
Lake	catcher	18	49	15	2	0
Mahoney	catcher	1	1	0	0	0
Yeager	catcher	13	54	10	2	0
Ganzel	first base	2	10	1	1	1
Stivetts	first base	2	16	1	1	2
Tenney	first base	128	1,248	81	16	69
Tucker	first base	4	41	4	2	0
Allen	second base	1	3	2	0	0
Duffy	second base	6	9	10	1	0
Lowe	second base	123	270	404	34	33
Stivetts	second base	2	2	5	1	0
Yeager	second base	4	7	16	3	1
Collins	third base	134	214	303	47	20
Yeager	third base	1	1	3	5	0
Allen	short stop	32	78	117	16	12
Duffy	short stop	2	2	4	0	1
Long	short stop	107	274	353	66	40
Allen	outfield	1	1	0	0	0
Bergen	outfield	1	2	0	1	0
Duffy	outfield	129	266	12	7	2
Hamilton	outfield	126	296	10	12	0
Klobedanz	outfield	2	2	0	0	0
Long	outfield	1	0	0	0	0
Stahl	outfield	111	164	17	14	4
Stivetts	outfield	29	47	3	4	1
Tenney	outfield	4	2	1	0	0
Yeager	outfield	10	15	2	1	0

PASSED BALLS	AVERAGE	LEFT	CENTER	RIGHT
	1.000			
	.965			
	.945			
	1.000			
	.968			
	.951			
	.909			
20	.963			
3	.942			
4	.970			
0	1.000			
4	.970			
	.917			
	.944			
	.988			
	.957			
	1.000			
	.950			
	.952			
	.875			
	.885			
	.917			
	.444			
	.924			
	1.000			
	.905			
	1.000	0	1	0
	.667	0	1	0
	.975	129	0	0
	.962	0	126	0
	1.000	0	0	2
		1	0	0
	.928	1	0	110
	.926	6	10	14
	1.000	0	0	4
	.944	2	1	7

Notes

1. Baseball's Original Evil Empire

1. Jack Kavanagh and Norman Macht, *Uncle Robbie* (Cooperstown NY: Society for American Baseball Research, 1999).

2. Charles Alexander, *John McGraw* (Lincoln: University of Nebraska Press, 1988).

3. For information related to Baltimore history, see the Web site of the Baltimore City Historical Society, http://www.historicbaltimore.org. For information regarding immigration during the period, see projects.vassar.edu/1896/immigration.html.

4. Alexander's biography of McGraw is one of numerous sources that refer to the illness that shortened McGraw's playing time in 1895. See Alexander, *John McGraw*.

5. U.S. Census Bureau report for the city of Baltimore, 1890.

6. Hanlon's philosophy of management, "baseball as she is played," is discussed in several works pertinent to the era, including Alexander, *John McGraw*; Kavanagh and Macht, *Uncle Robbie*; and Burt Solomon, *Where They Ain't: The Fabled Life and Untimely Death of the Original Baltimore Orioles* (New York: The Free Press, 1999).

7. Alexander, *John McGraw*.

8. Solomon, *Where They Ain't*.

9. Alexander, *John McGraw*.

10. Solomon, *Where They Ain't*.

11. Solomon, *Where They Ain't*.

12. Jack Smiles, *Ee-yah, The Life and Times of Hughie Jennings* (Jefferson NC: McFarland, 2005).

13. Smiles, *Ee-yah*.

14. Solomon, *Where They Ain't*.

15. The stories of Hanlon's spring training reconstruction of the 1894 Orioles are vividly recalled in Alexander, *John McGraw*; Solomon, *Where They Ain't;* and Smiles, *Ee-yah*.

16. Alexander, *John McGraw*.

17. The most complete contemporary retelling of the Petersburg story appears in Alexander, *John McGraw*.

18. Alexander speculates that an anonymous Oriole teammate—possibly reserve infielder Joe Quinn—is the source of the McGraw-Keeler shower fight story, which first appeared in the February 1899 edition of the *Sporting News*.

19. Alexander, *John McGraw*.

20. *Sporting News*, May 12, 1894.

21. *Sporting News*, June 30, 1894.

22. Retrosheet, http://www.retrosheet.org.

23. *Sporting News*, May 10, 1894.

24. Retrosheet, http://www.retrosheet.org.

25. *Sporting News*, August 11, 1894.

26. *Sporting News*, May 21, 1894.

27. *Sporting News*, July 21, 1894.

28. *Sporting News*, July 21, 1894.

29. Alexander, *John McGraw*.

30. Solomon, *Where They Ain't*.

2. The Royal Rooters

1. Peter J. Nash, *Boston's Royal Rooters* (Mount Pleasant sc: Arcadia Publishing, 2005).

2. Nash, *Boston's Royal Rooters*.

3. Nash, *Boston's Royal Rooters*.

4. *Sporting Life*, June 26, 1897.

5. The term "Royal Rooters" appears to have taken hold gradually during the summer of 1897. The earliest reference appears to occur almost as an afterthought in an article by Tim Murnane that was published in late June; "'Make 'em be good,' sang out a royal rooter, as Collins went up to the cannon's mouth for business in the ninth." An August 28 *Boston Globe* article refers to James Connally as a "loyal rooter." By September 10, when plans were announced for the Baltimore excursion, the group was more formally referred to as the "Rooters." The term "Boston Rooters" began to show up on the medallions

cast by Boston newspapers and worn by participants in the Baltimore trip and appeared again in headlines on September 24, the morning of the first game of the decisive series. After a short time the name became "Roxbury Rooters," in deference to the location of Nuf Ced McGreevy's 3rd Base tavern, and then "Royal Rooters."

6. Nash, *Boston's Royal Rooters*.

7. *Boston Globe*, June 17, 1897.

8. Nash's book, *Boston's Royal Rooters*, contains the most comprehensive analysis of the demographics of the Royal Rooters.

9. Kid Nichols file, A. Bartlett Giamatti Research Center, National Baseball Hall of Fame and Museum, Cooperstown NY.

10. Richard Selee, Hall of Fame induction speech for Frank Selee (Cooperstown NY, July 25, 1999).

11. Herman Long file, A. Bartlett Giamatti Research Center, National Baseball Hall of Fame and Museum, Cooperstown NY.

12. The Lowe story has been recounted in many places, including—in greatest detail—Joe Reichler and Ben Olan, *Baseball's Unforgettable Games* (New York: Ronald Press, 1960).

13. Hugh Duffy file, A. Bartlett Giamatti Research Center, National Baseball Hall of Fame and Museum, Cooperstown NY.

14. Explanations of the immigration issue in the 1890s are contained at http://www.bgsu.edu/departments/acs/1890s/ellisisland/nativism1 and http://projects.vassar.edu/1896/immigration.html.

15. Frank Selee file, A. Bartlett Giamatti Research Center, National Baseball Hall of Fame and Museum, Cooperstown NY.

16. J. C. Morse, from Frank Selee file, A. Bartlett Giamatti Research Center, National Baseball Hall of Fame and Museum, Cooperstown NY.

17. Robert L. Tiemann and Mark Rucker, *Nineteenth Century Stars* (Cleveland: Society for American Baseball Research, 1989).

18. *Boston Globe*, April 26, 1897.

19. *Boston Globe*, May 2, 1897.

20. Jimmy Collins file, A. Bartlett Giamatti Research Center, National Baseball Hall of Fame and Museum, Cooperstown NY.

21. Jimmy Collins file, A. Bartlett Giamatti Research Center, National Baseball Hall of Fame and Museum, Cooperstown NY.

22. Marty Bergen file, A. Bartlett Giamatti Research Center, National Baseball Hall of Fame and Museum, Cooperstown NY.

23. Tiemann and Rucker, *Nineteenth Century Stars*.

24. Tiemann and Rucker, *Nineteenth Century Stars*.

25. Ted Lewis file, A. Bartlett Giamatti Research Center, National Baseball Hall of Fame and Museum, Cooperstown NY.

3. Spring Thunderbolts

1. Between 1895, when he purchased the Giants, and 1900, Freedman changed managers eleven times, beginning with his firing of Monty Ward before the start of the 1895 season. Two men were fired and then rehired. The chronological list of managers, along with their win-loss records, is as follows: George Davis (17-17), Jack Doyle (31-31), Harvey Watkins (18-17); Arthur Irwin (38-53), Bill Joyce (132-81), Cap Anson (9-13), Bill Joyce (45-39), John Day (30-40), Fred Hoey (30-50), Buck Ewing (21-41), and George Davis (39-37).

2. *New York Times*, February 17, 1895.

3. Harold Seymour, *Baseball: The Early Years* (New York: Oxford University Press, 1960).

4. Andrew Freedman file, A. Bartlett Giamatti Research Center, National Baseball Hall of Fame and Museum, Cooperstown NY.

5. *New York Times*, January 9, 1897.

6. *Boston Journal*, April 12, 1897.

7. *Sporting Life*, April 17, 1897.

8. Andrew Freedman file, A. Bartlett Giamatti Research Center, National Baseball Hall of Fame and Museum, Cooperstown NY.

9. *Sporting Life*, April 17, 1897.

10. Freedman adopted this stance in an article published under his own byline in the *New York Journal* on April 10, 1897.

11. *New York Times*, April 7, 1896.

12. Albert G. Spalding, *America's National Game* (1911; reprint Lincoln: University of Nebraska Press, 1992), 302.

13. *Boston Globe*, March 18, 1897.

14. *Boston Globe*, March 18, 1897.

15. *Boston Journal*, March 22, 1897.

16. *Boston Globe*, March 30, 1897.

17. *Boston Globe*, March 30, 1897.

18. *Boston Globe*, April 2, 1897.

19. *Boston Globe*, April 3, 1897.

20. *Boston Globe*, April 5, 1897; and *Sporting Life*, April 17, 1897.

21. *Boston Globe*, April 11, 1897.

22. *Boston Journal*, April 19, 1897.

23. *Sporting News,* September 25, 1897.

24. *Boston Journal,* April 20, 1897.

4. Parade of Champions

1. *Sporting Life,* April 17, 1897.

2. *Baltimore Sun,* April 21, 1897.

3. *Boston Globe,* April 21, 1897.

4. *Sporting Life,* May 1, 1897.

5. *New York Clipper,* January 9, 1897, and January 30, 1897; cited in Alexander, *John McGraw.*

6. *Baltimore American,* March 19, 1897.

7. *Baltimore Sun,* March 29, 1897.

8. *Baltimore Sun,* April 2, 1897.

9. The Orioles' spring schedule included the following games and scores—March 27: Baltimore 13, Columbus (Georgia) 1; March 29: Baltimore 25, Columbus (Georgia) 2; April 3: Baltimore 21, Charlotte (North Carolina) 1; April 6: Baltimore 22, Newport News 5; April 7: Baltimore 22, Hampton (Virginia) 0; April 12: Baltimore 8, Norfolk 1; April 13: Baltimore 12, Norfolk 2; April 15: Baltimore 10, Princeton 1; April 17: Baltimore 10, Toronto 4; April 19: Baltimore 10, Toronto 2.

10. *Baltimore Sun,* April 12, 1897.

11. *Boston Journal,* April 19, 1897; *Baltimore American,* April 20, 1897; and *Baltimore Sun,* April 20, 1897.

12. Testament to the general dislike of Doyle is not hard to come by. Books on the Orioles by Fred Lieb, Charles Alexander, Jack Smiles, and Burt Solomon all agree on this point. So do Web site resources such as Baseball Reference, http://www.baseball-reference.com. Likewise, many contemporary accounts make note of Doyle's bad reputation; among them is Henry Chadwick's article in the *Sporting News* in September 1897, in which Chadwick notes that umpire Tom Lynch intended to "prefer charges" against Doyle at that winter's league meeting.

13. *Sporting Life,* May 1, 1897.

14. *Sporting Life,* May 1, 1897.

15. *Sporting Life,* May 1, 1897.

16. *Sporting Life,* May 1, 1897.

17. *Baltimore Sun,* April 27, 1897.

18. *Baltimore Sun,* April 27, 1897.

19. *Sporting Life,* May 1, 1897.

20. *Boston Journal*, April 24, 1897.

21. *Boston Globe*, April 24, 1897.

22. *Boston Globe*, April 24, 1897.

23. *Boston Globe*, April 24, 1897.

24. *Boston Globe*, April 24, 1897.

25. *Boston Journal*, April 26, 1897.

26. The most succinct explanation for and analysis of the coaching rules implemented before the 1897 season is contained in *Spalding's Official Base Ball Guide* (Chicago and New York: A. G. Spalding, 1898).

27. *Boston Globe*, April 25, 1897.

28. *Boston Globe*, April 25, 1897.

29. *Sporting Life*, June 19, 1897.

30. *Baltimore American*, April 27, 1897.

31. *Baltimore Sun*, April 29, 1897.

32. *Baltimore Sun*, April 29, 1897.

33. *Baltimore Sun*, April 29, 1897.

34. *Baltimore Sun*, April 30, 1897.

35. *Baltimore American*, April 30, 1897.

36. *Baltimore Sun*, May 1, 1897.

37. *Boston Globe*, April 26, 1897.

38. *Boston Globe*, April 26, 1897.

39. *Boston Globe*, April 26, 1897.

40. *Boston Globe*, April 30, 1897.

41. *Boston Globe*, May 2, 1897.

42. *Boston Globe*, May 2, 1897.

5. Suspected Criminals

1. The most complete source for umpiring data during the 1897 (or any other) season is a directory of umpires maintained by Retrosheet, http://www.retrosheet.org. The Web site's section on umpires features a roster of every person known to have umpired a major-league game, including the dates, opponents, and scores of the games.

2. Retrosheet, http://www.retrosheet.org.

3. The full passage is as follows:

Worcester gives it thus: "Umpire—a suspected criminal; an open enemy of society; a man distasteful to the common people; an individual who has no right to live." And *Chambers Encyclopedia* is even more severe: "Umpire—an outlaw, a notorious robber; a convicted assassin." Had further search been made, another exchange adds, there would have been found in the *International*: "Umpire—Italian brigand, derivation from Umph, exclamation after each decision, and ira (in Latin, rage) in natural sequence. Species Lally, Sheridan (aggravated type, see home umpire). Definition: Usurpers of hereditary and alien rights, mostly the latter. Diamond sharps. The verb 'to Lynch' was derived from one of the species."

4. *Sporting Life*, August 4, 1894.

5. *Sporting News*, May 15, 1897.

6. Retrosheet, http://www.retrosheet.org.

7. Retrosheet, http://www.retrosheet.org.

8. *Boston Globe*, August 16, 1897.

9. Thomas Lynch file, A. Bartlett Giamatti Research Center, National Baseball Hall of Fame and Museum, Cooperstown NY.

10. Timothy Hurst file, A. Bartlett Giamatti Research Center, National Baseball Hall of Fame and Museum, Cooperstown NY.

11. Ironically, the 1909 incident with Collins occurred twelve years to the day after an even more notorious incident that took place in Cincinnati in which Hurst was arrested for throwing a beer stein at an unruly spectator. The beer stein incident is described in chapter 9.

12. Robert Emslie file, A. Bartlett Giamatti Research Center, National Baseball Hall of Fame and Museum, Cooperstown NY.

13. *Sporting News*, June 26, 1897.

14. *Sporting Life*, May 8, 1897.

15. *Boston Globe*, May 4, 1897.

16. *Boston Globe*, May 6, 1897.

17. *Boston Globe*, May 7, 1897.

18. *Boston Globe*, May 10, 1897.

19. *Boston Globe*, May 10, 1897.

20. *Baltimore Sun*, May 9, 1897.

21. *Baltimore Sun*, May 7, 1897.

22. *Baltimore Sun*, May 8, 1897.

23. *Washington Post*, May 11, 1897.

24. *Baltimore Sun*, May 12, 1897.

25. *Baltimore Sun*, May 17, 1897.

26. *Boston Globe*, May 17, 1897.

27. *Boston Globe*, May 24, 1897.

28. *Sporting Life*, May 8, 1897.

29. *Louisville Courier-Journal*, May 14, 1897.

30. *Boston Journal*, May 4, 1897.

31. *Baltimore Sun*, May 19, 1897.

32. *Baltimore Sun*, May 19, 1897.

33. *Baltimore Sun*, May 20, 1897.

34. *Louisville Courier-Journal*, May 14, 1897.

35. *Louisville Courier-Journal*, May 14, 1897.

36. *Baltimore Sun*, May 21, 1897.

37. *Baltimore Sun*, May 22, 1897.

38. *Baltimore Sun*, May 22, 1897.

39. *Cincinnati Enquirer*, May 22, 1897.

40. *Baltimore Sun*, May 22, 1897.

41. *Baltimore Sun*, May 24, 1897.

6. Streaks of June

1. *Boston Globe*, May 10, 1897.

2. *Boston Globe*, May 10, 1897.

3. *Baltimore Sun*, May 25, 1897.

4. *Baltimore Sun*, May 25, 1897.

5. *Baltimore Sun*, May 24, 1897.

6. The story of Hurst's run-in in Pittsburg is most thoroughly recounted in the *Pittsburg Post*, May 26, 1897, but detailed versions may also be found in the same day's *Baltimore Sun* and in the *Sporting News* of May 29, 1897.

7. *New York World*, June 2, 1897.

8. *New York World*, June 2, 1897.

9. *Sporting Life*, June 26, 1897.

10. *Baltimore Sun*, May 29, 1897.

11. *Baltimore Sun*, May 31, 1897.

12. *Baltimore Sun*, June 1, 1897.

13. *Boston Globe*, May 31, 1897.

14. *Boston Globe*, May 31, 1897.

15. *Boston Globe*, May 31, 1897.

16. *Boston Globe*, May 31, 1897.

17. *Boston Globe*, May 31, 1897.

18. *Boston Globe*, June 3, 1897.

19. *Boston Globe*, June 5, 1897.

20. *Boston Globe*, June 5, 1897.

21. *Sporting Life*, June 5, 1897.

22. *Baltimore Sun*, May 27, 1897.

23. *Baltimore Sun*, June 3, 1897.

24. *Baltimore Sun*, June 7, 1897.

25. *Baltimore American*, June 12, 1897.

26. *Baltimore American*, June 15, 1897.

27. *Boston Globe*, June 12, 1897.

28. *Boston Globe*, June 13, 1897.

29. *Chicago Tribune*, June 1, 1897.

30. *Sporting Life*, June 26, 1897.

31. *Baltimore Sun*, June 19, 1897.

32. *Boston Globe*, June 22, 1897.

33. *Boston Globe*, June 20, 1897.

7. Sunday Misdemeanors

1. The early history of League Park and the Robisons is most specifically detailed in Peter Jedick, *League Park* (Cleveland: Peter Jedick Enterprises, 1992).

2. Charlie Bevis, *Sunday Baseball* (Jefferson NC: McFarland, 2003).

3. Bevis, *Sunday Baseball*.

4. Bevis, *Sunday Baseball*.

5. Bevis, *Sunday Baseball*.

6. Bevis, *Sunday Baseball*.

7. *Sporting News*, March 27, 1897.

8. *Sporting Life*, February 13, 1897.

9. *Cleveland Plain Dealer*, May 17, 1897.

10. *Sporting Life*, June 19, 1897.

11. *Cleveland Plain Dealer*, July 10, 1897.

12. *Sporting Life*, July 17, 1897.

13. One must approach with trepidation the pronouncements by newspaper writers of a century ago, who often wrote from a perspective of bias or with evidence of a personal agenda. By far the best-researched and most helpful analysis of the errors and overstatements inherent in the reportage of this era is Howard Rosenberg, *Cap Anson 3: Muggsy John McGraw and the Tricksters Baseball Fun Age of Rule Bending* (Arlington VA: Tile Books, 2005).

14. *Baltimore Sun*, June 24, 1897.

15. *Baltimore Sun*, June 24, 1897.

16. *Boston Globe*, June 25, 1897.

17. *Boston Globe*, June 25, 1897.

18. *Boston Globe*, June 26, 1897.

19. *Baltimore Sun*, June 28, 1897.

20. *Boston Globe*, July 26, 1897.

21. There are various published estimates of the visitors' take from these games. In the July 17, 1897, issue of *Sporting Life*, J. C. Morse puts the total at $8,400. But in the July 3, 1897, issue of the *Sporting News*, the figure is put at $9,000.

22. *Boston Globe*, July 29, 1897.

23. *Sporting News*, June 26, 1897.

24. Cap Anson's contention is passed along by Henry Chadwick in the *Sporting News*, June 26, 1897.

25. *Sporting News*, June 26, 1897.

26. The story of Jennings's beaning played out over two days, most graphically in the *Baltimore Sun* of June 29–30, 1897.

27. *Boston Globe*, July 6, 1897.

28. The man who went down in baseball history as Doc McJames always claimed his name was the result of a misunderstanding. "My name is James, not McJames," he told the *Boston Globe* in 1897. The records show that his full name was actually James McCutcheon James, but in school he fell into the habit of shortening that signature to James Mc James. Over time, the space inadvertently disappeared. "When I came into baseball, the managers got my prefixes twisted," explained McJames. "So now I have two titles—James at home and McJames in baseball." *Boston Globe*, August 23, 1897.

29. *Baltimore Sun*, July 7, 1897.

30. *Boston Journal*, June 27, 1897.

8. The Rise and Fall of Louis Sockalexis

1. The Sockalexis myth has been told many times. It probably originated around the league's dugouts, but it gained credence in Detroit for two reasons. The first was that, in his retirement, Hughie Jennings passed the story along through his various newspaper columns. Concurrently, H. G. Salsinger, then one of the most prominent sports editors, also told it, likely based on stories he had heard while covering Jennings's Tigers. It has since cropped up in various books.

2. The story of the Holy Cross throw is related in the best and one of the most recent of numerous Sockalexis biographies; see Ed Rice, *Baseball's First Indian* (Windsor CT: Tidemark Press, 2003).

3. *Sporting Life*, April 10, 1897.

4. Details of Sockalexis's experiences at Notre Dame and South Bend are contained in the Louis Sockalexis file at the A. Bartlett Giamatti Research Center, National Baseball Hall of Fame and Museum, Cooperstown NY; and in Rice, *Baseball's First Indian*.

5. Louis Sockalexis file, A. Bartlett Giamatti Research Center, National Baseball Hall of Fame and Museum, Cooperstown NY.

6. The origin of this comment is Frederick John, "Sockalexis: The Greatest Baseball Player of Them All," *Bangor Daily News*, March 8, 1975. The origin of the comment is not more specifically referenced. In its original form, it is also not ascribed to a particular Delahanty brother, of whom five played in the major leagues. Three, however, had not yet arrived in the majors as of 1897 and thus can be ruled out. One of the other two, Ed, was among the front rank of stars, and his life has been recorded in detail with no mention of the comment. That leaves only Tom Delahanty, a major-league hanger-on beginning his third and final season, as the likely source.

7. *Sporting Life*, June 19, 1897.

8. *Sporting Life*, March 27, 1897.

9. *Boston Globe*, June 2, 1897.

10. *Sporting Life*, May 15, 1897.

11. *Sporting Life*, June 19, 1897.

12. *Sporting Life*, June 19, 1897.

13. Rice, *Baseball's First Indian*.

14. *Sporting Life*, May 15, 1897.

15. Rice, *Baseball's First Indian*.

16. *Sporting Life*, May 15, 1897.

17. *Sporting Life*, June 19, 1897.

18. *Sporting Life*, June 19, 1897.

19. *Boston Globe*, June 3, 1897.

20. *Boston Globe*, June 3, 1897.

21. *Boston Globe*, June 3, 1897.

22. *Baltimore Sun*, June 17, 1897.

23. Cleveland played the Colts in Chicago on June 24, 26, and 27, 1897. The Spiders won the first game 5–2 after scoring twice in the second inning and three times in the sixth. Cleveland lost the second game 9–3 and won the third 5–0. Box scores were published in the *Sporting News* and *Sporting Life* on July 3, 1897.

24. Tebeau's recollections of Sockalexis's drinking problem were first published in connection with Sockalexis's death in 1913. They continued to ap-

pear in accounts written by Hughie Jennings, H. G. Salsinger, and others. Jennings produced one of the first comprehensive recountings in a 1926 edition of his syndicated column "Rounding Third." In that column, he purported to relate what Tebeau—dead eight years at the time—had told him. In *The National League Story* (New York: Hill and Wang, 1961), historian Lee Allen related the same material, ascribing it to reporters. The voluminous Sockalexis file at the A. Bartlett Giamatti Research Center at the National Baseball Hall of Fame contains several iterations of essentially the same story. In *Baseball's First Indian*, Sockalexis biographer Ed Rice debunks the Jennings column, which he said "led to a veritable cascade of untruths and myths that have been repeated by journalists over the years." Readers may make their own judgments.

25. *Washington Post*, July 17, 1897.

26. *Cleveland Plain Dealer*, July 13, 1897.

27. *New York Clipper*, March 20, 1897.

28. *Boston Globe*, June 8, 1897.

29. *Boston Globe*, June 14, 1897.

30. *Boston Globe*, August 10, 1897.

31. *Boston Globe*, August 7, 1897.

32. *Boston Globe*, June 19, 1897.

33. *Chicago Tribune*, July 9, 1897.

34. *Boston Globe*, July 12, 1897.

35. *Boston Globe*, July 16, 1897.

36. *Louisville Courier-Journal*, July 17, 1897.

37. The Giants-Colonels brawl is reported on extensively in *Louisville Courier-Journal*, July 17, 1897, and in *Sporting Life*, July 24, 1897.

38. *Boston Journal*, July 20, 1897.

39. *Sporting Life*, July 24, 1897.

40. *Sporting Life*, July 24, 1897.

41. *Boston Globe*, July 26, 1897.

42. The results of Yanigans' games got local attention in Baltimore, despite the fact that the games were generally one-sided. The *Baltimore American* reported on a July 16 28–2 victory by the Yanigans over the Pennsylvania ball club, a team of "colored players from North Baltimore."

43. *Baltimore Sun*, July 8, 1897.

44. *Baltimore Sun*, July 8, 1897.

45. *Cincinnati Enquirer*, July 8, 1897. The allegations are subsequently dealt with in the *Baltimore Sun*, July 9, 1897, and in *Sporting Life*, July 17, 1897.

46. *Baltimore Sun*, July 9, 1897.

47. *Baltimore Sun*, July 16, 1897.

48. *Baltimore Sun*, July 19, 1897.

49. *Baltimore Sun*, July 19, 1897.

50. *Chicago Tribune*, July 19, 1897.

51. *Sporting Life*, July 31, 1897; and *Baltimore Sun*, July 23, 1897.

52. Rice, *Baseball's First Indian*.

53. *New York Times*, August 3, 1897.

54. *Sporting Life*, August 7, 1897.

55. *Sporting Life*, August 7, 1897.

56. *Baltimore American*, July 27, 1897.

57. *Sporting Life*, July 24, 1897.

58. *Boston Globe*, July 20, 1897.

9. Day Jobs for Garroters

1. The Hurst beer stein incident received substantial attention in the *Cincinnati Enquirer* of August 5, 1897, and in the August 7, 1897, edition of the *Sporting News*.

2. *Cincinnati Enquirer*, August 5, 1897.

3. *Sporting News*, September 4, 1897.

4. *Sporting News*, September 4, 1897.

5. *Sporting News*, August 21, 1897.

6. *Boston Journal*, August 13, 1897; quote attributed to Zuber, *Cincinnati Times-Star*, August 6, 1897.

7. *Baltimore American*, August 1, 1897.

8. *Baltimore American*, August 1, 1897.

9. *Sporting Life*, July 31, 1897.

10. *Boston Globe*, August 2, 1897.

11. *Boston Globe*, August 2, 1897.

12. *Boston Globe*, August 2, 1897.

13. The most accessible resource for biographical information on Doc McJames and Win Mercer—or virtually any other historical baseball figure, for that matter—is the Internet. See, for example, the Baseball Reference Web site, http://www.baseball-reference.com, and the Society for American Baseball Research's Baseball Biography Project, http://www.bioproj.sabr.org.

14. *Boston Globe*, August 4, 1897.

15. *Boston Journal*, July 4, 1897.

16. *Baltimore American*, July 27, 1897.

17. *Boston Globe*, August 4, 1897.

18. *Boston Globe*, August 4, 1897.

19. *Boston Globe*, August 5, 1897.

20. *Boston Globe*, August 6, 1897.

21. *Baltimore Sun*, August 7, 1897.

22. *Baltimore Sun*, August 7, 1897.

23. *Baltimore Sun*, August 7, 1897.

24. *Boston Globe*, August 6, 1897.

25. *Boston Globe*, August 6, 1897.

26. *Baltimore Sun*, August 7, 1897.

27. *Sporting Life*, August 14, 1897.

28. *Sporting Life*, August 14, 1897.

29. *Boston Globe*, August 7, 1897.

30. *Boston Globe*, August 7, 1897.

31. *Boston Globe*, August 7, 1897.

32. *Boston Globe*, August 7, 1897.

33. *Sporting Life*, August 14, 1897.

34. *Sporting News*, August 28, 1897.

35. *Sporting Life*, August 14, 1897.

36. *Sporting News*, August 14, 1897.

37. *Sporting Life*, August 21, 1897.

38. *Baltimore Sun*, August 10, 1897.

39. *Baltimore American*, August 11, 1897.

40. *Baltimore American*, August 11, 1897.

41. *Boston Globe*, August 9, 1897.

42. *Boston Globe*, August 9, 1897.

43. *Boston Globe*, August 12, 1897.

44. *Boston Globe*, August 12, 1897.

45. *Baltimore Sun*, August 13, 1897.

46. *Baltimore Sun*, August 13, 1897.

47. *Boston Globe*, August 19, 1897.

48. *Boston Globe*, August 17, 1897.

49. *Boston Globe*, September 7, 1897.

50. *Sporting Life*, August 28, 1897.

51. *Baltimore American*, August 23, 1897.

52. *Baltimore American*, August 24, 1897.

53. *Baltimore Sun*, August 24, 1897.

54. *Baltimore American*, August 24, 1897.

10. Don't They Keep Warm?

1. *Sporting Life*, September 4, 1897.
2. *Sporting Life*, September 4, 1897.
3. *Sporting Life*, September 4, 1897.
4. *Sporting Life*, September 18, 1897.
5. *Sporting Life*, September 18, 1897.
6. *Sporting Life*, September 25, 1897.
7. *Baltimore Sun*, August 28, 1897.
8. *Boston Globe*, August 28, 1897.
9. *Boston Globe*, August 28, 1897.
10. This remark, attributed to the *Boston Herald*, appears under the presumably erroneous headline "Indictment Against McGarr," in *Sporting Life*, September 18, 1897.
11. *Louisville Courier-Journal*, August 31, 1897.
12. *Baltimore Sun*, August 31, 1897.
13. *Baltimore Sun*, August 31, 1897.
14. *Baltimore Sun*, September 1, 1897.
15. *Boston Journal*, September 5, 1897.
16. *Boston Globe*, September 1, 1897.
17. *Chicago Tribune*, September 3, 1897.
18. *Baltimore Sun*, September 7, 1897.
19. *Boston Globe*, September 6, 1897.
20. *Sporting Life*, September 4, 1897.
21. *Sporting Life*, September 4, 1897.
22. *Sporting Life*, September 4, 1897.
23. *Baltimore American*, September 9, 1897.
24. *Boston Globe*, September 9, 1897.
25. *Baltimore Sun*, September 11, 1897.
26. *Baltimore Sun*, September 13, 1897.
27. *Baltimore Sun*, September 13, 1897.
28. *Sporting Life*, September 11, 1897.
29. *Sporting Life*, September 11, 1897.
30. *Boston Journal*, September 12, 1897.
31. Details of the proposed trip are reported in all of the major Boston newspapers circa September 12, 1897.
32. *Boston Globe*, September 12, 1897.
33. *Boston Globe*, September 12, 1897.
34. *Baltimore Sun*, September 14, 1897.

35. *Baltimore Sun*, September 14, 1897.

36. *Baltimore Sun*, September 15, 1897.

37. *Boston Globe*, September 16, 1897.

38. *Boston Globe*, September 17, 1897.

39. *Boston Globe*, September 18, 1897.

40. *Sporting Life*, September 25, 1897.

41. *Boston Globe*, September 18, 1897.

42. *Baltimore American*, September 20, 1897.

43. *Baltimore American*, September 20, 1897.

44. *Boston Globe*, September 21, 1897.

45. *Boston Globe*, September 22, 1897.

46. *Sporting Life*, September 18, 1897.

11. Fall in Baltimore

1. *Boston Globe*, September 23.

2. *Boston Globe*, September 24, 1897.

3. *Baltimore Sun*, September 24, 1897.

4. *Baltimore American*, September 24, 1897.

5. *Baltimore American*, September 24, 1897.

6. *Baltimore American*, September 24, 1897.

7. *Baltimore American*, September 24, 1897.

8. *Boston Globe*, September 25, 1897; and *Sporting Life*, October 2, 1897.

9. *Boston Globe*, September 24, 1897. As subsequent accounts make clear, the number of Rooters at the games fluctuated on any given day.

10. Nash, *Boston's Royal Rooters.*

11. *Boston Globe*, September 24, 1897.

12. *Boston Herald*, September 24, 1897.

13. *Boston Globe*, September 22, 1897.

14. *Baltimore American*, September 26, 1897.

15. *Los Angeles Times*, September 26, 1897.

16. *Boston Globe*, September 25 and 26, 1897.

17. *Boston Globe*, September 25, 1897.

18. *Boston Globe*, September 25, 1897.

19. *Boston Globe*, September 25, 1897.

20. *Boston Herald*, September 25, 1897; and *Boston Globe*, September 25, 1897.

21. *Baltimore Sun*, September 25, 1897.

22. Hamilton's superstitious nature and the blame he attached to the photo for the second-game defeat is related in Nash, *Boston's Royal Rooters*.

23. *Boston Herald*, September 28, 1897.

24. *Baltimore American*, September 28, 1897.

25. *Boston Herald*, September 17, 1897.

26. *Boston Globe*, September 26, 1897.

27. *Baltimore American*, September 26, 1897.

28. *Boston Globe*, September 26, 1897.

29. Fred Lieb, a sports writer and author who was popular in the first half of the twentieth century, told a marvelous tale, which he said he had borrowed from turn-of-the-century sports writer Hughie Fullerton, regarding the conclusion of the second game of the series. The tale, recorded in Lieb's *The Baltimore Orioles* (New York: Putnam, 1955), centered on Keeler's game-saving catch of Stahl's drive:

> Right field, Willie's pasture, was rough and weedy, and back of it was a high fence used for advertising purposes. Inside the fence sloped at an angle of 65 degrees, though it was straight on the outside. With two runners on base, Chick Stahl, the crack Boston center fielder, hit a long fly to right which looked like the winning clout for the Beaneaters. Fullerton reported that Keeler, running like a scared rabbit, mounted the fence higher and higher, and with a final thrust caught the ball just as it was clearing the fence. Then, according to Hughie, the little outfielder's momentum was so great that he ran for another fifteen feet on top of the fence before falling some distance to the street below. The umpire ruled he had made a legal catch before falling out of the park.

Sadly for the yarn, it comes up a bit short in the truth department. There is no evidence that the Baltimore fence slanted enough for a player to run up it, much less along it. Stahl, who played right field and not center, did not bat in a situation where he represented the tying run, much less the winning one. Nor did he hit a late-inning fly ball that was caught by Keeler, either in front of, atop, or over the fence.

30. *Boston Journal*, September 26, 1897.

31. *Baltimore Sun*, September 27, 1897.

32. *Boston Journal*, September 27, 1897.

33. *Boston Herald*, September 17, 1897.

34. *Baltimore Sun*, September 27, 1897.

35. The actual address of the Diamond Café is open to question. Both Alex-

ander (*John McGraw*) and Solomon (*Where They Ain't*) place it at 519 N. Howard, and out of respect to their research, that is the address used here. However, the 1898 Baltimore City Guide (Enoch Pratt Free Library, Baltimore) lists the location of the Diamond Café as 226 W. Lexington Avenue. One possibility is that McGraw and Robinson moved the restaurant after its first year; indeed, the locations are only a few blocks from one another in the city's central business district.

36. *Boston Globe*, September 27, 1897.

37. *Baltimore Sun*, September 27, 1897.

38. *Boston Globe*, September 28, 1897.

39. *Boston Herald*, September 28, 1897.

40. *Baltimore Sun*, September 28, 1897.

41. *Boston Globe*, September 28, 1897.

42. *Baltimore Sun*, September 28, 1897.

43. *Baltimore Sun*, September 28, 1897.

44. *Boston Globe*, September 28, 1897.

45. *Boston Globe*, September 28, 1897.

46. *Boston Globe*, September 28, 1897.

47. *Louisville Courier-Journal*, September 28, 1897.

48. *Baltimore Sun*, September 30, 1897.

49. *Brooklyn Eagle*, September 30, 1897.

50. *Boston Globe*, October 1, 1897.

51. *Boston Globe*, October 1, 1897.

52. *Boston Journal*, October 3, 1897.

53. *Boston Globe*, October 1, 1897.

54. *Boston Globe*, September 30, 1897.

55. *Baltimore Sun*, September 28, 1897.

56. *Boston Journal*, October 3, 1897.

Afterword

1. Allen, *The National League Story*.

2. Nash, *Boston's Royal Rooters*.

3. Marty Bergen file, A. Bartlett Giamatti Research Center, National Baseball Hall of Fame and Museum, Cooperstown NY.

4. Chick Stahl file, A. Bartlett Giamatti Research Center, National Baseball Hall of Fame and Museum, Cooperstown NY.

5. Chick Stahl file, A. Bartlett Giamatti Research Center, National Baseball Hall of Fame and Museum, Cooperstown NY.

6. Frank Selee file, A. Bartlett Giamatti Research Center, National Baseball Hall of Fame and Museum, Cooperstown NY.

7. Rice, *Baseball's First Indian.*

8. Allen, *The National League Story.*

9. Patsy Tebeau file, A. Bartlett Giamatti Research Center, National Baseball Hall of Fame and Museum, Cooperstown NY.

10. Ed Doheny file, A. Bartlett Giamatti Research Center, National Baseball Hall of Fame and Museum, Cooperstown NY.

11. Jimmy Collins file, A. Bartlett Giamatti Research Center, National Baseball Hall of Fame and Museum, Cooperstown NY.

12. Hugh Duffy file, A. Bartlett Giamatti Research Center, National Baseball Hall of Fame and Museum, Cooperstown NY.

13. Kid Nichols file, A. Bartlett Giamatti Research Center, National Baseball Hall of Fame and Museum, Cooperstown NY.

14. Bobby Lowe file, A. Bartlett Giamatti Research Center, National Baseball Hall of Fame and Museum, Cooperstown NY.

15. Ted Lewis file, A. Bartlett Giamatti Research Center, National Baseball Hall of Fame and Museum, Cooperstown NY.

16. The best of numerous biographies of McGraw remains Charles Alexander's *John McGraw.*

17. The best biography of Wilbert Robinson is *Uncle Robbie,* by Jack Kavanagh and Norman Macht.

18. Hughie Jennings file, A. Bartlett Giamatti Research Center, National Baseball Hall of Fame and Museum, Cooperstown NY.

19. Joe Kelley file, A. Bartlett Giamatti Research Center, National Baseball Hall of Fame and Museum, Cooperstown NY.

20. Solomon, *Where They Ain't.*

21. Jack Doyle file, A. Bartlett Giamatti Research Center, National Baseball Hall of Fame and Museum, Cooperstown NY.

22. Arlie Pond file, A. Bartlett Giamatti Research Center, National Baseball Hall of Fame and Museum, Cooperstown NY.

23. Bill Hoffer file, A. Bartlett Giamatti Research Center, National Baseball Hall of Fame and Museum, Cooperstown NY.

24. *New York Times,* July 30, 1959.

25. Ned Hanlon file, A. Bartlett Giamatti Research Center, National Baseball Hall of Fame and Museum, Cooperstown NY.

CPSIA information can be obtained
at www.ICGtesting.com
Printed in the USA
LVHW110337070721
692012LV00008B/717